PARENTAL DESCRIPTIONS OF CHILD PERSONALITY

Developmental Antecedents of the Big Five?

The LEA Series in
Personality and Clinical Psychology
Irving B. Weiner, Editor

Gacono/Meloy • *The Rorschach Assessment of Aggressive and Psychopathic Personalities*

Zillmer/Harrower/Ritzler/Archer • *The Quest for the Nazi Personality: A Psychological Investigation of Nazi War Criminals*

Sarason/Pierce/Sarason • *Cognitive Interference: Theories, Methods, and Findings*

Exner (Ed.) • *Issues and Methods in Rorschach Research*

Hy/Lovinger • *Measuring Ego Development, Second Edition*

Ganellen • *Integrating the Rorschach and the MMPI-2 in Personality Assessment*

Kelly • *The Assessment of Object Relations Phenomena in Adolescents: TAT and Rorschach Measures*

Meloy/Acklin/Gacono/Murray/Peterson (Eds.) • *Contemporary Rorschach Interpretation: A Casebook*

McCallum/Piper (Eds.) • *Psychological Mindedness: A Contemporary Understanding*

VanHasselt/Herson (Eds.) • *Handbook of Psychological Treatment Protocols for Children*

Handler/Hilsenroth • *Teaching and Learning Personality Assessment*

Loevinger (Ed.) • *Technical Foundations for Measuring Ego Development: The Washington University Sentence Completion Test*

Tedeschi/Park/Calhoun (Eds.) • *Posttraumatic Growth: Positive Changes in the Aftermath of Crisis*

Wong/Fry (Eds.) • *The Human Quest for Meaning: A Handbook of Psychological Research and Clinical Applications*

Kohnstamm/Halverson/Mervielde/Havill (Eds.) • *Parental Descriptions of Child Personality: Developmental Antecedents of the Big Five?*

PARENTAL DESCRIPTIONS OF CHILD PERSONALITY

Developmental Antecedents of the Big Five?

Edited by

Geldolph A. Kohnstamm
Leiden University

Charles F. Halverson, Jr.
University of Georgia

Ivan Mervielde
University of Ghent

Valerie L. Havill
University of Georgia

 LAWRENCE ERLBAUM ASSOCIATES, PUBLISHERS
1998 Mahwah, New Jersey   London

Lawrence Erlbaum Associates, Inc., Publishers
10 Industrial Avenue
Mahwah, NJ 07430

Cover design by Kathryn Houghtaling Lacey

Library of Congress Cataloging-in-Publication Data

Parental descriptions of child personality : developmental
antecedents of the big five? / edited by Geldolph A.
Kohnstamm ... [et al.].
    p. cm.
    Includes bibliographical references and indexes.
    ISBN 0-8058-2301-8
    1. Personality in children. 2. Temperament in chil-
dren. I. Kohnstamm, Geldolph A.
    BF723.P4P36 1998
    155.4'182—dc21   97-32503
                                 CIP

Books published by Lawrence Erlbaum Associates are
printed on acid-free paper, and their bindings are chosen
for strength and durability.

Printed in the United States of America
10 9 8 7 6 5 4 3 2 1

Contents

Preface   vii

1   Analyzing Parental Free Descriptions of Child Personality   1
Geldolph A. Kohnstamm, Charles F. Halverson, Jr.,
Ivan Mervielde, and Valerie L. Havill

2   Extraversion: Toward a Unifying Description   21
From Infancy to Adulthood
Eric Elphick, Charles F. Halverson, Jr., and
Magdalena Marzal-Wisniewska

3   Agreeableness as a Diachronic Human Trait   49
Valerie L. Havill, Elias Besevegis, and Sophia Mouroussaki

4   A Developmental Integration of Conscientiousness   65
From Childhood to Adulthood
Geldolph A. Kohnstamm, Yuching Zhang,
Anne-Marie Slotboom, and Eric Elphick

5   Emotional Stability: Developmental Perspectives   85
From Childhood to Adulthood
Alois Angleitner, Geldolph A. Kohnstamm, Anne-Marie
Slotboom, and Elias Besevegis

6   Linking Openness and Intellect in Childhood   105
and Adulthood
Ivan Mervielde, Filip De Fruyt, and Slawomir Jarmuz

7 Developmental Changes in Personality Descriptions of   127
   Children: A Cross-National Comparison of Parental
   Descriptions of Children
   Anne-Marie Slotboom, Valerie L. Havill,
   Vassilis Pavlopoulos, and Filip De Fruyt

8 Parental Personality Descriptions of Boys and Girls   155
   Filip De Fruyt, Alain Van Hiel, and Veerle Buyst

9 How African American Parents Describe Their Children   169
   James B. Victor, Harold E. Dent, Barbara Carter,
   Charles F. Halverson, Jr., and Valerie L. Havill

10 Validity of Results Obtained by Analyzing   189
   Free Personality Descriptions
   Ivan Mervielde

   Appendix: Composition of the Seven Samples   205
   Anne-Marie Slotboom and Eric Elphick

   Author Index   211

   Subject Index   217

Preface

The research reported in this book should be thought of as part of the continuing search for the main dimensions of temperament and personality in childhood. Several competing theoretical traditions exist, and each has generated a variety of instruments to measure dimensions of specific interest to the particular theory. Although the variety of theories and instruments is not as overwhelming as in adult personality psychology, progress in developmental psychology has been hampered by the fact that individual differences in temperament and personality are conceptualized and assessed in so many different ways. More often than not, the outcomes of research in which temperament measures play a major role cannot be compared because measures used to operationalize individual differences are themselves incomparable. Progress in this field would be facilitated if consensus were reached on what the most important and "basic" dimensions of temperament are in infancy, in childhood, and in adolescence.

One possible way to achieve such a goal is to bring theorists together at conferences and to attempt to reach consensus by discussing the merits of each individual theory. Although such conferences (e.g., the 12 successive Occasional Temperament Conferences held in the United States) have been very stimulating and rewarding, the goal of achieving consensus remains remote. While struggling to obtain uniformity in theory and assessment of temperament in childhood, however, we came across research documenting the emerging consensus in adult personality psychology that the domain of adult personality could be comprehensively represented by five factors.[1]

The Five-Factor Model (FFM) consensus among researchers of adult personality is stimulated by theory based on the study of language—more precisely on the study of adjectives that are used for denoting individual

---

[1] Historically, the terms *Big Five* and *Five-Factor Model* stem from different research traditions, the former being associated with the lexical approach (see Goldberg, 1993, for a short overview) and the latter with the NEO-PI personality inventory by McCrae and Costa. In this book, both terms are used interchangeably.

differences in personality. These adjectives have been selected from dictionaries, but also, in recent years, from free descriptions of personality given by adults. The five main dimensions are usually labeled as (I) Extraversion, (II) Agreeableness, (III) Conscientiousness, (IV) Emotional Stability or Instability, and (V) Intellect, Culture, or Openness to Experience.

Until recently, only the studies by Digman and his associates (Digman, 1963, 1990; Digman & Inouye, 1986) explored the validity of the FFM for assessing individual differences in personality among children. Now, the number of studies exploring child personality is rapidly growing (e.g., Digman & Shmelyov, 1996; Halverson, Kohnstamm, & Martin, 1994).

When we began to explore the possibility of adapting this approach to the field of temperament and personality in childhood, we were hampered by the fact that there was no compilation of terms to describe temperament and personality in children. A dictionary-based approach, as was used in adult personality psychology, seemed cumbersome and inadequate for studying individual differences in childhood because many of the words were clearly developmentally inappropriate. One of us had already experimented for some years with free parental descriptions of temperament characteristics of children. These characteristics had been categorized in a temporary category system that was in continuous development. Encouraged by the fact that John (1990a, 1990b) and Church and Katigbak (1989) had used a similar approach with free descriptions to validate some aspects of the FFM (in particular, the model's claim of comprehensiveness, i.e., that it covered the major dimensions of personality), we decided to collect parental free or natural-language descriptions of children in several languages and cultures.

The first goal of this project was to create an alternative dictionary (in each language) of expressions used by parents to describe the characteristics of their children. These lexicons are now being used in the second phase of the project to provide representative words and phrases to construct items for a series of age-related questionnaires in the various countries. Factor analyzing data from parental ratings of these questionnaires should then result in age-appropriate n-factor models summarizing the common variance in these questionnaires. The resemblance between these n-factor models for individual differences in children of different ages and the FFM in adulthood can then be studied. These are the goals we are pursuing.

Why have we emphasized different languages and cultures? We believe that the descriptions parents spontaneously use to characterize their children depend partly on the saliency of certain traits in their children and partly on what parents expect to see, based on family history, as well as on the prevailing belief systems about what traits are important for children in their particular cultures (Harkness & Super, 1996; Sigel, 1985). Parents in different cultures might use different personality traits to describe their children, but the evidence as to whether they do so remains sketchy. Dictionary-based studies in psychological research of adult personality have now been done or are underway in many different countries and languages. Data from these studies seem to be pointing toward the cultural universality of the Big Five for *adult* individual differences psychology. Our work, however, is directed at the question of cultural universality of major dimensions of temperament and personality *in childhood*. From our developmental interest follows the next question: How do the major dimensions of infancy and childhood gradually evolve into adult personality structure?

The intent of this volume is to lay a foundation to answer these questions. We present and discuss the results of the first phase of an ambitious project: the analysis of the contents of the free descriptions collected in seven different countries. In the first chapter we describe the research method and samples that provided the data. Chapters 2 through 6 then present results for the five major categories of the coding scheme. In chapter 7, cross-sectional age comparisons of samples from seven countries are analyzed. This chapter is followed by one discussing child gender effects. In chapter 9, results are summarized from a sample of African American parents living in Virginia. The last chapter deals with the validity of the data collected in this international project.

Throughout the book, the samples are named by country names (for example: "the Dutch sample"). This practice does not imply that the authors pretend that the samples are representative for the country populations. In the Appendix the demographic details of all samples are presented.

ACKNOWLEDGMENTS

Support for the Belgian part of the project came from Grant No. OZF-0112792 from the University of Ghent and from a NATO Collaborative Research Grant (941239) awarded to I. Mervielde. Support for the Chinese part of the project came from the Child Development Center of China, Beijing, the Netherlands Royal Academy of Sciences and Leiden University. Support for the Dutch part came from Leiden University. The German part was partially financed through funds from a Max Planck Research Prize given to A. Angleitner and J. Strelau (No. 27 360). The Greek part was funded by the Research Committee of the University of Athens. The Polish part was supported by the Committee for Scientific Research (Komitet Badan Naukowych), the University of Wroclaw, and the Institute of Psychology of the Polish Academy of Sciences. Finally, support for the U.S. part of the project came from National Institute of Mental Health Grant No. MH 50302 to C. F. Halverson, Jr., and National Institute of Mental Health Grant No. MH53272 to J. Victor.

REFERENCES

Church, A. T., & Katigbak, M. S. (1989). Internal, external and self-reward structure of personality in non-Western culture: An investigation of cross-language and cross-cultural generalizability. *Journal of Personality and Social Psychology, 57*, 857–872.

Digman, J. M. (1963). Principal dimensions of child personality as inferred from teachers' judgments. *Child Development, 34*, 43–60.

Digman, J. M. (1990). Personality structure: Emergence of the five-factor model. In M. R. Rosenzweig & L. W. Porter (Eds.), *Annual Review of Psychology* (Vol. 41, pp. 417–440). Palo Alto, CA: Annual Reviews.

Digman, J. M., & Inouye, J. (1986). Further specification of the five robust factors of personality. *Journal of Personality and Social Psychology, 50*, 116–123.

Digman, J. M., & Shmelyov, A. G. (1996). The structure of temperament and personality in Russian children. *Journal of Personality and Social Psychology, 7*, 341–351.

Goldberg, L. R. (1993). The structure of phenotypic personality traits. *American Psychologist, 48*, 1, 26–34.

Halverson, C. F., Jr., Kohnstamm, G. A., & Martin, R. P. (Eds.). (1994). *Development of the structure of temperament and personality from infancy to adulthood.* Hillsdale, NJ: Lawrence Erlbaum Associates.

Harkness, S., & Super, C. M. (Eds.). (1996). *Parents' cultural belief systems: Their origins, expressions, and consequences.* New York: The Guilford Press.

John, O. P. (1990a). The "Big Five" factor taxonomy: Dimensions of Personality in the natural language and in questionnaires. In L. A. Pervin (Ed.), *Handbook of personality: Theory and research* (pp. 66–100). New York: The Guilford Press.

John, O. P. (1990b). Towards a Taxonomy of Personality Descriptors. In D. M. Buss & N. Cantor (Eds.), *Personality psychology: Recent trends and emerging directions* (pp. 261–271). New York: Springer Verlag.

Sigel, I. E. (Ed.). (1985). *Parental belief systems: The psychological consequences for children.* Hillsdale, NJ: Lawrence Erlbaum Associates.

Analyzing Parental Free Descriptions of Child Personality

Geldolph A. Kohnstamm
Leiden University

Charles F. Halverson, Jr.
University of Georgia

Ivan Mervielde
University of Ghent

Valerie L. Havill
University of Georgia

Since Thomas and Chess popularized the concept of temperament in childhood (e.g., 1977), many studies devoted to temperamental differences among children have been published, and the nine-dimensional structure devised by Thomas, Chess, and their collaborators has attained textbook status. Applied initially to the study of infants, but later to older children as well, this approach categorizes temperamental differences based on clinical experience into nine more or less independent traits: Activity Level, Rhythmicity, Approach-Withdrawal, Adaptability, Threshold of Responsiveness, Intensity of Reaction, Quality of Mood, Distractibility, and Persistence. Beyond these first-order constructs, second-order constructs of three clusters—easy, difficult, and slow to warm up—have been proposed based on factor analyses of the nine scales.

Because of their clinical usefulness, the temperament scales developed by Thomas and Chess and later by Carey and others (e.g., Carey & McDevitt, 1978) became well-known instruments for assessing temperamental differences in infancy and childhood. We have begun with this brief history to emphasize that temperament measures currently in use, regardless of format, are top-down, theoretically derived instruments, with items reflecting the concerns of the child-care specialists. Even when some form of factor analysis has been used to summarize dimensions statistically—as opposed to clinically—the final result has still depended on item selection done in constructing the instruments. In the case of the scales by Thomas and Chess and by Carey (e.g., McDevitt & Carey, 1978), other authors have shown that the original nine dimensions have not been recovered from factoring at the item level. Instead, from five to seven factors not closely resembling the original nine have emerged (see Martin, Wisenbaker, & Huttunen, 1994). We have emphasized here how the theoretical and clinical concerns of the Thomas and Chess group have shaped the temperament field. We have no quarrel with the usefulness of the nine-dimensional structure for many clinical assessments or research programs, but the dimensions might not be comprehensive, coherent statistically, or robust across ages and cultures. There are other ways to develop items, as we next propose, and there is a pressing need to assess the cross-cultural generality of constructs developed largely in one language or culture. Anthropologists and cross-cultural researchers have begun to demand justification for such cross-cultural applications of psychological instruments (e.g., Malpass & Poortinga, 1986; Shwalb, Shwalb, & Shoji, 1994).

Although it might seem that cultural homogeneity is on the increase at the same time that cultural uniqueness is on the decrease, a world where cultural differences have vanished in one big melting pot has not yet arrived. Thus, the appropriateness of translation and application of psychological instruments across cultures should be questioned more frequently than is presently done. Thus far, cross-cultural studies in the field of temperament have consisted mostly of comparisons of means and variances on scales originating in England (e.g., Eysenck Personality Questionnaire [EPQ], Eysenck & Eysenck, 1975) or the United States and translated into other languages. Although this work has produced many interesting results, we decided to follow a different approach.

FREE DESCRIPTIONS OF PERSONALITY

We were originally motivated by John (1990a), who called for more studies using free descriptions of personality to test for the possibility that the reliance on top-down, theorist-imposed descriptors was "too parochial":

> . . . given that the Big Five were intended to represent the major dimensions of natural-language personality descriptions, another option is to investigate the characteristics people use in free descriptions of themselves and others. Would the Big Five be replicated if the set of descriptors factored was based

on the content of subjects' free descriptions, rather than on those sets of terms selected by the taxonomers themselves? (p. 92)

To explore this question, John and Chaplin (John, 1990a, 1990b) asked more than 300 U.S. college students to describe their own personalities and to generate terms for both their desirable *and* their undesirable characteristics. This first phase of collecting, categorizing, and counting descriptors was then followed by a second phase in which the 60 most frequently used descriptors were put in a questionnaire and given to a new sample of subjects. Factor analyses of self-ratings yielded five factors that closely resembled the conceptual definitions of the Five-Factor Model (FFM), a finding supporting the hypothesis that these five factors are indeed the most salient dimensions of personality for U.S. college students.

The FFM free-description methodology has been used cross-culturally as well. For example, Church, Katigbak, and Castaneda (1988) conducted in-depth, open-ended interviews with 41 Filipino bilingual (English and Tagalog) college students. The students provided general descriptions of healthy and unhealthy Filipinos in several broad areas of functioning (e.g., attitudes and feelings toward others; actions with others; attitudes and feelings toward humans in general; attitudes, feelings, or thoughts about themselves; goals or values; and mood). Responses were recorded verbatim and transcribed.

The 1,516 nonredundant descriptors obtained were inductively reduced to 54 semantic categories. The authors could allocate almost all of these 54 categories to one of the five dimensions of the FFM. There were, however, additional dimensions not easily summarized by the FFM. For example, a dimension relating to nationalism and societal awareness emerged. Although these descriptors might fit in Category III (Conscientiousness) in the FFM, the authors suggested that their saliency in the personality descriptions was in response to the emphasis on social and political awareness in the Philippines during the time of the research.

In these studies, spontaneously mentioned personality characteristics were valued because it is assumed that people frequently mention those characteristics that they think are most important or basic. Further, it is assumed that aggregating these spontaneously mentioned descriptors over groups of individuals yields a set of perceptions specific to the culture of the informants.

Coding Free Descriptions

The collection and categorization of free descriptions of personality are the first steps in our research program. When many people have been interviewed, the large collection of personality descriptors obtained must be ordered. This is done by judges using a well-tested categorization system with good interjudge reliability.

When the system of categories has been applied, we can assess category frequency. Then, assuming that frequency of category use indicates the degree of saliency of each personality category in a particular culture, we choose exemplars from the high-frequency categories to prepare for the second phase. In this phase, the representative selection of descriptors is put into a questionnaire format that is then given to new samples of people from the particular culture involved. They may be asked to rate themselves or others on the items selected. Finally, factor analyses of the items are used to summarize the underlying dimensions in the set of characteristics.

Free Descriptions of Child Personality

In the late 1980s, in his own search for the major dimensions in parental perceptions of temperament and personality in children, Kohnstamm and his students did some pilot work using parental free descriptions. These pilot studies served to develop and refine the methodology of eliciting and coding parental free descriptions. The studies demonstrated the sensitivity of the free-response format to detecting both social class and informant differences (e.g., mother versus father) in the Dutch language and culture, and they also revealed the potential of the FFM for categorizing parental descriptors. Until 1990, only one investigator had explored the structure of perceived personality in late childhood and adolescence from a FFM perspective (Digman, 1963, 1990; Digman & Inouye, 1986).

During a sabbatical year together at the Netherlands Institute for Advanced Study (NIAS) in 1990–1991, Kohnstamm and Halverson formulated the idea for the project described in this volume. An international group of researchers was formed with the goal of collecting free descriptions of children of different ages, in different languages and cultures. We assumed that our method of collecting free descriptions would tell us whether we would get the same or different personality dimensions over different languages and cultures. To quote from Church and Katigbak (1989): "By starting with a taxonomy of personality concepts generated independently in each culture, culture-relevant dimensions are allowed to emerge independently, providing a more convincing test of universality when comparable dimensions emerge" (p. 870).

Although the societies represented in the present study are all modern, the families involved live in differing social and economic circumstances, with large differences in household income and in future prospects for the children described. With the samples of differing cultures and circumstances, we can assess whether the parents in these societies generate temperament and personality descriptors with differing emphases, frequencies, and evaluations. When questionnaire items are distilled from the variety of terms, we can assess whether different dimensions emerge from parents' perceptions of their children's personalities in these different cultures.

METHOD

In all participating countries, personality descriptions were collected from parents of children between 2 and 13 years of age. In some samples, parents were simply asked to tell us about their children. In other samples, after an introduction in which the word "personality" was mentioned, the parents were asked, "Can you tell me what you think is characteristic of your child?" All interviews were audiotaped and subsequently transcribed verbatim. The coders used elaborate coding manuals that included instructions about units of analysis, division of phrases, dealing with repetitions, and synonymy.

For our purposes, a unit of analysis was defined as an adjective, verb, noun, or phrase referring to a description of behavior, personality characteristic, or ability. Phrases referring to situational causes of behavior or to physical attributes were not coded. Because a unit of analysis could be a phrase, it was sometimes helpful to split phrases into simple, easily codable parts. Adjacent words or phrases could be divided and coded separately as two individual units if the meaning of each part was understood when considered independently. If a coder judged that meaning or context was lost by splitting the phrase, the unit was coded as one single description. For example, the phrase "She likes to play outdoors with neighbor kids" can be separated into two distinct parts: "She likes to play outdoors" and "Plays with neighbor kids." The first phrase would be coded as referring to physical activity level, and the second phrase would be coded as indicating extraversion or sociability. The phrase "She's so quick; her head works very, very fast" would be coded as a single unit because breaking the description into two parts could conceivably lead the coder to misinterpret "She's so quick" as referring to physical activity instead of cognitive proficiency.

In free-language interviews, respondents often elaborated on a single characteristic by mentioning concrete, situation-specific behaviors to illustrate the personality characteristic. In such cases, the elaborative phrase or phrases were taken with the descriptive word or phrase and were coded as one unit of analysis. Respondents might also mention a descriptive characteristic in the past tense and contrast this with a similar descriptive characteristic in the present tense to illustrate the way a child is now with respect to a younger age. In this case, the past-tense phrase was not coded separately, but was included in one unit with the present-tense phrase. The part of the phrase in the present tense was the subject of analysis; the past-tense word or phrase, however, might have helped the coder to assess the meaning or importance of the unit as a whole.

Words and phrases that were not coded as descriptive phrases included those referring to a person other than the target child or to children in general. These were considered nonrelevant phrases. Phrases about peripheral information were also excluded; these included information connected to the main issue, but so remote as to have no immediate relevance to the target child (e.g., "Her parents are friends of mine" or "You have a lot of temper tantrums and things with all kids, you know; that is not specific to Susie, but that is something that would bother me about her"). If there was reasonable doubt as to whether a respondent was referring to the target child directly, then the word or phrase was not coded.

When words or phrases were repeated verbatim or if phrases expressing the same literal meaning were used more than once in a single interview, these units were recorded and coded as repetitions, but were not included in frequency analyses more than once.

The Categorization System

To categorize the expressions generated by the parents, a coding system was developed. Although the system of categories was inspired by the FFM framework, with several subcategories in each of the five dimensions, an additional eight categories were added. Each major category was designated by a Roman numeral. The first five were numbered according to conventions in the FFM literature. The subcategories or facets were inductively derived. Responses are coded as Positive, Neutral, or Negative as well. For example: "Enthusiastic" is coded as IA+; "Tends to shut herself off" is coded IA−. Table 1.1 shows the total system. No examples are given for responses coded as Neutral. Decisions were made on which utterances were to be used as units for coding and which utterances could be discarded. Detailed instructions were developed for this step in applying the categorization scheme.

Rationale for Categories Included

The origin of the first five main categories has already been explained. The subcategories within these five are our own inventions, based on clusters of high-loading items, or "facets," as published in several FFM studies. For the location of some of the subcategories (e.g., Manageable for Parents and Teachers—Category II), we had no empirical basis: No

TABLE 1.1
Categories for Coding Descriptors From "Free"
Personality Descriptions and Examples of Descriptors

I.—Extraversion	

1A: Sociability—outgoing versus shy

1A+	1A−
Enthusiastic	Tendency to shut self off
Totally thrilled to be alive	Inhibited and withdrawn
Likes to be with others	Shy, prefers to play alone

1B: Dominance, Leadership, Assertiveness

1B+	1B−
A leader	Passive
Strong character	Follows everyone
Assertive	Does not stand up for self

1C: Activity, Pace, Tempo, Energy, Restlessness, Vitality

1C+	1C−
Active	Quiet
Energetic	Not physically active
Always on the move	Does not do much

II.—Agreeableness	

2A: Helpfulness, Cooperation, Amiability

2A+	2A−
Loving, sweet	Selfish
Good natured	Impatient
Caring	Not a good helper
	Initiates aggression

2B: Manageable for Parents and Teachers

2B+	2B−
Well behaved	Argumentative
Never belligerent	Stubborn
Cooperative	Rebellious

2C: Honest, Sincere

2C+	2C−
Sincere	Lies
Honest	Can be deceiving
Trustworthy	Insincere

III.—Conscientiousness	

3A: Carefulness

3A+	3A−
Long attention span	Forgetful
Good concentration	Daydreams, easily distracted
Responsible	Careless, indifferent
Neat, tidy	Sloppy, chaotic

(Continued)

(Continued)

3B: Faithfulness, Loyalty

3B+	3B–
Very loyal to friends	No enduring friendships
Stands up for friends	
Reliable	

3C: Diligence, Industriousness, Persevering

3C+	3C–
Determined	Needs motivation
Hard working	Lazy
Competitive	Unwilling to work
Wants to do things well, perfectionist	

IV.—Emotional Stability

4A: Emotional Reactivity and Stability

4A+	4A–
Under control	Cries a lot
Very resilient	Sensitive to words from others
Rarely loses temper	Needs to control temper

4B: Self-Confidence

4B+	4B–
Confident	Lacks self-confidence
Self-assured	Insecure
Certain	Tentative in assessing own abilities

4C: Anxious, Fearful

4C+	4C–
Does not exhibit a lot of fears or nervousness of dogs, etc.	Afraid of the dark, fearful

---

V.—Openness to Experience, Intelligence

5A: Openness to Experience, Adventure Seeking

5A+	5A–
Curious	Afraid of failure
Inquisitive	Not too open (to new things or ideas)
Easily interested in new things	Hesitant to do things

5B: Interested in Things, Good at . . .

5B+	5B–
Interested in computers	Dislikes reading
Likes music, plays piano very well	Not interested in . . .

5C: Intelligence, Language Proficiency, Reasoning Capacities

5C+	5C–
Bright	Difficulty in understanding
Quick to learn	Slow to learn

(Continued)

TABLE 1.1
(Continued)

VI.—Independence, Ability to Do Things Independently	
6+	6–
Independent	Does not do things on his or her own
Often involved in activities	
Likes to do things on his or her own	Too dependent on mom

VII.—Mature for Age	
7+	7–
Mature	Babyish behavior
Precocious	Emotionally immature
Intelligent for his or her age	Young for his or her peer group

VIII.—Illness, Handicaps, and Health	
8+	8–
Healthy	Sickly
	Severe allergy problems, attention-deficit disorder

IX.—Rhythmicity of Eating, Sleeping, etc.	
9+	9–
Likes things to run on regular schedule	No examples

X.—Gender Appropriate, Physical Attractiveness	
10+	10–
He is all boy; she is all girl	He only likes to play with girls
Attractive, handsome	She only likes to play with boys

XI.—School Performance, Attitudes Toward School	
11+	11–
Eager about school	Talks when not supposed to in school
Excellent student, self-motivated at school	Not challenged at school

XII.—Contact Comfort, Desire to Be Cuddled, Clinging	
12+	12–
Cuddly, huggable	Does not like to be touched

XIII.—Relationships With Siblings and Parents	
13A: Sibling Relationships	
13A+	13A–
Helps with siblings	Ignores sister
Watches out for brother, problems with siblings	Will not play with brother
13B: Interaction With Parents and Family	
13B+	13B–
Likes to do things with family	Not too eager to do things with family
Oriented to the family	
Good father–daughter relationship	

(Continued)

TABLE 1.1
(Continued)

XIV.—Ambiguous Phrases and Descriptions That Cannot Be Coded in Other Categories

---

Strong spiritual character
Persnickety
Too materialistic
Big

---

adjectives for Manageability were included in FFM adjective studies as they did not deal with children. In the instrumentation phase of this project, items dealing with Manageability might not cluster with a higher order factor recognizable as the FFM's Agreeableness. We emphasize here that we do not necessarily expect to find a neat FFM structure once new samples of parents have rated their children on the items derived from the categories.

As for the rationale for the coding in our pilot studies for the categories additional to the FFM (i.e., Categories VI through XIV), we coded the Independence (VI) category separately from the Big Five for two reasons. First, when parents described their children as being independent (or as being too dependent), they might mean something different from being simply high or low on Extraversion, Conscientiousness, Emotional Stability or Instability, or Openness to Experience. Second, in the FFM literature about adults, a factor labeled as Autonomy or Independence has been repeatedly seen as having independent status. So, on rational grounds, John (1990a, 1990b) made a separate category for Independence when categorizing personality descriptors generated by his students. Also, Costa and McCrae (1988), on empirical grounds, saw sufficient indications for a separate factor of Autonomy in the Personality Research Form (PRF). Whether being independent and autonomous *in childhood* will attain independent factorial status remains to be determined in the following phases of our project.

Mature for Age (VII) is a category specific to children. Very few adjectives of this kind have ever been included in FFM adjective studies using self- or other ratings of adults, and it is therefore impossible to tell if and where Mature for Age would fit in the factor analytically derived model. The category is included for coding comprehensiveness and possible links to other categories.

It is questionable whether a person's being often or never ill or having a disability is a personality characteristic in the strict sense. We have included Illness, Handicaps, and Health (VIII) in our system because parents of children who are ill or disabled often mentioned this fact first when beginning the interview. These parents considered their children's condition as fundamental background information for understanding the youngsters' other characteristics.

Rhythmicity (IX) is included as a coding category because it is one of the nine dimensions of the Thomas–Chess model. In the Thomas–Chess-derived DOTS-R questionnaire (Revised Dimensions of Temperament Survey; Windle & Lerner, 1986), Rhythmicity is even operationalized in three separate scales (for eating, sleeping, and daily habits). Angleitner and Ostendorf (1994) demonstrated that when students rate themselves on many different personality questionnaires, including the DOTS-R, Rhythmicity obtains independent status as a sixth factor outside the FFM domain. We found, however, that only a very small proportion of the descriptors had to do with Rhythmicity. Parents from other cultures might possibly generate more descriptors indicating aspects of Rhythmicity than we have found so far.

Gender-Appropriate Behavior and Physical Attractiveness (X) are concepts not usually included in the measurement of temperament and personality, although they are important personal characteristics that could cluster with other major personality traits in childhood. Usually parents, at least in Western cultures, do not mention physical attractiveness (or lack thereof) in a conversation with a stranger. Nevertheless, we coded descriptors for physical attractiveness because of its importance for both children and adults. For example, Lanning (1994) found an independent attractiveness factor, the first one after the Big Five, when factoring a sample of 940 California Adult Q-Set (CAQ) ratings of students in California.

We also included a category for descriptors indicating how well children are doing in school, for example, whether their marks are good, average, or bad (XI). Typically, in the history of personality testing such qualities are measured by instruments other than personality questionnaires. By keeping school performance and attitudes apart in our category system, we have, however, somewhat reduced the number of "descriptors" coded in Category III, Conscientiousness, notably those describing a child as being industrious or lazy at school.

The concept of Cuddliness and Clinging Behavior (XII) was included because of the history of the concept in literature on temperament (e.g., Bates, Freeland, & Lounsbury, 1979). Thus far, few descriptors have been given in this area. The low frequency might not warrant the inclusion of cuddliness and clinging behavior in the second phase of this project.

A separate category (XIII) was included to code descriptions of relationships between the target child and his or her siblings, parents, or both. As for the category School Performance, by creating a separate category we might have reduced the number of descriptors that otherwise would have been coded as I, II, or IV. The last category, XIV, consisted of

Ambiguous Phrases That Cannot Be Coded in Our System. All phrases were retained, however, to allow for the emergence of a category if parents mentioned unanticipated traits.

Why Differentiate Between Positive and Negative Descriptors?

As indicated previously, the characteristics mentioned by parents were also coded as High, Low, or Neutral on the dimensions presumably underlying the categories (see + and − signs in Table 1.1). High or Low can at times be thought of as Positive or Negative as on many dimensions the positive pole can be thought of as the more desirable. Care must be exercised here: Many of these high and low distinctions might be somewhat arbitrary and not isomorphic with evaluation. At times, High might mean more of a (hypothetical) dimension and Low less of one. For example, children described as active (IC+) could be considered by their parents and teachers as being too active (amount), or their activity could be a positively valued trait. Thus the coding generally means positively valued or negatively valued, with some caveats and ambiguities remaining for some phrases.

For all categories separately and for the total of all characteristics together, the percentages of Negative and Positive characteristics were computed. Some teams also distinguished a Neutral category for cases in which it could not be decided from the context of the interview whether the descriptor was high or low on the hypothetical dimension.

Categories differed widely in the proportions of Negative codes. Category IV (Emotional Stability or Instability) received the most. About 75% of all characteristics mentioned by parents and coded in this category referred to emotional instability and neurotic behavior. At the other extreme, descriptors in Category V (Openness to Experience) were coded as negative only about 5% of the time. In later chapters we also document some considerable category differences in the negative–positive ratio by country.

Differences in the Conceptual Span or Width of the Categories

In this book, we report large differences in proportions over categories. Although we could say that these differences reflect dissimilarities in how broadly we defined the various categories, we favor another more interesting explanation: that the differences among categories reflect the salience of these dimensions for parents when they talked about their children. Because what was coded were sentences (or parts of sentences), we can rule out the explanation of frequency of personality words in the lexicon as the major reason for differential use of the categories. Frequency of use mostly reflects saliency, which is in part due to the behavioral frequencies of these dimensions in the children as well as the cultural values emphasizing some categories over others.

Important differences in contents of descriptions also surely have to do with the ages of the children described. For instance, in Conscientiousness, the proportions of descriptors suddenly increased when the children went to school. This sort of difference is certainly not dependent on either width of categories or availability of words in the lexicon, but rather on the developmental saliency and relevance of the behavioral characteristics (for parents) for children at different ages. Chapter 7 is devoted to analyzing the age trends found in the seven countries.

Training of Coders and Coding Reliability

Intensive communication among the coding teams has helped to find solutions to most of the discrepancies and uncertainties encountered in coding the verbal protocols. After training, coders' agreement over the 14 main categories was between 80% and 90%. When the agreement over the 15 subcategories in the first five (Big Five) main categories was also analyzed, reliabilities ranged between 70% and 80%. In the Appendix, more detailed information is given about the interjudge reliability of the coding procedure.

Samples Involved

Throughout this book, the samples are designated with the names of the countries in which they were collected. This does not mean that we assumed that our samples were in any way representative of the populations of these countries. In the Appendix, a demographic description of each sample is given.

In five of the seven countries, parents were interviewed in their homes, sometimes separately, sometimes with others present. In Poland, parents were interviewed in a room of the school attended by their children. In the United States, parents were interviewed separately in a number of settings, including day-care centers, schoolrooms, rooms where parents had come to register their children for various activities, and several other settings outside the home. Because the samples can be grouped by whether the interviews were done inside or outside the home, some results obtained with the five inside-the-home samples are grouped together from west to east, beginning in Europe: Belgium, Netherlands, Germany, Greece, and China. The two outside-the-home samples were grouped together when reporting some analyses. In the Appendix, the samples sizes are described in each country, separately for the four age groups, and divided by gender. The number of child descriptions varied from 193 (Netherlands) to 427 (Belgium). About equal numbers of boys and girls were described. In Belgium and the United States, somewhat more girls were described, and in China somewhat more boys. Overall, many more mothers than fathers were accessible to describe their children. Because in some samples both mothers and fathers were asked to describe the same child and because one parent might have been asked to describe more than one child, the totals for parents interviewed and children described as presented in the Appendix do not always correspond.

SOME GENERAL RESULTS

Number of Descriptors per Interview and Breadth of Coverage

The interviews varied considerably in length as operationalized by the number of descriptors that could be coded from the interview protocols. In Table 1.2, the means and variances for the seven samples are presented. These samples form three groups, according to the average number of descriptors coded: Germany; Belgium, Greece, and the Netherlands; and Poland, China, and the United States. In each of these groups, there were no significant differences in length. All sample comparisons *between* countries in the three groups were significantly different from each other (analysis of variance with Scheffé test; $p < .05$).

Methodologically, we expected that the length of an interview would be modestly correlated with the number of categories that parents mentioned at least once during the interview. Computed over the first five categories, the average correlation was .54 ($p < .01$), with correlations ranging from .41 to .62 for the different samples. We also analyzed the relation between length of interview and frequency of codes in each category. It might be expected that our largest categories, like I, II, and V, would be mentioned earlier and more often in the interviews and that shorter interviews would be biased against the less frequently coded dimensions. For example, if a parent said only a few things, there could be a systematic bias against categories that came only later in longer interviews, like negative or infrequent descriptors or both. Our analyses, however, revealed no consistent relation between length and category frequency in any country. Correlations were all near zero for each category, whether coded as positive or negative. Thus, length of interview

TABLE 1.2
Mean Number of Descriptors Given by Parents in Seven Countries

	Germany	Belgium	Greece	Netherlands	Poland	China	U.S.A.
M	37.1	22.5	21.2	20.7	12.7	11.1	10.8
SD	14.7	10.4	11.3	10.0	7.3	4.2	4.8

had no systematic effect on the differences in category frequencies in or between countries.

Table 1.2 shows that German parents on average produced more than three times as many descriptors as did Chinese parents and significantly more than any other country in our study. Although both German and Chinese interviews were conducted in the home, these robust and large differences indicated that other factors, including cultural ones, combined to determine interview length. Some of the U.S. interviews were not considered long enough for the analyses used in this book. Some parents used a very limited range of categories. To prevent possible distorting influences of one- or two-category interviews, the U.S. team selected those interviews that had at least one descriptor coded in at least three of the first five main categories. For the other samples no such selection procedure was used.

Proportions of Descriptors Over the 5 + 9 Main Categories of the Coding Scheme

In this research program, two alternative methods of computing proportions were used. Method 1 used as a base all coded descriptors for a sample. This total, over all subjects, constituted 100%. Individual categories were then computed as a percentage of the total. For example, in the Belgian sample, a total of 9,607 descriptors was obtained, and 27% of this total was coded in Category I, Extraversion. Method 2 used the individual as the unit of analysis. Each person's proportions for the categories summed to 100%. This method allowed us to compute mean proportions and variances for each category between and in countries and also allowed us to examine the magnitude of differences with ANOVA and MANOVA. To compensate for skewness of distributions (many parents had zero entries in the smaller categories), arcsine transformations were used when tests of significance were applied to the data. In Table 1.3, Method 1 average proportions are shown for the main categories for all seven samples.

These two methods necessarily yield identical marginal totals except for the small deviations in Method 2 produced by rounding at the individual level. In some of the earlier publications on this project, Method

TABLE 1.3
Proportions of Descriptors Categorized in Main Categories of Coding Scheme:
Average Proportions Over All Individual Descriptions

		Belgium	Netherlands	Germany	Greece	China	Poland	U.S.A.
N of child descriptions		427	322	246	459	401	359	202
N of descriptors		9,607	6,660	9,135	9,744	4,458	4,567	2,184
		%	%	%	%	%	%	%
I.	Extraversion	27.7	28.5	29.9	25.0	27.2	29.7	29.5
II.	Agreeableness	19.6	18.9	21.3	25.5	17.4	23.7	17.8
III.	Conscientiousness	7.9	6.8	8.3	10.7	19.4	8.1	7.3
IV.	Emotional Stability	9.2	9.9	8.0	8.7	7.1	8.4	8.6
V.	Openness, Intellect	12.6	12.2	17.6	11.1	14.1	11.5	21.2
VI.	Independence	3.5	3.9	2.4	1.3	5.9	2.8	1.2
VII.	Mature for Age	2.4	3.0	1.8	1.8	1.4	1.5	1.6
VIII.	Illness, Health	0.6	0.8	0.3	0.2	1.2	1.6	0.8
IX.	Rhythmicity	0.8	1.0	0.1	0.7	0.5	0.7	0.2
X.	Gender Appropriate	0.9	1.3	1.8	1.6	0.4	1.0	2.5
XI.	School Performance	4.3	3.8	2.2	3.6	2.0	3.0	2.8
XII.	Contact Comfort	1.7	1.1	0.2	1.0	0.0	0.5	0.5
XIII.	Family Relations	4.3	3.6	4.4	6.0	0.3	3.6	2.0
XIV.	Ambiguous	4.5	5.3	1.7	2.6	3.2	3.9	4.0

1 was used (Kohnstamm, Halverson, Havill, & Mervielde, 1996; Kohnstamm, Mervielde, Besevegis, & Halverson, 1995). Where there are differences between the data presented here and those published earlier, however, they mostly arise from differences in sample size and sample composition, rather than from method of computation.

An overview of Method 1 proportions presented in Table 1.3 shows the following trends:

1. The vast majority of descriptors in all countries were coded in the first five categories, corresponding to the Big Five personality factors in the adult literature.

2. Extraversion received the most descriptors in all samples. There was a remarkable consistency across samples.

3. Two other categories, Agreeableness (II) and Openness and Intellect (V), also received large proportions of descriptors. The proportional use of these two categories varied by country (see chapters 2 and 5 for specific analyses).

4. The proportions coded in the categories of Conscientiousness (III) and Emotional Stability (IV) were both of intermediate size, only exceeding 10% in some samples. A notable exception was the large proportion of Conscientiousness descriptors in the Chinese sample (see chapter 4). Consistency across countries was high for these two dimensions.

5. The best filled categories in the group of small categories invented specifically for children's characteristics were Independence (VI), School Performance (XI), Family Relations (XIII), and Ambiguous (XIV).

6. Rhythmicity (IX), well known from the Thomas–Chess scheme of temperament dimensions, received only 1% or less of the descriptors.

7. An analysis of the consistency of use of the Ambiguous (XIV) category indicated some differences among coding teams. Largest differences were only between 3% and 4% (for the Dutch and German teams).

Overall, the similarities in proportions among the seven samples strike us more than the differences do. The concordance in results presented in Table 1.3 is remarkable when taking into consideration the large cultural and language differences between the samples involved; the different settings in which the interviews were held; the different coding teams working independently; the large differences in interview length and resulting numbers of descriptors. We had not expected such a concordance when we started this project.

TABLE 1.4
Average Proportions (Rounded) of Descriptors Coded
as Positive, Neutral, and Negative in Seven Countries[a]

	Belgium	Netherlands	Germany	Greece	China	Poland	U.S.A.
Positive	64	65	67	67	58	68	77
Neutral	7	4	—	—	—	—	2
Negative	30	30	33	33	42	32	21

[a]Computed over Categories I through XIII, excluding XIV (Ambiguous Phrases).

Descriptors Coded as Positive, Neutral, and Negative

As explained earlier, descriptors were also coded as at either the high or
the low end of each dimension that presumably underlies each category
and associated facets. In Table 1.4, it can be seen that only three of the
seven coding teams used a Neutral code. The Belgian team used this
coding option most. The varied use of the Neutral coding category makes
it hazardous to compare the proportions of positive and negative codings
over samples. A preliminary comparison can be done, however, by dividing the Neutral codes equally between Positive and Negative descriptors in those countries using the Neutral code and then comparing the
use of Positive and Negative descriptors with the Neutral category controlled for. When this procedure is done, it seems that a group of European
countries use the Negative code moderately, with proportions ranging
between 32% and 33%. The United States was lowest and China the
highest in the use of Negative coding categories.

In the next five chapters, the results obtained with codings in the five
main categories are analyzed in more detail.

REFERENCES

Angleitner, A., & Ostendorf, F. (1994). Temperament and the Big Five Factors of Personality.
    In G. A. Kohnstamm, C. F. Halverson, & R. P. Martin (Eds.), *The developing structure of
    temperament and personality from infancy to adulthood* (pp. 69–90). Hillsdale, NJ: Lawrence
    Erlbaum Associates.
Bates, J. E., Freeland, C. A. B., & Lounsbury, M. L. (1979). Measurement of infant difficultness.
    Child Development, 50, 794–803.
Carey, W. B., & McDevitt, S. C. (1978). Revision of the Infant Temperament Questionnaire.
    Pediatrics, 61, 735–739.
Church, A. T., & Katigbak, M. S. (1989). Internal, external and self-reward structure of
    personality in non-Western culture: An investigation of cross-language and cross-cultural
    generalizability. *Journal of Personality and Social Psychology, 57,* 857–872.

Church, A. T., Katigbak, M. S., & Castaneda, I. (1988). The effects of language of data collection on derived conceptions of healthy personality with Filipino bilinguals. *Journal of Cross-Cultural Psychology, 19,* 178–192.

Costa, P. T., & McCrae, R. R. (1988). Personality in adulthood: A 6-year longitudinal study of self-reports and spouse ratings on the NEO Personality Inventory. *Journal of Personality and Social Psychology, 54,* 116–123.

Digman, J. M. (1963). Principal dimensions of child personality as inferred from teachers' judgments. *Child Development, 34,* 43–60.

Digman, J. M. (1990). Personality structure: Emergence of the five-factor model. In M. R. Rosenzweig & L. W. Porter (Eds.), *Annual Review of Psychology* (Vol. 41, pp. 417–440). Palo Alto, CA: Annual Reviews.

Digman, J. M., & Inouye, J. (1986). Further specification of the five robust factors of personality. *Journal of Personality and Social Psychology, 50,* 116–123.

Eysenck, H. J., & Eysenck, S. B. G. (1975). Manual of the Eysenck Personality Questionnaire. Loughton, Essex, England: Hodder & Stoughton.

John, O. P. (1990a). The "Big Five" factor taxonomy: Dimensions of personality in the natural language and in questionnaires. In L. A. Pervin (Ed.), *Handbook of personality: Theory and research* (pp. 66–100). New York: Guilford Press.

John, O. P. (1990b). Towards a taxonomy of personality descriptors. In D. M. Buss & N. Cantor (Eds.), *Personality psychology: Recent trends and emerging directions* (pp. 261–271). New York: Springer Verlag.

Kohnstamm, G. A., Halverson, C. F., Jr., Havill, V. L., & Mervielde, I. (1996). Parents' free descriptions of child characteristics: A cross-cultural search for the developmental antecedents of the Big Five. In S. Harkness & C. M. Super (Eds.), *Parents' cultural belief systems: Cultural origins and developmental consequences* (pp. 27–55). New York: Guilford Press.

Kohnstamm, G. A., Mervielde, I., Besevegis, E., & Halverson, C. F., Jr. (1995). Tracing the Big Five in parents' free descriptions of their children. *European Journal of Personality, 9,* 283–304.

Lanning, K. (1994). Dimensionality of observer ratings on the California Adult Q-set. *Journal of Personality and Social Psychology, 67,* 151–160.

Malpass, R. S., & Poortinga, Y. H. (1986). Strategies for design and analysis. In W. J. Lonner & J. W. Berry (Eds.), *Field methods in cross-cultural research* (pp. 47–86). Beverly Hills, CA: Sage.

Martin, R. P., Wisenbaker, J., & Huttunen, M. (1994). Review of factor analytic studies of temperament measures based on the Thomas–Chess structural model: Implications for the Big-Five. In C. F. Halverson, Jr., G. A. Kohnstamm, & R. P. Martin (Eds.), *The developing structure of temperament and personality from infancy to adulthood* (pp. 157–172). Hillsdale, NJ: Lawrence Erlbaum Associates.

McDevitt, S. C., & Carey, W. B. (1978). The measurement of temperament in 3- to 7-year old children. *Journal of Child Psychology and Psychiatry, 19,* 245–253.

Shwalb, B. J., Shwalb, D. W., & Shoji, J. (1994). Structure and dimensions of maternal perceptions of Japanese infant temperament. *Developmental Psychology, 30,* 131–141.

Thomas, A., & Chess, S. (1977). *Temperament and development.* New York: Brunner/Mazel.

Windle, M., & Lerner, R. M. (1986). Reassessing the dimensions of temperament individuality across the life span: The Revised Dimensions of Temperament Survey (DOTS-R). *Journal of Adolescent Research, 1,* 213–230.

2

Extraversion: Toward a Unifying Description From Infancy to Adulthood

Eric Elphick
Leiden University

Charles F. Halverson, Jr.
University of Georgia

Magdalena Marszal-Wisniewska
Polish Academy of Sciences

Extraversion is clearly one of the core concepts of trait psychology. Some form of the Extraversion dimension can be found in *all* widely used multidimensional personality scales. Further, the concepts of extraversion can usually be recovered in one form or another from temperament scales and inventories not specifically designed to measure personality directly, such as those designed to measure behavioral dysfunction. An examination of the literature over the past 75 years reveals that Extraversion is central to the complete description of adult personality.

The history of the extraversion construct can be traced back to the writings of Hippocrates, who enunciated the Greco-Roman belief in the balance of four humors that produced inner dispositions that, in turn, caused differences in the emotions and behavior. In the 2nd century, Galen, a Greek physician, expanded the notions of the Greeks and Romans and derived four temperamental types that resulted in the excess of one of the four humors. For our purposes, two of the types map directly onto 20th-century conceptions of extraversion and introversion. The first type, characterized by an excess of black bile, was the *melancholic*, the modern-day introvert. The second type was characterized by an excess of blood, hence called the *sanguine* type, and was the early characterization of the modern-day extravert.

In this brief chapter, we cannot review the detailed history of the Extraversion construct from Galen to the present century. Suffice it to say that a number of theorists (e.g., Bain, 1861; Stewart, 1887) described the concept of Extraversion in various guises in the 19th century. Indeed, even Freud (see Diamond, 1957, for a discussion of the early writings on temperament and personality, including Extraversion) discussed the sanguine and melancholic types as basic "emotional types" in his theory of individual development. William James (1907) also described characterological types that can be identified with the Extraversion–Introversion typology.

The modern history of the concept of Extraversion–Introversion began with Carl G. Jung (1921), who has been commonly acknowledged as the originator of the modern personality typology (see, e.g., Carrigan, 1960; Guilford & Braley, 1930; Hildebrand, 1970; Zuckerman, 1991). For Jung, Extraversion was defined as "an outward turning of libido denoting a manifest relatedness of subject to object in the sense of a positive movement of subjective interest towards the object" and Introversion as "a turning inward of the libido whereby a negative relation of the subject to the object is expressed" (Jung, 1921, p. 543). In Jung's theory, extraversion and introversion were not really personality traits but were instead enduring orientations toward the world, with introverts being directed inward toward subjective experience and extraverts directed outward toward other people and the world around them.

In the 1930s, Jung's personality typology elicited much research focused on characterizing the multidimensionality of Extraversion and linking Extraversion with physiological processes and various perceptual and cognitive dimensions (see Carrigan, 1960; Guilford & Braley, 1930). During this period, many instruments were developed to measure both Extraversion and Introversion (see, e.g., Gilliland, 1970). For example, J. P. Guilford and R. B. Guilford (1934, 1936) used the then new technique of factor analysis to organize Extraversion–Introversion items into facets of sociability, impulsivity, and masculinity–femininity, among others.

H. J. Eysenck's model of Extraversion flowed directly from the early work of the Guilfords. The Maudsley Personality Inventory (H. J. Eysenck, 1958) contained Eysenck's original Extraversion scale that was built from items earlier used by the Guilfords in their Guilford–Zimmerman Temperament Survey (1949) and featured aspects of both sociability and impulsivity.

In the rest of this chapter, we concentrate on the various conceptualizations and operationalizations of Extraversion. Although there has been extensive theorizing about the psychobiological nature of Extraversion (see, e.g., H. J. Eysenck & M. W. Eysenck, 1985; Zuckerman, 1991), we focus only on phenotypic personality. First, we discuss several conceptualizations developed on the basis of studies of adult personality. Second, we discuss concepts from infancy and childhood literature with implications for the Extraversion construct. We conclude with a description of

Extraversion that is based on parental free descriptions of their children's personalities, descriptions obtained in seven different countries.

CONCEPTIONS OF ADULT EXTRAVERSION

In the 1940s and 1950s, the number of researchers investigating Extraversion (or closely related concepts) increased rapidly. It is beyond the scope of this chapter to give an exhaustive review of all these studies. Instead, we focus on three adult personality taxonomies. Each taxonomy is touted as completely covering the personality domain. Each differs, however, in the number of personality dimensions believed necessary to describe all personality traits.

Cattell's Model

Working separately from early theorists like Eysenck and Guilford, Cattell was one of the main proponents of the trait approach to personality. Cattell was convinced that the discovery of the major dimensions of personality embodied in the natural language would lead to a comprehensive model of personality structure. Beginning with Allport and Odbert's (1936) effort to compile a complete list of trait-related terms in the English language, Cattell applied various selection procedures that enabled him to use a pool of 35 clusters. These 35 clusters were assumed to give a comprehensive summary of the whole domain of personality differences. (For an extensive review of the selection procedures applied by Cattell, see John, Angleitner, & Ostendorf, 1988.)

Using this 35-variable list, Cattell conducted a series of factorial studies that culminated in his structural model of personality (John et al., 1988). The structural model contained eight second-order factors and 16 primary factors. The first second-order factor (in Questionnaire data or Q data) mentioned by Cattell (1957) was labeled Extraversion versus Introversion, or as Cattell would probably prefer, Exvia versus Invia. Before his 1957 model, Cattell did not seem to be convinced of the need for a concept of extraversion-introversion as a unitary trait. Based on repeated experiments that showed a clear, second-order simple structure factor among the Q data, he commented:

> With this possibility of defining extraversion-introversion, as a unique second-order factor, instead of as a rough correlation cluster or a vaguely conceived mixture of the personality primaries—surgency, cyclothymia, and parmia—it is perhaps worthwhile to make a determined attempt to rescue the label "extravert-vs-introvert" from the scientific disrepute and useless-

ness into which it has fallen through popular adoption. (Cattell, 1957, p. 267)

Repeated factor analyses of Cattell's 16PF (Cattell, Eber, & Tatsuoka, 1980) have, for the most part, rather consistently confirmed that Extraversion is a higher order dimension composed of primary traits describing extraverted individuals as warmhearted and easygoing (A), dominant (E), enthusiastic (F), bold (H), and socially connected (Q_2), while introverted individuals were described as being reserved, submissive, taciturn, shy, and timid.

Eysenck's Model

H. J. Eysenck has been another major advocate of a trait approach to personality. The personality taxonomy developed by Eysenck was not, however, based on an analysis of the "personality" language as was Cattell's. Eysenck has argued that the analysis of the natural language of trait description is not able to yield conclusive evidence about basic personality dimensions (H. J. Eysenck, 1994). Although he has often stressed the need to base his constructs on some version of "psychobiology" (H. J. Eysenck, 1994), the construction of his personality measures has relied largely on earlier empirical work on personality, mostly that of the Guilfords. In 1958 Eysenck first published the Maudsley Personality Inventory (MPI), which was designed to measure the personality dimensions that Eysenck himself judged important: Neuroticism (N, or emotionality) and Extraversion (E). The development of the Eysenckian Extraversion–Introversion scale started with an item pool from the Guilford inventories (see H. J. Eysenck, 1977; Guilford, 1975), which were (according to North, 1948) based in turn on a list of descriptive sentences compiled by Freyd (1924). The Extraversion scale in the MPI was composed of 12 R items, 10 S items, 1 A item, and 1 G item. In Table 2.1, we summarize the Guilford scales R, S, A, and G, which were Eysenck's original Extraversion scale. After a number of modifications, the MPI was given a new name: the Eysenck Personality Inventory (EPI). Like the MPI, the EPI set out to measure Eysenck's favorite two dimensions of personality, E and N (S. B. Eysenck, 1965).

A "final" revision of his questionnaire, named the Eysenck Personality Questionnaire (EPQ), included a scale to measure Psychoticism (H. J. Eysenck & S. B. Eysenck, 1975). The creation of the Psychoticism scale had consequences for Eysenck's version of Extraversion. The earlier EPI Extraversion scale contained elements of both sociability and impulsivity. Attempting to maintain orthogonality among the three scales of Extraversion, Neuroticism, and Psychoticism, Eysenck discarded some items

TABLE 2.1
Description of Traits of Guilford–Zimmerman
Temperament Survey Involved in MPI

Symbol	Name and Definition
R	Restraint and seriousness versus rhathymia and impulsiveness
S	Sociability and social interest versus seclusiveness and shyness
A	Ascendance and social boldness versus submissiveness and timidity
G	General activity versus slowness and lack of energy

and reassigned others to other scales (based on their changing primary loadings). Zuckerman (1991) concluded: "The result has been that the new Extraversion scale is almost entirely composed of sociability type items. The impulsivity items have either gravitated to the new psychoticism scale or been dropped" (Zuckerman, 1991, p. 12).

The traits making up the most recent Eysenckian concept of Extraversion are Sociable, Lively, Active, Assertive, Sensation Seeking, Carefree, Dominant, Surgent, and Venturesome (H. J. Eysenck & M. W. Eysenck, 1985, p. 15).

The Big Five Model

The subtle and sometimes not-so-subtle differences in the various meanings of extraversion documented thus far are typical for the whole field of personality psychology. As John pointed out: "Researchers, as well as practitioners in the field of personality assessment are faced with a bewildering array of personality scales from which to choose, with little guidance and no overall rationale at hand" (John, 1990, p. 66). Such a state of affairs impedes progress partly because of a lack of accumulation of solid empirical findings based on a shared taxonomy. Recent efforts to resolve this problem have guided researchers toward a descriptive taxonomy that appears capable of representing the many different personality theories currently in use. Such a taxonomic structure, gaining quickly in common acceptance, has become known as the Big Five-Factor Model (FFM).[1] Like Cattell's taxonomy, the Big Five Model is derived from analyses of the natural-language terms that people use to describe themselves and others. In the following section, we briefly describe the major proponents and researchers of this model and the taxonomic structures they have created. Almost all the research endeavors started from natural language as the most comprehensive pool of personality descrip-

---

[1]We are aware of the distinction between the "Big Five" personality model (see, e.g., Goldberg & Saucier, 1995) and the "Five-Factor Model" of personality (see, e.g., Costa & McCrae, 1995). In this chapter, however, both terms are used interchangeably.

tors. (For an extensive historical review of the development of the Big Five Model, see John, 1990; John, Angleitner, & Ostendorf, 1988.)

The Early Big Five Attempts

Tupes and Christal are commonly described as the originators of the Big Five structure, also known as the FFM (see Goldberg, 1993). They conducted now-classic studies in which they analyzed the intercorrelations among trait-ratings on the 35 personality-descriptive bipolar adjectives selected earlier by Cattell as traits representative of the whole personality domain. (Actually, Tupes and Christal did not use Cattell's original variables, but instead used abbreviated Cattell scales.) Five robust and recurrent factors emerged from each of their eight analyses. In every analysis they conducted, a factor they labeled as Surgency emerged. The nine adjective pairs describing Surgency were Silent versus Talkative, Secretive versus Frank, Cautious versus Adventurous, Submissive versus Assertive, Self-Contained versus Sociable, Languid or Slow versus Energetic, Shy or Bashful versus Composed, Slight versus Marked Interest in Opposite Sex, and Depressed versus Cheerful.

Norman conducted four peer nomination studies (Norman, 1963) in which he attempted to replicate the five-factor structure found in the Tupes and Christal studies. Norman selected four scales with the highest median factor loadings for each of the five factors found by Tupes and Christal (1961/1992). They are summarized in Table 2.2.

Norman found clear evidence for the existence of five relatively orthogonal, interpretable personality factors. He seemed to be impressed by the replicability of the FFM structure, but did not believe that his FFM was an *adequate* taxonomy of personality attributes. Norman quoted Tupes and Christal about the comprehensiveness of the five-factor structure: "It is unlikely that the five factors are the *only* fundamental personality factors. There are quite likely other fundamental concepts involved among the Allport–Odbert adjectives on which the variables used in the present study were based [p. 12]" (Norman, 1963, pp. 581–582).

Following the Tupes and Christal critical note, Norman investigated the structure of a more comprehensive set of personality terms that were based on 2,800 trait terms distilled from several unabridged English dictionaries. Norman asked university students to provide for each term a definition, its social desirability, and one self-rating and three peer ratings. On the basis of this information, he reduced the original set of 2,800 trait terms to 1,431 terms, which were then classified by Norman himself into 75 categories based on *his* understanding of the similarity in meaning of these terms. In Table 2.3 we summarize examples of Norman's trait adjectives for Extraversion or Surgency.

TABLE 2.2
Personality Descriptive Marker Scales for Factor of Extraversion
in Norman's Peer Nomination Studies (1963) and Their
Averaged Factor Loadings From Two Independent Samples

Silent, Introspective	*vs.*	*Talkative*	*Loading*
Says very little; gives the impression of being introspective and occupied with thoughts.		Talks a lot, to everybody.	.90
Frank, Expressive	*vs.*	*Secretive, Reserved*	*Loading*
Readily expresses his or her real feelings on various questions, so that others know where they stand.		Keeps thoughts and feelings to her- or himself. Often leaves others puzzled about the motives for his or her actions. Inscrutable.	.78
Cautious, Retiring, Timid	*vs.*	*Adventurous, Bold*	*Loading*
Avoids the strange and new. Looks at all aspects of a situation overcautiously. Keeps clear of difficulties. Uninquiring, lacking in desire to try new things.		Rushes in carefree fashion into new experiences, situations, emergencies. Ascendant: ready to meet anything. Happy-go-lucky. Has a great appetite for life.	.79
Gregarious, Sociable	*vs.*	*Self-Contained*	*Loading*
Likes to be in large groups. Seeks people for the sake of company. Likes parties as often as possible. Not fond of being alone.		Does not seem to miss others' company. Goes own way.	.88

Although Norman compiled this "new" comprehensive list of trait adjectives, he never tested whether other fundamental personality factors beyond the Big Five could be discerned. Not until Goldberg (1990) attempted to demonstrate the generality of the FFM was the 75-category Norman taxonomy put to a rigorous empirical test. Goldberg used several factor analytic algorithms to investigate the robustness of the factorial structures. He found considerable support for the FFM when using Norman's 75 categories. None of the different factor analytic procedures Goldberg employed led to any substantial change in the FFM structure.

Goldberg, however, noted two disadvantages to using Norman's 75 categories. First, the 1,431 terms in Norman's taxonomy made it practically impossible to administer the list in a single testing session, and second,

TABLE 2.3
Extraversion Categories in Norman's Taxonomy
of 1,431 Trait-Descriptive Adjectives

Factor Pole	Trait Adjectives	Total Number of Adjectives
I+		
Spirit	Jolly, merry, witty, lively, peppy	26
Talkativeness	Talkative, articulate, verbose, gossipy	23
Sociability	Companionable, social, outgoing	9
Spontaneity	Impulsive, carefree, playful, zany	28
Boisterousness	Mischievous, rowdy, loud, prankish	11
Adventure	Brave, venturous, fearless, reckless	44
Energy	Active, assertive, dominant, energetic	36
Conceit	Boastful, conceited, egotistical	13
Vanity	Affected, vain, chic, dapper, jaunty	5
Indiscretion	Nosy, snoopy, indiscreet, meddlesome	6
Sensuality	Sexy, passionate, sensual, flirtatious	12
I–		
Lethargy	Reserved, lethargic, vigorless, apathetic	19
Aloofness	Cool, aloof, distant, unsocial, withdrawn	26
Silence	Quiet, secretive, untalkative, indirect	22
Modesty	Humble, modest, bashful, meek, shy	18
Pessimism	Joyless, solemn, sober, morose, moody	19
Unfriendliness	Tactless, thoughtless, unfriendly	20

Note. From "An Alternative 'Description of Personality' . . . ," by L. R. Goldberg, 1990, *Journal of Personality and Social Psychology, 59*(6), p. 1218. Copyright 1990 by ADA. Reprinted with permission.

the classification of the 1,431 trait-descriptive adjectives was made only by Norman himself. Goldberg then provided a more objective classification of Norman's original list of 1,431 terms by reducing them to a set of 133 synonym clusters based on 479 trait adjectives (for more details on the classification, see Goldberg, 1990). These 133 synonym clusters were further refined by internal-consistency analysis into a set of 100 clusters derived from 339 trait adjectives, and the set is still remarkably similar to Norman's original list of adjectives for Extraversion (see Goldberg & Rosolack, 1994, for the list of adjectives).

Costa and McCrae did not rely on the lexical approach to develop their version of the FFM but instead developed their model in the context of their ongoing studies of personality and aging. They have become two of the most cited proponents of the FFM. McCrae and Costa described Extraversion as a trait that concerns differences in preference for social interaction and lively activity. They argued that distinctions can be made among six facets of Extraversion, which can be grouped into three inter-personal and three temperamental facets (McCrae & Costa, 1990). The facet scales for Extraversion were partly based on the structure and content of several inventories, including Buss and Plomin's EASI (Emotionality, Agreeableness, Sociability & Impulsivity, 1975) and items from the 16PF (Sixteen Personality Questionnaire), GZTS (Guilford Zimmerman Temperament), and EPI (Eysenck Personality Inventory).

The first facet, Warmth or Attachment, refers to a friendly, compassionate, intimately involved style of personal interaction. McCrae and Costa recognized that this facet is close in meaning to another FFM factor, Agreeableness. They argued, however, that Attachment is distinguished from Agreeableness by cordiality and warmth. Attachment and Gregariousness (the desire to be with other people) constitute the dimension of Sociability or Affiliation. The Assertive facet describes people who are natural leaders, easily taking charge, making up their own minds, and readily expressing their feelings and desires.

The three facets of Extraversion referred to as temperamental in nature are Activity, Excitement Seeking, and Positive Emotions. According to McCrae and Costa, "Extraverts like to be busy, acting vigorously and talking rapidly; they are energetic and forceful, and also prefer environments that stimulate them, often going in search of excitement. . . . The active and exciting life of extraverts is reflected emotionally in the experience of positive emotions" (McCrae & Costa, 1990, pp. 43–44).

Costa and McCrae (1994) have found in college samples that all six facets loaded positively on the Extraversion dimension. Other theorists, particularly Hogan (1983), saw compelling reasons for dividing Extraversion into two separate but related constructs. Hogan labeled these Surgency and Sociability: Surgent individuals are status seekers characterized by ambition and tenacity, while sociable individuals are friendly, expressive, and concerned about people. The complex nature of the Extraversion construct is also revealed by the controversy about the placement of the Impulsivity trait (see our discussion of Eysenck's taxonomy). It is interesting to note the positioning of this trait by McCrae and Costa. In the NEO-Personality Inventory-Revised (NEO-PI-R), McCrae and Costa placed Impulsivity in a Neuroticism facet group. Describing their Impulsiveness scale, they mentioned that in the NEO-PI-R Impulsiveness refers to the inability to control cravings and urges and should not be confused with spontaneity, risk taking, or rapid decision time (Costa & McCrae, 1992, p. 16). Others (e.g., Zuckerman, 1991) saw Impulsivity as more linked to a general sensation-seeking dimension. Similarly, Eysenck has altered his original formulation of Extraversion with its saturation of both Sociability and Impulsivity. On the basis of findings of the relative independence of Impulsivity (e.g., Zuckerman, Kuhlman, & Camac, 1988), many people have placed Impulsivity on dimensions other than those with the facets of Extraversion dealing with Sociability and Activity.

To test the generalizability of the FFM across cultures, several studies have been conducted in countries such as Germany (Ostendorf, 1990), Netherlands (Hofstee & De Raad, 1991), Hungary (Szirmák & De Raad, 1994), and Russia (Digman & Shmelyov, 1996; Shmelyov & Pokhil'ko, 1993). Although the results of these studies are interesting in their own right, we specifically want to mention the research program conducted in the Netherlands by Hofstee and colleagues.

During the 1970s, Hofstee and colleagues (Brokken, 1978; Hofstee, 1976; Hofstee & De Raad, 1991) initiated an elaborate research program aimed at the development of a trait taxonomy of individual differences based on the Dutch language. Their research efforts, conducted over almost 25 years, have resulted in a personality taxonomy based on the FFM but deviating from this model in one important aspect. According to De Raad, Hendriks, and Hofstee (1994, p. 90), the main problem with a simple structure model (like the FFM) is that the majority of trait variables can best be described by two factors. If this argument holds, a logical consequence would be that using a simple structure model leads to a disregard of a large amount of information. As an alternative to the simple structure model, they developed a model that represents all possible orthogonal dimensions of the Big Five taken two at a time to describe 10 circumplex models. In this model, named the Abridged Big Five Circumplex Model (AB5C), the trait variables are represented on the basis of their two highest factor loadings. (Specific details about the application of the AB5C principle can be found in De Raad et al., 1994.) On the basis of ratings of many people on many descriptors, De Raad et al. classified these trait descriptors (using their AB5C procedure) according to their primary and secondary loadings. In Table 2.4 the numbers of trait terms (in the Dutch language) are given for those having their primary loading on Extraversion.

From the viewpoint of a simple structure model, inspection of Table 2.4 summarizing the AB5C model of Extraversion leads to a curious conclusion: Only 14 trait terms turn out to be factor-pure trait terms (I+I+ and I–I–). In other words, out of the 222 trait terms found to have a primary loading on Extraversion, 93.7% also had a significant secondary loading on one of the other four factors of the FFM. Even more interesting is that among the 10 highest (either positive or negative) loading terms on Extraversion, only 4 terms turn out to be factor-pure trait descriptors according to the AB5C classification.

De Raad et al. therefore concluded "that a simple structure approach to personality structure is too simple to arrive at a fair, economical, and comprehensive representation of the meanings of the personality domain" (De Raad et al., 1994, p. 104). Instead, De Raad et al. argued that the AB5C system can be useful in clarifying many disputes about the nature of factors and their proper interpretations. For example, trait adjectives found to be

TABLE 2.4
AB5C Representation: Numbers of Trait Terms for Those Trait Terms
With Their Primary Loading on Extraversion

Secondary Loading	Primary Loading	
	I+	I–
I+	4	—
II+	35	3
III+	3	6
IV+	16	3
V+	22	7
I–	—	10
II–	6	21
III–	9	8
IV–	8	31
V–	1	29
Totals	104	118

Note. Adapted from "The Big Five . . . ," by B. De Raad, A. A. J. Hendriks, and W. K. B. Hofstee, 1994, in *The Developing Structure of Temperament and Personality* (pp. 101–103), by C. F. Halverson, Jr., G. A. Kohnstamm, and R. P. Martin (Eds.), 1994, Hillsdale, NJ: Lawrence Erlbaum Associates. Copyright © 1994 by Lawrence Erlbaum Associates.

factor-pure terms for the factor Extraversion (De Raad et al., 1994) are (from the Dutch) Exuberant, Spontaneous, Open, and Funny (for the positive pole); and Uncommunicative, Introverted, Difficult, Unyielding, Surly, and Impersonal (for the negative pole). The AB5C scheme also describes facets of the core meaning of Extraversion as blends of Extraversion and Agreeableness. For example, the trait adjectives Cheerful, Joyous, Sunny, Gay, High Spirited, and Pleasant have a primary loading on Extraversion and a secondary loading on Agreeableness. Thus, differences in meaning of the personality dimension Extraversion and its overlap with other Big Five dimensions found by different researchers might be explained by the measurement of different facets of this personality dimension. For example, there are *agreeable* ways to be extraverted (e.g., sociable, enthusiastic, vibrant) and *disagreeable* ways to be extraverted (rough, manipulative, gruff) in addition to "pure" extraversion or introversion.

EXTRAVERSION IN CHILDHOOD

In view of the somewhat different conceptualizations of adult Extraversion, we now briefly review what traits of children and adolescents resemble these adult conceptualizations. To make such comparisons, we review factor analytic studies of child and adolescent temperament and personality. In this review, we show how childhood factors might be conceptualized as analogous to one or more facets of adult Extraversion. We focus on infancy and childhood, including early adolescence.

With a construct as broad as Extraversion, the research done in the early part of this century is too voluminous to be easily summarized here. Many investigators (e.g., Burt, 1915; Webb, 1915) collected data on children at the same time as they did on adults. Burt (1948) used factor analysis to describe both Extraversion and Introversion in children between 9 and 13 years of age. About the same time, Cattell attempted to describe the nature of child personality using factor analytic approaches to personality description (e.g., Cattell & Coan, 1957). Digman, more than any investigator, can be thought of as a pioneer in the description of child personality. He began his program of research by reanalyzing the Cattell and Coan (1957) study (see Digman, 1963, 1965). From this work has come the most clearly articulated treatment of the FFM for child personality. Through many studies and interpretive reviews, Digman could say with confidence: "A wide sampling of rated personality characteristics of children will typically produce from five to seven factors, of which five will almost invariably be recognized as the Big Five found in adults" (1989, p. 144).

No brief history of Extraversion could be complete without mentioning the central role of the Eysencks' research. Like Cattell, the Eysencks measured Neuroticism and Extraversion with questionnaires and applied their system of E and N to children with some success (see, e.g., S. B. Eysenck, 1965; Morris, 1979).

Thomas and Chess's nine-dimensional temperament model (Thomas & Chess, 1977) inspired and stimulated many researchers trying to characterize individual differences in infancy and early childhood. Martin, Wisenbaker, and Huttunen (1994) reviewed 12 studies in which parents or teachers rated their children or pupils on questionnaires based on the nine-dimensional Chess and Thomas temperament model.

Four of these studies were factor analyses of parental ratings of infants. Martin et al. (1994) suggested that the factorial structures found across these studies could be summarized by five major dimensions that they labeled Activity Level, Negative Emotionality, Task Persistence, Adaptability-Agreeableness, and Inhibition (as well as two lesser factors that they labeled Rhythmicity and Threshold). Among the five major factors, Activity Level was most often associated with Extraversion (see our discussion of the conceptualization of Extraversion in adulthood and also, e.g., Hagekull, 1994). Martin et al. noted, however, that especially in infancy some manifestations of Activity Level were associated with arousal and negative emotional experience. Therefore, unlike the close linkage to Extraversion in adults, Activity Level in infancy might be more closely linked to negative emotionality. Martin et al. suggested that not until later in childhood might Activity Level be linked to Extraversion. We expand on the relations of Activity Level to personality later in this chapter.

A second factor in children, clearly related to adult Extraversion, has been labeled Social Inhibition by some (Garcia-Coll, Kagan, & Resnick, 1984; Martin et al., 1994) and Approach-Withdrawal by many others (e.g., Hagekull, Lindhagen, & Bohlin, 1980; McClowry, Hegvik, & Teglasi, 1993). This discovery reflects the empirical findings that social approach and withdrawal consistently load on the same factor in the many studies of the factor structure obtained in infants and young children.

Rothbart and her associates have often related temperament in childhood to the Big Five (Ahadi & Rothbart, 1994; Rothbart, 1989; Rothbart & Ahadi, 1994). Focusing on Extraversion (Rothbart used the labels Extraversion, Surgency, and Positive Emotionality), she proposed that infant positive affect and approach would be the most likely developmental precursors of later Extraversion. Her focus on approach and positive affect has clear parallels with the theorizing of Tellegen (1985) and particularly of Watson and Clark (1997) who speculated that the core of extraversion throughout life can be characterized as affect, specifically as positive affect, which might be a good candidate to link the facets of extraversion like enthusiasm, joy, energy, and other terms connoting warm and affiliative emotion.

Buss and Plomin (1984) have suggested that Extraversion is a combination of Sociability and Shyness with impulsivity playing only a minor role. For Buss and Plomin, the Impulsivity factor typically found among Extraversion items should more properly be called Liveliness (recall our remarks about Eysenck's conceptualization of Extraversion and the shifting role of Impulsivity). For Buss and Plomin, Impulsivity is not a unitary trait, and thus they dropped the construct of Impulsivity as a basic aspect of temperament. In view of their belief that Impulsivity is more properly called Liveliness, it is not surprising that they did not mention their third personality trait, Activity, when they discussed the constituents of Extraversion. In relation, however, to the adult Extraversion scales already discussed (see, e.g., Eysenck [Active], Cattell [Languid, Slow versus Energetic], Norman [Energy], Goldberg [Energy Level], and McCrae and Costa [Activity]), it seems likely that Activity assessed in infancy and childhood is linked to Extraversion in adulthood. This suggestion has also been made by several researchers (see, e.g., Eaton, 1994; Hagekull, 1994; Martin et al., 1994). Rothbart and her associates have consistently recovered three broad factors in scale-level analyses of the Children's Behavior Questionnaire (CBQ), for children between 3 and 8 years old (Rothbart & Ahadi, 1994). One of these factors, labeled Surgency or Extraversion, was defined primarily by the CBQ scales of Approach, High-Intensity Pleasure, Activity Level, Impulsivity, and Shyness.

Using a simplified version of the California Child Q-sort (CCQ), John, Caspi, Robins, Moffitt, and Stouthamer-Loeber (1994) analyzed 350 mothers' descriptions of their 12- to 13-year-old sons. The CCQ was constructed to provide comprehensive descriptions of children's personalities. Developing the CCQ, "Block [who originally developed the CCQ] sought to devise a generally applicable, *clinically* based language for describing all important aspects of personality" (John, 1990, p. 82). Using Block's choice of content domain (that is, clinically relevant personality descriptions), John et al. (1994) set out to explore whether the Big Five structure could be recaptured from the CCQ. They first constructed preliminary scales guided by consensual definitions of the Big Five dimensions in adulthood and ended with 48 CCQ items assigned to the final Big Five scales (John et al., 1994, p. 166). Submitting the descriptions of the 350 mothers on all 100 CCQ items to principal component analysis resulted in a seven-factor solution.

To aid in the interpretation, the empirical factors were then correlated with the rationally constructed Big Five scales. The third factor correlated .87 with the Extraversion scale constructed by John et al. (1994). The content of the items loading on the third factor referred primarily to elements of Sociability and Expressiveness and was interpreted as Sociability, which can be described as a more narrow version of Extraversion that lacks any reference to Energy and Activity Level. The researchers also found a sixth factor correlated with their Extraversion scale ($r = .26$). This factor included many of the Extraversion items missing from the third factor labeled Sociability. On the basis of the content of the items, such as Energy, Activity Level, and Social Presence, they labeled this factor Positive Activity (or Approach). John et al. concluded that the broad construct of Extraversion typically found in adults was represented by two factors, Sociability and Activity, in young adolescents (see also Buss & Plomin, 1975). They suggested that "it is possible that Sociability and Activity, being distinct in early adolescence, may continue to be integrated in later development into the adult trait of Extraversion, which contains both Sociability and Activity" (John et al., 1994, p. 173).

In the Netherlands, van Lieshout and Haselager (1994) factored a Dutch version of the CCQ, with 720 children and adolescents described by parents, teachers, and, in the case of adolescents, with self- and peer descriptions. They obtained an Extraversion factor that was very similar to the U.S. Extraversion factor reported by John et al. (1994). Out of the nine high-loading scales in the United States, the Dutch factor was the same on six scales. The difference arose primarily because in the Dutch analysis the Activity Level items formed a factor separate from Extraversion.

To summarize and synthesize the conceptualizations of Extraversion described in this chapter are complex tasks. Summarizing across different levels of abstraction in the relevant literature (item, scale, and even factor level) mitigated against concise results. Therefore, in this section we do not focus on the ample overlap in the areas of High Approach and Pleasure. Instead, we highlight three constructs that still arouse controversy about whether they are constituents of an Extraversion construct. Those constructs are Impulsivity, Shyness or Inhibition, and Activity.

Impulsivity

There appears to be little agreement among different measures of Impulsivity. For example, White, Moffitt, Caspi, Bartusch, Needles, and Stouthamer-Loeber (1994) noted: "Personality researchers assume that impulsivity is an enduring dimension of behavior that is manifest in distractibility, high levels of behavioral activity, an inability to delay gratifications, short-lived interpersonal relationships, and anti-social behavior" (White et al., 1994, p. 194). The concept of Impulsivity thus seems to be implicated in at least three of the Big Five factors: Extraversion, Conscientiousness, and Neuroticism. In a study conducted by Angleitner and Ostendorf (1994), even a fourth factor of the FFM appeared to be related to Impulsivity. Analyzing *adult* temperament and personality scales, they found that the different scales of Impulsivity, as measured by the EASI, had their highest loadings respectively on Neuroticism (Noninhibition Control), Openness to Experience (Short Decision Time and Sensation Seeking), and Conscientiousness (Nonpersistence). Trying to resolve this problem by limiting the meaning attached to the construct of Impulsivity (like Costa & McCrae, 1992) has proved inconclusive. Costa and McCrae distinguished Impulsivity as a facet of Neuroticism. In the NEO-PI-R, this facet refers to the inability to control cravings and urges (e.g., food, cigarettes). They stated that NEO-PI-R impulsiveness should not be confused with spontaneity, risk taking, or rapid decision time. In a recent study, however, Costa and McCrae (1995) correlated Eysenck's Personality Profile Scales with the NEO-PI-R scales and found significant correlations between the NEO-PI-R facet scale Impulsiveness and Eysencks' Expressive-Inhibited scale (Extraversion, $r = .35$) and Impulsive-Controlled scale (Psychoticism, $r = .45$).

Buss and Plomin (1984) dealt with the multiple components of Impulsivity by dropping the construct as a unifying dimension. Instead, they kept two lower level constituents, Inhibitory Control and Excitement Seeking. These were included in a preliminary form of the revised questionnaire. Further, results with college students showed a clear Excitement-Seeking factor. Items included to measure Inhibitory Control, however, were spread across factors involving the other temperaments traits, in particular Activity and Emotionality. Buss and Plomin finally resolved the complexities surrounding the trait of Impulsivity by referring to one of their criteria of temperament, the early appearance of a trait. Because they found no evidence of the early appearance of Impulsivity as a personality trait (at least not until the 4th or 5th year of life), they dismissed Impulsivity as being a temperament trait.

In literature discussing both adult and child personality, the role of Impulsivity is far from clear, and the subject needs more research. In terms of the AB5C model discussed earlier (De Raad et al., 1994; Hofstee & De Raad, 1991), we think a case can be made for Impulsivity's being a blend of the positive pole of Extraversion (I+) and the negative pole of Conscientiousness (III–). The reason for its checkered history is that the trait is not a good exemplar of any of the major dimensions but is rather a derivative construct, based on blends of several dimensions. One other possibility bears brief mention. It might be possible to better conceptualize Impulsivity negatively—that is, by its absence—and instead recogize the presence of the dimension of Effortful Control as identified by Rothbart (1989) in her work with infants and children. Children characterized as high on Effortful Control might, by definition, not be impulsive. This dimension might, in childhood, be a moderator that is linked to several major dimensions, including Extraversion (I) and Conscientiousness (III), and possibly others as well. Ahadi and Rothbart (1994), for example, showed that there might be "effortful" ways to be agreeable (for those children for whom being agreeable must be achieved by overcoming basic disagreeable tendencies). Such a moderator could work for most major dimensions. Only more research can tell.

Shyness

The second topic that is still unclear in relation to Extraversion is the way that Shyness is linked to Extraversion and Neuroticism. From our previous discussion, it is clear that there is disagreement about the position of Shyness as well as Impulsivity. In Cattell's taxonomy, Shyness belongs to Extraversion. For Eysenck, Shyness is a facet of Neuroticism (H. J. Eysenck & M. W. Eysenck, 1985). Goldberg (1990) found Shyness to be a constituent of Extraversion. Recently, theoretical and empirical accounts have lent support to the notion that Shyness is not simply low Extraversion but is an empirically distinct construct. For example, Jones, Briggs, and Smith (1986) summarized a series of studies showing that Shyness measures were valid and that Shyness was definable as a major dimension of personality in its own right.

Commenting on the relation between Sociability and Shyness, Buss and Plomin (1984) also believed that Sociability and Shyness can (and should) be defined independently. They defined Sociability as "the tendency to affiliate with others and to prefer being with other rather than being alone," whereas they regarded Shyness as "one's behavior when with people who are casual acquaintances or strangers: inhibited and awkward, with feelings of tension and distress and a tendency to escape from social interaction" (p. 77). Considering the dual nature of Shyness, Buss and Plomin stated:

> Fear of strangers, the early developing form, starts in infancy and continues through adulthood; it appears to consist largely of a combination of high fearfulness and low sociability. Self-conscious shyness, the later developing form, starts at roughly the fourth or fifth year of life; it appears to consist largely of acute awareness of oneself as a social object. (Buss & Plomin, 1984, p. 79)

If their theoretical account holds true, the only Shyness seen in infants is fearful Shyness. In older children and adults there should be two kinds of Shyness: the fearful kind, which continues throughout development, and the self-conscious kind. Questioning the unitary nature of Guilford's factor of Social Shyness, Eysenck hypothesized a difference between introverted Social Shyness and neurotic Social Shyness. He suggested "that introverts do not care for people . . . but if necessary can effectively take part in social situations, whereas the neurotic is anxious and afraid when confronted with social situations. . . . In other words, the introvert does not care to be with other people; the neurotic is afraid of being with other people" (H. J. Eysenck & M. W. Eysenck, 1985, p. 25). Putting his hypothesis to a test, Eysenck correlated the Guilford Social Shyness scale with measures of Extraversion and Neuroticism. Indeed, the two almost unrelated groups of items reflected the distinction made between introverted and neurotic Social Shyness. This division between Shyness items might very well reflect the differentiation made by Buss and Plomin between fearful Shyness and self-conscious Shyness.

If we are able to identify Extraversion and Neuroticism constructs in childhood, only further research can clarify the links of Shyness to these general dimensions. Much research on inhibition (see, e.g., Kagan, Resnick, & Snidman, 1988) and social withdrawal has been published in literature on social development (see, e.g., Rubin, Stewart, & Coplan, 1995). Theorists like Rubin et al. (1995) and Asendorpf (1991, 1993) have described differences among children who show different forms of solitude (reticence, passive withdrawal, and active solitary play). Each of these might have different links to major personality dimensions to be discovered in future research. In most temperament research (see Martin et al., 1994), the single empirical dimension of approach and withdrawal that is repeatedly obtained appears to be a direct sociability antecedent of Extraversion. Clearly, further empirical analyses are needed.

Activity Level

The third and last concept we discuss here is Activity Level. "Activity level (AL) is one of the focal noncognitive dimensions of individual differences in infancy and childhood (Buss & Plomin, 1975; Goldsmith et al., 1987; Thomas & Chess, 1977), but its status as a dimension of adult difference is far less clear" (Eaton, 1994, p. 174). The literature on Activity Level suggests that Activity is logically a constituent of Extraversion (see, e.g., Ahadi & Rothbart, 1994; Hagekull, 1994; Martin et al., 1994). A close look at the empirical evidence for this relation, however, gives a murkier picture. In a study by Angleitner and Ostendorf (1994) mentioned earlier, five factors in a six-factor solution were judged to represent the FFM based on their convergent correlations with Costa and McCrae's NEO-Five-Factor Inventory (NEO-FFI) scales. Angleitner and Ostendorf found that activity scales from the EASI-III (Tempo and Vigor) loaded primarily (.45 and .59 respectively) on a factor labeled Conscientiousness. In addition, a third activity scale (Activity Level, General) from the DOTS-R (Windle & Lerner, 1986) loaded primarily (−.41) on Agreeableness. Reviewing studies on the position of Activity Level in the FFM in adulthood, Eaton concluded: "The consistent theme that emerges from the studies of the Big Five in adulthood is that AL is a second-tier trait, one primarily related to Extraversion and secondarily to several other traits, most notably Conscientiousness" (Eaton, 1994, p. 177). We think it noteworthy that Activity emerges as a *separate factor* in all the scales of infancy and childhood. It is *not* subsumed by some other dimension. In fact in many of the studies, Activity does not correlate with ostensibly Extraversion precursors like Sociability or Approach (e.g., Halverson & Post-Gorden, 1984; Martin, 1988; McClowry et al., 1993). By adolescence, the positive correlations with Sociability mirror the possible adult structure of Extraversion (see, e.g., Lanthier, 1994). Obviously, more research is needed in this area as well.

Developmentally, the three concepts we have discussed show complicated, differential relations with at least two of the Big Five factors. We can attempt to resolve these ambiguities by using either a hierarchical approach to the trait universe in which these constructs may be subordinate facets of superfactors (see Digman, 1990), or we can conceptualize these dimensions as blends of the superfactors (from the circumplex tradition, see Hofstee, DeRaad, & Goldberg, 1992). Here the constructs of Impulsivity, Shyness or Inhibition, and Activity Level are not thought of as primary traits but rather as blends of primary traits. In fact, we think it likely that much of the extensive literature on Sociability in childhood will be characterized as blends of I (Extraversion) and II (Agreeableness) when the empirical data can be collected.

EXTRAVERSION IN PARENTS' FREE DESCRIPTIONS OF THEIR CHILDREN'S PERSONALITY CHARACTERISTICS

The content analysis of the free descriptions was made possible by our categorization system. This categorization system (see chapter 1) distinguishes three subcategories comprising the dimension of Extraversion: Sociability, Dominance or Assertiveness, and Activity. The relative proportions of Extraversion are given in Table 1.3 in chapter 1. From this table, we can see that in all countries except Greece, Extraversion was the most frequently used category. In Greece, both Agreeableness and Extraversion were essentially equal in importance. In all countries, these first two dimensions accounted for about 50% of all descriptions used by parents in describing their children (Goldberg's compilation of personality adjectives in the first two categories summed to 58%; Goldberg & Rosolack, 1994).

In Table 2.5 and Figures 2.1, 2.2, 2.3, and 2.4, we summarize the proportion of descriptors from seven different countries referring to Extraversion as well as the proportions in facets we coded as subsumed under Extraversion. In total, the averaged percentage of descriptors classified as referring to the main category of Extraversion was 27.9%. In comparing countries, we can see that there were no differences among Germany, the Netherlands, the United States, Poland, Belgium, and China in total Extraversion descriptors (based on ANOVAs of arcsined proportions). Greece, however, was different, but only from Germany and the Netherlands. The magnitude of these differences was small, and the most reasonable conclusion about the overall proportions was that these coun-

TABLE 2.5
Proportions of Descriptors Coded in Extraversion (Across Age)

	Belgium	Netherlands	Germany	Greece	China	Poland	U.S.A.	Total
Extraversion (Total)	27.7	28.4	29.9	25.0	27.2	29.6	29.5	27.9
Facets:								
Sociability	15.2	17.1	16.4	13.7	14.0	13.4	15.8	14.9
Dominance	6.2	6.4	6.0	4.8	2.2	3.4	2.2	4.5
Activity	6.3	4.9	7.5	6.5	11.0	12.8	11.5	8.4

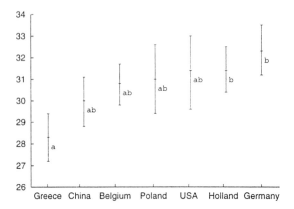

FIG. 2.1. Arcsine transformed means and 95% confidence intervals for
Category I, Extraversion. *Note.* a, b, ab, etc. = Means of samples sharing a
common letter *not* significantly different from one another according to
post hoc Scheffé tests.

tries were remarkably similar in their proportions of Extraversion descriptions.

Closely examining the distribution of the personality descriptors across
the three facets does reveal some differences among countries. First, Table
2.5 and Figure 2.2 reveal some differences among countries in the facet
of Sociability. Three countries were relatively high on Sociability: the
Netherlands, Germany, and Belgium; three were low: Poland, China, and
Greece, with the United States in the middle of the group, not significantly
different from either the low or the high group. These results were rep-

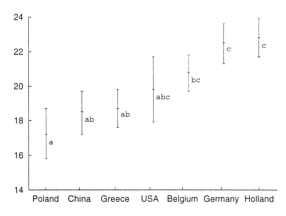

FIG. 2.2. Arcsine transformed means and 95% confidence intervals for
Category Ia, Sociability. *Note.* a, b, ab, etc. = Means of samples sharing a
common letter are *not* significantly different from one another according
to post hoc Scheffé tests.

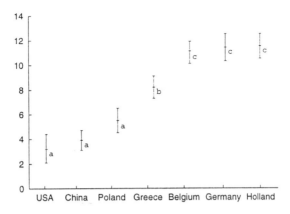

FIG. 2.3. Arcsine transformed means and 95% confidence intervals for Category Ib, Dominance. *Note.* a, b, ab, etc. = Means of samples sharing a common letter are *not* significantly different from one another according to post hoc Scheffé tests.

licated when the Sociability category was divided into high and low (see Table 2.6). Poland and China formed a low pair, and the Netherlands and Germany a high pair, with the other countries being statistically equal. Clearly, parents in the lowland countries of the Netherlands and Belgium, along with Germany, found Sociability a most salient dimension for describing children.

Table 2.5 and Figure 2.3 also revealed interesting differences among countries for the Dominance facet. The Netherlands, Germany, and Belgium again formed a group with higher percentages on Dominance than

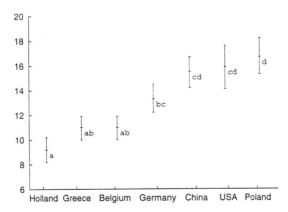

FIG. 2.4. Arcsine transformed means and 95% confidence intervals for Category Ic, Activity. *Note.* a, b, ab, etc. = Means of samples sharing a common letter are *not* significantly different from one another according to post hoc Scheffé tests.

TABLE 2.6
Portions of Descriptors Coded in Extraversion as High or Low

		Belgium	Netherlands	Germany	Greece	China	Poland	U.S.A.
Extraversion	High	20.1	20.2	20.9	19.0	18.4	22.0	24.1
	Low	6.4	7.4	9.0	6.1	8.8	7.6	5.1
Sociability	High	10.0	11.4	10.8	9.7	8.7	9.4	12.3
	Low	4.7	5.2	5.6	4.0	5.3	4.0	3.4
Dominance	High	5.2	5.2	4.9	3.7	1.5	2.2	1.5
	Low	0.6	1.1	1.1	1.1	0.7	1.2	0.6
Activity	High	4.9	3.7	5.2	5.6	8.2	10.4	10.3
	Low	1.1	1.1	2.3	0.9	2.8	2.5	1.1

Note. Descriptors coded as Neutral were not taken into account. Small deviations occur between the proportions reported in this table and the proportions reported in Table 2.5.

did the other countries (with Greece being neither high nor low). The United States, China, and Poland formed a contrasting group of low-scoring countries on Dominance. Like Sociability, Dominance was relatively important for the three Western European countries in contrast to the other countries.

A similar but reversed pattern was obtained for the Activity facet. As shown in Table 2.5 and Figure 2.4, Poland, the United States, and China were the highest group relative to Activity, while Belgium, the Netherlands, and Greece formed the low group of countries, with the Netherlands being the lowest, different from four other countries, including Germany. Unlike the patterns for Sociability and Dominance, Activity showed the reverse pattern. These results demonstrate how, for Extraversion in particular, the overall score is much less informative of differences among countries than are the facet scores. We did not find many differences in overall Extraversion because the relatively equal totals were comprised of *high* Sociability and Dominance and *low* Activity for the Western European countries, while for the other countries these totals were made from *low* levels of Sociability and Dominance and high levels of Activity. These differences were substantial and substantive and may represent real differences of emphasis on the facets of Extraversion among the participating countries, which nevertheless showed agreement on the overall importance of the construct.

A comparison of the descriptors coded as high or low (Table 2.6) does not reveal anything different from the results just discussed. In fact, only the Sociability category contained a large enough fraction of low-end descriptors to analyze, and these findings mirrored the analyses for scores summed across high and low. For both Activity and Dominance, there were very few low-end descriptors, mostly around 1% or lower. Parents overwhelmingly used high-end descriptors to describe their children in all three facet categories.

CONCLUSIONS

The predominant role ascribed to the personality dimension of Extraversion in trait psychology (next to Neuroticism) is certainly validated by finding that, across seven different countries, 25% to 30% of the personality-relevant utterances mentioned in free-response descriptions could be classified as referring to this dimension. At the main category level no consistent differences existed among the seven samples.

In our content analysis (see chapter 1), three facets were distinguished under the assumption that they constituted the overall category of Extraversion. This assumption was based on clusters of high-loading items published in several adult personality studies, which have been described in the first section of this chapter. The question of whether this assumption holds true in studying child personality can be answered only after we have developed questionnaires based on the free descriptions and have factor analyzed the ratings of children on these questionnaires. We have described in this chapter the literature on adult extraversion clearly supporting the coding of distinct categories of Sociability, Dominance or Assertiveness, and Activity as facets of Extraversion. The temperament literature, however, is more equivocal on this topic.

Generally, when we examined proportions for the facets, two groups of countries were distinguished, one consisting of the Western European countries of Belgium, the Netherlands, and Germany, the second of China, Poland, and the United States. For Dominance, Greece was positioned between both groups; in the case of Activity, Greece joined the group of Western European countries (Belgium, the Netherlands, and Germany).

Clearly, we found Extraversion to be a salient, important dimension for parents when describing their children. This importance mirrors the prominent place that extraversion occupies in the descriptions of adult personality. Extraversion has been identified in virtually every important multidimensional inventory for adults (Watson & Clark, 1997).

At the core of the construct is the view that people high in extraversion are gregarious and outgoing individuals. Recent conceptualizations have also added the ideas that extraverts are happy, energetic individuals as well. Clearly, Extraversion should play a role in adaptive social functioning. Those who are positive, happy, and outgoing might be at diminished risk for anxiety disorders like dysphoria and depression. Further, when combined with high levels of Agreeableness, we might be able to identify those well-functioning, mentally resilient people who cope well and are versatile in the interpersonal domain. Of course, the developmental trajectory of Extraversion remains an important topic. Many analyses await the formulation of a set of personality measures based on the descriptions of extraversion provided by the interviewed parents. When we can better define and delineate the Extraversion construct in childhood, we will be better able to examine developmental processes that link Extraversion in childhood to Extraversion in adulthood and to examine how Extraversion and its facets are linked to major developmental outcomes.

REFERENCES

Ahadi, S. A., & Rothbart, M. K. (1994). Temperament and the Big Five. In C. F. Halverson, Jr., G. A. Kohnstamm, & R. P. Martin (Eds.), *The developing structure of temperament and personality from infancy to adulthood* (pp. 189–207). Hillsdale, NJ: Lawrence Erlbaum Associates.

Allport, G. W., & Odbert, H. S. (1936). Trait names: A psycholexical study. *Psychological Monographs, 47*(1, Whole No. 211).

Angleitner, A., & Ostendorf, F. (1994). Temperament and the Big Five Factors of personality. In C. F. Halverson, Jr., G. A. Kohnstamm, & R. P. Martin (Eds.), *The developing structure of temperament and personality from infancy to adulthood* (pp. 69–90). Hillsdale, NJ: Lawrence Erlbaum Associates.

Asendorpf, J. B. (1991). Development of inhibited children's coping with unfamiliarity. *Child Development, 62,* 1460–1474.

Asendorpf, J. B. (1993). Abnormal shyness in children. *Journal of Child Psychology and Psychiatry and Allied Disciplines, 34,* 1069–1081.

Bain, A. (1861). *On the study of character.* London: Parker Son & Bourn.

Brokken, F. B. (1978). *The language of personality.* Unpublished doctoral dissertation, University of Groningen, Netherlands.

Burt, C. (1915). General and specific factors underlying the primary emotions. *British Association Anthropometrical Reports, 80,* 694–696.

Burt, C. (1948). The factorial study of temperamental traits. *British Journal of Psychology, Statistical Section, 1,* 178–203.

Buss, A. H., & Plomin, R. (1975). *A temperament theory of personality development.* New York: Wiley.

Buss, A. H., & Plomin, R. (1984). *Temperament: Early developing personality traits.* Hillsdale, NJ: Lawrence Erlbaum Associates.

Carrigan, P. M. (1960). Extraversion-Introversion as a dimension of personality: A reappraisal. *Psychological Bulletin, 57*(1), 329–360.

Cattell, R. B. (1947). Confirmation and clarification of primary personality factors. *Psychometrika, 12*(3), 197–220.

Cattell, R. B. (1957). *Personality and motivation: Structure and measurement.* New York: World Book.

Cattell, R. B., & Coan, R. A. (1957). Child personality structure as revealed in teachers' ratings. *Journal of Clinical Psychology, 13,* 315–327.

Cattell, R. S., Eber, H. W., & Tatsuoka, M. M. (1980). *Handbook for the Sixteen Personality Questionnaire (16PF).* Champaign, IL: Institute for Personality and Ability Testing.

Costa, P. T., & McCrae, R. R. (1992). *Revised NEO Personality Inventory (NEO PI-R) and NEO Five-Factor Inventory (NEO-FFI): Professional manual.* Odessa, FL: Psychological Assessment Resources.

Costa, P. T., & McCrae, R. R. (1994). Stability and change in personality from adolescence through adulthood. In C. F. Halverson, Jr., G. A. Kohnstamm, & R. P. Martin (Eds.), *The developing structure of temperament and personality from infancy to adulthood* (pp. 139–150). Hillsdale, NJ: Lawrence Erlbaum Associates.

Costa, P. T., & McCrae, R. R. (1995). Solid grounds in the wetlands of personality: A reply to Block. *Psychological Bulletin, 117*(2), 216–230.

De Raad, B., Hendriks, A. A. J., & Hofstee, W. K. B. (1994). The Big Five: A tip of the iceberg of individual differences. In C. F. Halverson, Jr., G. A. Kohnstamm, & R. P. Martin (Eds.), *The developing structure of temperament and personality from infancy to adulthood* (pp. 91–109). Hillsdale, NJ: Lawrence Erlbaum Associates.

Diamond, S. (1957). *Personality and temperament.* New York: Harper.

Digman, J. M. (1963). Principal dimensions of child personality as seen in teachers' judgments. *Child Development, 34,* 43–60.

Digman, J. M. (1965). Child behavior ratings: Further evidence of a multiple-factor model of child personality. *Educational and Psychological Measurement, 25,* 787–798.

Digman, J. M. (1990). Personality structure: Emergence of the five factor model. *Annual Review of Psychology, 41,* 417–440.

Digman, J. M., & Shmelyov, A. G. (1996). The structure of temperament and personality in Russian children. *Journal of Personality and Social Psychology, 71,* 341–351.

Eaton, W. O. (1994). Temperament, development, and the Five-Factor Model: Lessons from activity level. In C. F. Halverson, Jr., G. A. Kohnstamm, & R. P. Martin (Eds.), *The developing structure of temperament and personality from infancy to adulthood* (pp. 173–187). Hillsdale, NJ: Lawrence Erlbaum Associates.

Eysenck, H. J. (1958). *Manual of the Maudsley Personality Inventory.* London: University of London Press.

Eysenck, H. J. (1977). Personality and factor analysis: A reply to Guilford. *Psychological Bulletin, 84,* 3, 405–411.

Eysenck, H. J. (1994). The Big Five or Giant Three: Criteria for a paradigm. In C. F. Halverson, Jr., G. A. Kohnstamm, & R. P. Martin (Eds.), *The developing structure of temperament and personality from infancy to adulthood* (pp. 37–51). Hillsdale, NJ: Lawrence Erlbaum Associates.

Eysenck, H. J., & Eysenck, S. B. (1975). *Manual of the Eysenck Personality Questionnaire.* London: Hodder & Stoughton.

Eysenck, H. J., & Eysenck, M. W. (1985). *Personality and individual differences: A natural science approach.* New York: Plenum Press.

Eysenck, S. B. (1965). *The Junior Eysenck Personality Inventory.* London: University of London Press.

Freyd, M. (1924). Introverts and extroverts. *Psychological Review, 31,* 74–87.

Garcia-Coll, C., Kogan, J., & Resnick, J. S. (1984). Behavioral inhibition in young children. *Child Development, 55,* 1005–1009.

Gilliland, A. R. (1934, reprinted 1970). What do introversion–extraversion tests measure? In H. J. Eysenck (Ed.), *Readings in extraversion-introversion: 1: Theoretical and methodological issues* (pp. 29–34). London: Staples Press. (Reprinted from *Journal of Abnormal and Social Psychology, 28,* 407–412)

Goldberg, L. R. (1990). An alternative "description of personality": The Big-Five Factor structure. *Journal of Personality and Social Psychology, 59*(6), 1216–1229.

Goldberg, L. R. (1993). The structure of phenotypic personality traits. *American Psychologist, 48*(1), 26–34.

Goldberg, L. R., & Rosolack, T. (1994). The Big Five structure as an integrative framework: An empirical comparison with Eysenck's P-E-N model. In C. F. Halverson, Jr., G. A. Kohnstamm, & R. P. Martin (Eds.), *The developing structure of temperament and personality from infancy to adulthood* (pp. 7–35). Hillsdale, NJ: Lawrence Erlbaum Associates.

Goldberg, L. R., & Saucier, G. (1995). So what do you propose we use instead? A reply to Block. *Psychological Bulletin, 117,* 221–225.

Goldsmith, H. H., Buss, A. H., Plomin, R., Rothbart, M. K., Thomas, A., Chess, S., Hinde, R. A., & McCall, R. B. (1987). Roundtable: What is temperament? Four approaches. *Child Development, 58,* 505–529.

Guilford, J. P. (1975). Factors and factors of personality. *Psychological Bulletin, 82*(5), 802–814.

Guilford, J. P., & Braley, K. W. (1930). Extroversion and introversion. *Psychological Bulletin, 27,* 96–107.

Guilford, J. P., & Guilford, R. B. (1934). An analysis of the factors in a typical test of introversion-extroversion. *Journal of Abnormal and Social Psychology, 28,* 377–399.

Guilford, J. P., & Guilford, R. B. (1936). Personality factors S, E, and M and their measurement. *Journal of Personality, 2,* 109–127.

Guilford, J. P., & Zimmerman, W. S. (1949). *The Guilford–Zimmerman temperament survey: Manual.* Beverly Hills, CA: Sheridan Supply.

Hagekull, B. (1994). Infant temperament and early childhood functioning: Possible relations to the Five-Factor Model. In C. F. Halverson, Jr., G. A. Kohnstamm, & R. P. Martin (Eds.), *The developing structure of temperament and personality from infancy to adulthood* (pp. 227–240). Hillsdale, NJ: Lawrence Erlbaum Associates.

Hagekull, B., Lindhagen, K., & Bohlin, G. (1980). Behavioral dimensions in 1-year-olds and dimensional stability in infancy. *International Journal of Behavioral Development, 3,* 351–364.

Halverson, C. F., Jr., & Post-Gorden, J. C. (1984). Measurement of open-field activity in young children. In E. Pollitt & P. Amante (Eds.), *Energy intake and activity* (pp. 185–206). New York: Alan Liss.

Hildebrand, H. P. (1970). A factorial study of introversion-extraversion. In H. J. Eysenck (Ed.), *Readings in extraversion-introversion: 1: Theoretical and methodological issues* (pp. 128–144). London: Staples Press. (Reprinted from *British Journal of Psychology, 1958, 49,* 1–11)

Hofstee, W. K. B. (1976). *Dutch traits: The first stages of the Groningen taxonomy study of personality descriptive adjectives.* Unpublished manuscript, University of Groningen, Netherlands.

Hofstee, W. K. B., & De Raad, B. (1991). Persoonlijkheidsstructuur: De AB5C taxonomie van Nederlanse eigenschapstermen [Personality Structure: The AB5C taxonomy of Dutch traits]. *Nederlands Tijdschrift voor de Psychologie, 46,* 262–274.

Hofstee, W. K. B., De Raad, B., & Goldberg, L. R. (1992). Integration of the Big-Five and circumplex approaches to trait structure. *Journal of Personality and Social Psychology, 63,* 146–163.

Hogan, R. (1983). A socioanalytic theory of personality. In M. M. Page (Ed.), *1982 Nebraska Symposium on Motivation-Personality: Current theory and research* (pp. 55–89). Lincoln: University of Nebraska Press.

James, W. (1907). *Pragmatism.* New York: Henry Holt.

John, O. P. (1990). The "Big Five" factor taxonomy: Dimensions of personality in the natural language and in questionnaires. In L. A. Pervin (Ed.), *Handbook of personality: Theory and research* (pp. 66–100). New York: Guilford Press.

John, O. P., Angleitner, A., & Ostendorf, F. (1988). The lexical approach to personality: A historical review of trait taxonomic research. *European Journal of Personality, 2,* 171–203.

John, O. P., Caspi, A., Robins, R. W., Moffitt, T. E., & Stouthamer-Loeber, M. (1994). The "Little Five": Exploring the nomological network of the Five-Factor Model of personality in adolescent boys. *Child Development, 65,* 160–178.

Jones, W. H., Briggs, S. R., & Smith, T. G. (1986). Shyness: Conceptualization and measurement. *Journal of Personality and Social Psychology, 51,* 629–639.

Jung, C. G. (1921). *Psychological types.* New York: Harcourt Brace.

Kagan, J., Resnick, J. S., & Snidman, N. (1988). Biological bases of childhood shyness. *Science, 240,* 167–171.

Lanthier, R. (1994). *The big five dimensions of personality in middle childhood and adolescence.* Unpublished doctoral dissertation, University of Denver, Denver, CO.

Martin, R. P. (1988). *Assessment of personality and behavior problems.* New York: Guilford Press.

Martin, R. P., Wisenbaker, J., & Huttunen, M. (1994). Review of factor analytic studies of temperament measures based on the Thomas–Chess structural model: Implications for the Big Five. In C. F. Halverson Jr., G. A. Kohnstamm, & R. P. Martin (Eds.), *The developing structure of temperament and personality from infancy to adulthood* (pp. 157–172). Hillsdale, NJ: Lawrence Erlbaum Associates.

McClowry, S. G., Hegvik, R. L., & Teglasi, H. (1993). An examination of the construct validity of the Middle Childhood Temperament Questionnaire. *Merrill–Palmer Quarterly, 39,* 279–283.

McCrae, R. R., & Costa, P. T. (1990). *Personality in adulthood.* New York: Guilford Press.

Morris, L. W. (1979). *Extraversion and introversion.* Washington, DC: Hemisphere.

Norman, W. T. (1963). Toward an adequate taxonomy of personality attributes: Replicated factor structure in peer nomination personality ratings. *Journal of Abnormal and Social Psychology, 66,* 574–583.

North, R. D. (1948). An analysis of the personality dimensions of introversion-extroversion. *Journal of Personality, 17,* 352–367.

Ostendorf, F. (1990). *Sprache und Persönlichkeitsstruktur; Zur Validität des Fünf-Faktoren Modells der Persönlichkeit.* Regensburg, Germany: Roderer Verlag.

Rothbart, M. K. (1989). Temperament and development. In G. A. Kohnstamm, J. E. Bates, & M. K. Rothbart (Eds.), *Temperament in childhood* (pp. 187–247). New York: Wiley.

Rothbart, M. K., & Ahadi, S. A. (1994). Temperament and the development of personality. *Journal of Abnormal Psychology, 103*(1), 55–66.

Rubin, K. H., Stewart, S., & Coplan, R. J. (1995). Social withdrawal in childhood: Conceptual and empirical perspectives. *Advances in Clinical Child Psychology, 17,* 157–196.

Shmelyov, A. G., & Pokhil'ko, V. I. (1993). A taxonomy-oriented study of Russian personality-trait names. *European Journal of Personality, 7,* 1–17.

Stewart, A. (1887). *Our temperaments.* London: Crosby Lockwood.

Szirmák, Z., & De Raad, B. (1994). Taxonomy and structure of Hungarian personality traits. *European Journal of Personality, 8,* 95–117.

Tellegen, A. (1985). Structures of mood and personality and their relevance to assessing anxiety, with an emphasis on self-report. In A. H. Tuma & J. D. Maser (Eds.), *Anxiety and the anxiety disorders* (pp. 681–706). Hillsdale, NJ: Lawrence Erlbaum Associates.

Thomas, A., & Chess, S. (1977). *Temperament and development.* New York: Brunner/Mazel.

Tupes, E. C., & Christal, R. E. (1992). Recurrent personality factors based on trait ratings. *Journal of Personality, 60,* 225–251. (Reprinted from Tech. Rep. No. ASD-TR-61-97, 1961, Lackland Air Force Base, TX: U.S. Airforce.)

Van Lieshout, C. F. M., & Haselager, G. J. T. (1994). The Big Five personality factors in Q-sort descriptions of children and adolescents. In G. A. Kohnstamm, C. F. Halverson, & R. P. Martin (Eds.), *The developing structure of temperament and personality from infancy to adulthood* (pp. 293–318). Hillsdale, NJ: Lawrence Erlbaum Associates.

Watson, D., & Clark, L. A. (1997). Extraversion and its positive emotional core. In R. Hogan, J. Johnson, & S. Briggs (Eds.), *Handbook of personality psychology* (pp. 767–793). San Diego, CA: Academic Press.

Webb, E. (1915). Character and intelligence. *British Journal of Psychology, Monograph Series,* 1(Whole No. 3).

White, J. L., Moffitt, T. E., Caspi, A., Bartusch, D. J., Needles, D. J., & Stouthamer-Loeber, M. (1994). Measuring impulsivity and examining its relationship to delinquency. *Journal of Abnormal Psychology, 103*(2), 192–205.

Windle, M., & Lerner, R. M. (1986). Reassessing the dimensions of temperament individuality across the lifespan: The Revised Dimensions of Temperament Survey (DOTS-R). *Journal of Adolescent Research, 1,* 213–230.

Zuckerman, M. (1991). *Psychobiology of personality*. Cambridge, England: Cambridge University Press.

Zuckerman, M., Kuhlman, D. M., & Camac, C. (1988). What lies beyond E and N? Factor analyses of scales believed to measure basic dimensions of personality. *Journal of Personality and Social Psychology, 54*, 96–107.

Agreeableness as a Diachronic Human Trait

Valerie L. Havill
University of Georgia

Elias Besevegis
University of Athens

Sophia Mouroussaki
University of Athens

The concept of agreeableness (and disagreeableness) has permeated much of the world's literature. In the first pages of the Bible (Gen. 4:8), Cain, the first offspring of Adam and Eve, murdered his brother Abel in a fit of jealousy. Two chapters later, "The Lord saw that the wickedness of man was great in the earth, and that every imagination of his heart was only evil continually" (Gen. 6:5). In Greek mythology, many characters epitomized agreeable or disagreeable behaviors (e.g., Poseidon's mean-spirited treatment of Odysseus). Agreeable and disagreeable traits were also assigned to characters in Shakespeare's plays (e.g., *The Taming of the Shrew*). Contemporary literature and films have continued the tradition, and the essence of a character is often defined in terms of agreeableness or disagreeableness. How kind, caring, and cooperative or how selfish, cruel, and manipulative a person is has been very salient throughout written history: Both writers and audience have long been intrigued by variations in the characteristics summarized by the concept of agreeableness.

Goldberg (1981) suggested that people ask what are perhaps five universal questions about individuals whom they meet, and the five dimensions of personality encompass possible answers to these questions. One question is: "Is X *agreeable* (warm and pleasant) or disagreeable (cold and distant)?" (p. 161). If agreeableness is a universal concern, then words to describe agreeable or disagreeable people and behaviors should be encoded in the world's languages (Goldberg, 1981). Hogan (1983) has argued that personality language emerges from group processes. His social competency perspective was founded on evolutionary theory, which maintains that people always live in groups and that every group is organized by a status hierarchy. Our ancestors were group-living hominids, dependent on each other for survival. Hogan argued that certain behavioral dispositions or traits were more important for survival (i.e., intelligence, cooperativeness) than were others, and these essential traits would become salient and encoded in language. For a member of a social group, it would be crucial to evaluate others' enduring personality traits to survive. As Hogan so eloquently put it, "The lackadaisical should not be left to guard the flock, the lecherous should not guard the harem, nor the larcenous guard the treasury" (p. 59).

Recognizing Agreeableness as a trait might facilitate the study of intimate relationships. Cooperative social exchanges have been linked to reproductive competition (Cosmides, 1989). Buss (1992) found that Pleasure Induction and Coercion were used as manipulation tactics in interpersonal relationships. Individuals rated high on Agreeableness were more likely to use Pleasure Induction and those rated low on Agreeableness were more likely to use Coercion to reach their goals. Yet, a society consisting of only highly agreeable people might not survive in competition with antagonistic societies. From a society's viewpoint, all people are necessary (McCrae & Costa, 1989): aggressive warriors, assertive lawyers, and skeptical stockbrokers are as important as charitable leaders, compassionate health care providers, and sympathetic teachers. Individual differences might cause certain people stress or unhappiness, but still promote the survival of a culture or society.

The concept of Agreeableness should thus show a universal salience across cultures, although different levels or aspects of Agreeableness might be valued differently by different groups in a culture (e.g., by age or gender), and values might vary from culture to culture (e.g., collective versus individualistic groups). For example, Mead (1972) described the Mundugumor, a group residing in New Guinea, as follows: "Fierce possessive men and women were the preferred type; warm and cherishing men and women were culturally disallowed" (p. 206).

Indeed, in research on adult individual differences, Agreeableness, or a very similar factor, has usually been the first to emerge from factor analyses. Cattell (1945) labeled his largest factor Cyclothyme versus Paranoid Schizothyme. The traits contained in this factor could also be seen as warmth versus coldness, or friendliness. Digman and Takemoto-Chock (1981) found "friendly compliance versus hostile non-compliance" to be the first factor to emerge when data from six large-scale studies were reanalyzed. Graziano and Eisenberg (1997) suggested that there has been a research bias against conceptualizing Agreeableness as a personality construct; thus the emergence of Agreeableness as a first factor in a factor analysis is downplayed or ignored, and the actual salience and importance of the concept are underestimated. Even so, many English-language-based personality inventories have measured a construct that is a close approximation to the Agreeableness dimension measured by the Five-Factor Model (FFM). Eysenck (1994), however, has consistently maintained that adherents of the FFM err by not recognizing that Agreeableness is actually a facet of his higher order Psychoticism factor. Yet, Goldberg and Rosolack (1994) argued that Eysenck's Psychoticism is itself a blend of the two higher order factors of Agreeableness and Conscientiousness. Most factor analytic data have supported the latter interpretation, thereby maintaining the independence of the Agreeableness construct as a major personality dimension.

The studies based on natural-language personality descriptors have consistently found an Agreeableness factor. Some researchers and their labels for factors that could be reasonably considered Agreeableness include Fiske (1949), Social Adaptability; Tupes and Christal (1961), Agreeableness; Borgatta (1964), Likability; Goldberg (1981), Agreeableness; Conley (1985), Agreeableness; De Raad, Mulder, Kloosterman, and Hofstee (1988), Agreeableness versus Coldheartedness; and Digman (1990), Love.

The construct of Agreeableness is not simply an artifact of the lexical model. Analyses of Leary's (1957) Interpersonal Circumplex combined Extraversion and Agreeableness. The Hogan Personality Inventory (Hogan, 1986) measured Likability. The Myers–Briggs Type Indicator (Myers & McCaulley, 1985), inspired by Jungian typology, measured some aspects of Agreeableness (tough versus tender-minded) although the trait was labeled Thinking versus Feeling. The Feeling typology did not, however, encompass other interpersonal facets of Agreeableness such as trust, cooperation, and generosity (McCrae & Costa, 1989). McCrae, Costa, and Busch (1986) extracted five factors from the California Q-Set (Block, 1961), one of which, labeled Femininity, also resembled Agreeableness. Wiggins (1991) argued that two motivational systems, agency and communion, drive interpersonal systems. He defined communion as the striving for intimacy, union, and solidarity with others. Johnson and Ostendorf (1993) labeled one of their five factors Softness in place of Agreeableness. These constructs can be seen as sharing the same conceptual (and empirical) underpinnings as Agreeableness. Thus although these various personality measures were derived from a variety of theoretical perspectives, an Agreeableness construct consistently has emerged.

AGREEABLENESS IN THE FFM

The authors of chapter 1 present a clear overview of the development of the FFM, beginning with Cattell's taxonomy as well as the work by Tupes and Christal. We do not review the literature again here, but we present Norman's (1963) Agreeableness categories as reported by Goldberg (1990).

TABLE 3.1
Categories in Norman's Taxonomy for Agreeable Domain

Factor Pole/Category	Examples	Number of Terms
II+		
Trust	Democratic, friendly, genial, cheerful	20
Amiability	Generous, charitable, indulgent	29
Generosity	Trustful, unsuspicious, unenvious	18
Agreeableness	Conciliatory, cooperative, agreeable	17
Tolerance	Tolerant, reasonable, impartial	19
Courtesy	Patient, moderate, tactful, polite	17
Altruism	Kind, loyal, unselfish, helpful	29
Warmth	Affectionate, warm, tender	18
Honesty	Moral, honest, just, principled	16
II–		
Vindictiveness	Sadistic, vengeful, cruel	13
Ill Humor	Bitter, testy, crabby, sour	16
Criticism	Harsh, severe, strict, critical	33
Disdain	Derogatory, caustic, sarcastic	16
Antagonism	Negative, contrary, argumentative	11
Aggressiveness	Belligerent, abrasive, unruly	21
Dogmatism	Biased, opinionated, stubborn	49
Temper	Irritable, explosive, wild	29
Distrust	Jealous, mistrustful, suspicious	8
Greed	Stingy, selfish, ungenerous	18
Dishonesty	Scheming, sly, wily, insincere	29

Note. Terms from an inventory of 1,710 trait-descriptive adjectives. Adapted from "An Alternative 'Description of Personality' . . . ," by L. R. Goldberg, 1990, *Journal of Personality and Social Psychology, 59*, p. 1218. Copyright © 1990 by the American Psychiatric Association. Reprinted by permission.

The adjectives in Table 3.1 help define the dimension of Agreeableness as discussed in the Big Five literature.

To demonstrate the flavor and ubiquitous nature of the Five Factors, comparisons reported by McCrae and John (1992) of adjectives, Q sort items, and scales to define the Five Factors are summarized in Table 3.2. The adjectives came from a checklist used by psychologists to rate 280 men and women. The Q sort items consisted of the California Q set (Block, 1961) self-sorted by 403 participants in the Baltimore Longitudinal Study of Aging (McCrae, Costa, & Busch, 1986), and the scales were the facet scales from the Revised NEO Personality Inventory (NEO-PI-R; Costa, McCrae, & Dye, 1991).

Throughout the history of assessment of personality, most researchers seemed to prefer to generate new measures rather than to attempt to reach consensus about measures already available. We have shown that independent researchers, in attempting to test their own theories of personality,

TABLE 3.2
Examples of Factor Definers of Adjectives, Q Sort Items,
and Questionnaire Scales Defining Agreeableness

Adjectives	Q Sort Items	Scales
Appreciative	Not critical, skeptical	Trust
Forgiving	Behaves in giving way	Straightforwardness
Generous	Sympathetic, considerate	Altruism
Kind	Arouses liking	Compliance
Sympathetic	Warm, compassionate	Modesty
Trusting	Basically trustful	Tendermindedness

have indeed come to a consensus about at least one dimension of personality: Agreeableness emerged as a core concept in the assessment of individual differences. In our research, we are investigating the developmental antecedents of adult Agreeableness. When does the concept of Agreeableness emerge as a useful schema to differentiate individual differences?

DEVELOPMENTAL ANTECEDENTS
OF AGREEABLENESS

Researchers have widely agreed that individual differences in temperament have biological roots (Bates & Wachs, 1994; Goldsmith et al., 1987). Yet, biology need not be destiny: Bates and Wachs (1994) warned that there is as much continuity as discontinuity in the development of temperament. When a developmental perspective is taken, many possible precursors to Agreeableness appear. One of most widely used concepts in childhood temperament literature is Difficultness (Bates, 1986). Difficultness typically refers to a collection of attributes in young children. At the core, the construct refers to frequent and intense expression of negative emotion. The term *Difficult* refers to more than a temperament trait (Bates, 1986): It encompasses the interpersonal challenge that these kinds of child characteristics create for caregivers (Thomas, Chess, & Birch, 1968).

These early-emerging individual differences in temperament and behavioral characteristics are especially important because they have been linked to later personality and behavior problems (Rutter, 1987). Several studies have suggested that behavior problems remain stable in preschool and early grade school years (Campbell, 1991; Killeen, Ayoub, & Frame, 1993; McGee, Partridge, Williams, & Silva, 1991). For Agreeableness in childhood, theorists have shown a continuity between disruptive and externalizing problems in preschool years and externalizing problems in adolescence (Loeber, 1990; Rutter, 1985). Although externalizing behavior might encompass more than low Agreeableness (e.g., hyperactivity), children who are disruptive, disobedient, resistant, and unable to get along with other children (low agreeable) in first grade have been found to be 50% more likely than other children to become delinquents in adolescence (Offord, Boyle, Racine, & Fleming, 1992). Caspi, Elder, and Bem (1987) have identified many life-course risks for ill-tempered children. Boys with a pattern of frequent temper tantrums at ages 8 to 10 years were more likely to experience downward occupational mobility and divorce in adulthood. This negative trajectory was correlated with being undercontrolled, irritable, and moody. Similarly, girls who were disagreeable were more likely to become ill-tempered mothers who married men with low occupational status and then divorced.

The biological antecedents of Agreeableness were considered by Rothbart, Derryberry, and Posner (1994). They discussed the role of positive social orientation in controlling how children experience situations as well as how they express emotional and behavioral responses. In literature on adult temperament, positive social orientation is part of the construct of Agreeableness. Rothbart et al. argued that positive social orientation and the expression of emotional responses have specific neural underpinnings (regulating inhibition and excitation) and are temperamental in nature albeit heavily influenced by experience. Ahadi and Rothbart (1994) proposed that effortful control moderates the expression of love and hate (Agreeableness). Rothbart and her colleagues, as well as many other researchers, attempted to identify psychophysiological and genetic processes that influence personality development by focusing their investigations on the basic, constitutional substrates of personality.

Agreeableness in children might also be the result of the ability to inhibit disagreeable behaviors. This process might include cognitive inhibition mechanisms that have been hypothesized to have evolved to promote cooperation, group cohesion, and political success (Bjorklund & Harnishfeger, 1995), as well as behavioral inhibition that controls aggressive responses and allows for delay of gratification and resistance to temptation (Bjorklund & Kipp, 1996). Kindness often requires a person's inhibiting immediate or "selfish" needs to nurture another. (For thorough reviews of the adult literature on Agreeableness as well as consideration of some developmental antecedents, see Graziano [1994], Graziano & Eisenberg [1997], and John [1990].)

As emphasized in chapter 1, until recently there has been very little research on the relevance of the FFM for children's personality traits. A notable exception is the work of Digman and colleagues (1989; Digman & Inouye, 1986). They found the FFM to be appropriate for describing children's personalities when analyzing teachers' behavior ratings of children ages 12 and 13. Graziano and Ward (1992) also found that school counselors perceived differences in Agreeableness in children ranging from 11 to 14 years of age and that Agreeableness ratings were related to indices of adjustment. Van Lieshout and Haselager (1994) translated the California Q set (Block, 1961) into Dutch and had parents and teachers rate children (ages 3 to 17). The most robust factor to emerge from their data was Agreeableness. Agreeableness remained robust from ratings of preschoolers to adolescents, across gender, as well as across observers. Mervielde (1994) found that, when teachers generated characteristics illustrating individual differences in their Belgian students (ages 4 to 12 years), Agreeableness was the most prominent factor.

Research by Victor (1994) provided possible reasons that teachers recognized Agreeableness as a salient trait. He had teachers provide personality ratings of fifth- and sixth-grade students using Digman and Inouye's (1986) Hawaii Scales for Judging Behavior. A second teacher then completed a behavior problem questionnaire (RBPC; Quay & Peterson, 1961). Victor first replicated the Five-Factor solution reported by Digman and Inouye (1986) and then refactored the data combining the RBPC and the personality inventory. Agreeableness showed strong loadings on the Conduct Disorder factor. Victor's findings supported Digman's (1989) speculation that the low end of Agreeableness suggests psychopathology and noncompliance. In any case, it was clear that differences in Agreeableness accounted for much of the variance in behavior disorders for middle-school children.

AGREEABLENESS IN PARENTS' FREE-LANGUAGE DESCRIPTIONS OF CHILDREN

The lexical tradition focused on the basic description of individuality rather than on investigations of biological or environmental correlates of individual differences. The results from our cross-national study of parents' free-language descriptions of their children have shown that the concept of Agreeableness (as coded using the manual described in chapter 1) is very salient for parents. As described in chapter 1, we divided the dimension of Agreeableness into three facets: Kind and Helpful, Manageable for Caregivers, and Honest and Sincere. These categories were not formed empirically; we hoped that they would prove to be a useful classification of many of the descriptors given by teachers and parents.

The proportion of descriptors coded as Agreeable based on the total number of codable phrases used by parents to describe their children is summarized in Fig. 3.1. It can be seen that the Agreeable dimension accounts for between 17.3% and 25.5% of all descriptors given by parents. Most descriptions were coded in the facets Kind and Helpful and Man-

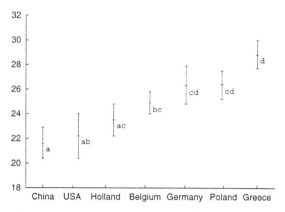

FIG. 3.1. Arcsine transformed means and 95% confidence intervals for Category II, Agreeableness. *Note.* Means of samples sharing a common letter are *not* significantly different from one another according to post hoc Scheffé tests.

ageable (see Figs. 3.2 & 3.3). The Honesty facet was used infrequently. Of the total of 2,416 parents included in this study, only 300 ever used a descriptor that could be coded in the Honesty subcategory. This is not to say that parents do not value honesty. Baldwin, Baldwin, and Cole (1990) reported that when parents made ratings of Kohn's (1977) 13 values, they endorsed Honesty as the most important. We speculate that traits such as Honesty might become more salient to parents as their children approach adolescence and adulthood. An alternative hypothesis is that parents assume honesty in their children. Thus Honesty is a characteristic

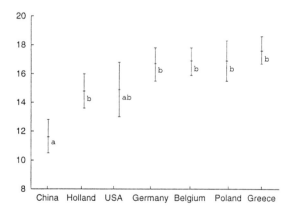

FIG. 3.2. Arcsine transformed means and 95% confidence intervals for Category IIa, Helpfulness. *Note.* Means of samples sharing a common letter are *not* significantly different from one another according to post hoc Scheffé tests.

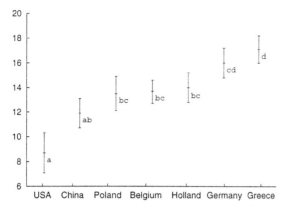

FIG. 3.3. Arcsine transformed means and 95% confidence intervals for Category IIb, Manageability. *Note.* Means of samples sharing a common letter are *not* significantly different from one another according to post hoc Scheffé tests.

that is highly valued by parents, but it is only mentioned when absent. For example, a parent might report that a child tells lies or has been caught cheating at school, yet it is unlikely that the parent would mention that the child does not lie, cheat, or steal.

Greek parents provided the greatest percentage of Agreeable phrases, while Chinese parents used the fewest. Greek respondents differed significantly at $p < .05$ on the Scheffé Multiple Range test, with an effect size of $\eta^2 > .05$, from the U.S. sample as well as the Chinese sample. This finding was hypothesized by the U.S. team when it went in search of research funding (National Institute of Mental Health grant proposal No. 50302). We based our hypothesis on the work by Triandis (1972), who found that the term *philotemo* was used by 74% of Greeks when asked to describe themselves. *Philotemo* is not easily translated into English, but describes a person who is "polite, virtuous, proud, has 'a good soul,' behaves correctly, meets obligations, does his duty, is truthful, generous, self-sacrificing, tactful, respectful, and grateful" (Triandis, 1972, pp. 308–309). Because of this emphasis on *philotemo* and because most descriptors used to define the term are coded in the dimension of Agreeableness in our coding system, we speculated that Greeks might find these characteristics to be more important, or salient, than did people from other countries participating in this study. Although other significant differences can be seen in Figs. 3.1, 3.2, and 3.3, the effect sizes were less than $\eta^2 > .05$, and we judged them as too small to merit meaningful interpretation.

A different picture is portrayed when the Agreeableness category is divided into descriptors coded as either positive or negative (see Table

TABLE 3.3
Proportions of Descriptors Coded Positive or Negative for Agreeableness

		U.S.A.	Netherlands	Belgium	Germany	Poland	Greece	China	Total
A: Positive	M	13.1_{ab}	11.3_{ab}	12.0_{ab}	11.8_{ab}	15.9_{ab}	15.6_a	10.9_b	13.0
B: Negative	M	4.6_{ab}	6.9_a	6.9_a	9.5_{ac}	7.7_a	10.0_{ac}	6.7_a	7.2

Note. Means in the same row that do not share subscripts differ at $p < .05$ in the Scheffé Multiple Range test and have an effect size (η^2) larger than .05. Analyses based on arcsine transformed data.

3.3). Unlike some of the other dimensions (e.g., Extraversion), descriptors coded as positive with respect to Agreeableness (e.g., kind, helpful, cooperative, sweet) are positive in evaluation, while those coded as negative instances of Agreeableness (e.g., selfish, mean, argumentative, evil) are negative in evaluation. The percentage of descriptors in the dimension of Agreeableness coded as high are presented by country. The percentage of descriptors coded positively ranged from 10.9 to 15.9. Tests for mean differences showed that Greece and China differed significantly with an $\eta^2 > .05$. Greek parents used proportionally more positive terms to describe their children than did Chinese parents. Further, the percentage of negative descriptors ranged from 4.6 (United States) to 10 (Greece). Both German and Greek samples of parents used more negative descriptors than did the U.S. sample, another instance of the importance of agreeable traits for Greek parents. They discussed their children in terms of both kind and prosocial behavior as well as in terms of selfish and uncooperative characteristics.

SALIENCE OF AGREEABLENESS
ACROSS INFORMANTS

Thus far we have reported only on parental descriptions of children. Does the FFM provide an adequate representation of children's perception of themselves and their peers? This area, like the general area of personality structure in children, has remained nearly an empty set. There were early studies of children's perceptions of parents (e.g., Kagan, 1961; Kagan & Lemkin, 1963) and children's descriptions of others, the most notable being Donahue (1994), Lively and Bromley (1973), and Yarrow and Campbell (1963). The major conclusion from these studies of children's cognitions about social concepts (Peevers & Secord, 1973; Prentice, 1990; Wylie, 1990) is that children used many structural forms in addition to traits to describe self and others (e.g., fact, habits, skills, appearance). Younger children (less than about 10 years old) were more concerned with readily observable external features of people. This complex problem of trait perception is embedded in the more general area of the development of person perception. The lexical and cognitive traditions must both be considered when using children's free descriptions of self and others to provide the basis of instrument development.

Lanthier (1993) had children (aged 10 to 14 years) rate themselves on a Big Five Personality Questionnaire (BFPQ), which he constructed from a list of adjectives found in Goldberg (1990), Norman (1963), and McCrae and Costa (1987). Lanthier extracted seven factors. Factor I resembled the positive pole of Agreeableness with items such as Cooperative, Sincere, and Trusting loading highly. The sixth factor was reported to resemble the negative pole of Agreeableness with items such as Selfish, Stubborn, and Rude as high loaders. Lanthier's findings provide evidence that children can use the FFM to describe themselves in middle childhood and that they make a distinction between the positive and negative poles of Agreeableness.

To explore children's spontaneous use of the FFM to describe others, Havill and the University of Georgia team interviewed 140 fourth- and fifth-grade students. The procedure was very similar to the parent interviews described in chapter 1. We recorded all interviews and asked the children to describe themselves, to describe a same-sex peer, and to describe a peer of the other gender. They were told that the peer that they described could be a friend, a classmate, or someone of the same age from their neighborhood. It was made clear that children did not have to like the peers whom they chose to describe. They were given prompts such as: "How are you the same as or different from other boys or girls your age?" and "What are you like on the inside?"

We found that 81% of the descriptions provided by the children could be coded in the first five dimensions of our category system. As can be seen in Table 3.4, the Agreeableness dimension accounted for 21% of the descriptions. Fifteen percent of all descriptions provided by the children were coded on the positive or high pole of Agreeableness. The facet used most often was Helpful and Kind. Eighteen percent of their descriptors

TABLE 3.4
Children's Free-Language Descriptions of Self and Others

Agreeableness Facet	Percentage of High Agreeableness Descriptors	Percentage of Low Agreeableness (Disagreeable) Descriptors
Helpful, Kind	14	4
Manageable	1	1
Honest	0	0

Note. Percentages are based on the total number of descriptors.

were coded in that facet of Agreeableness. The descriptors in that category were coded mostly on the high pole of Agreeableness. The children described themselves and others in words such as nice, gentle, kind and in phrases referring to sharing. The negative (low) terms included teasing, picks on people, annoying. It was quite obvious that the third facet, Honesty, was not used at all. None of the children described themselves or others as being honest or dishonest. This facet was the same one that parents used infrequently.

This study provides evidence that the FFM can account for a substantial proportion of what children say is important to know about themselves and their peers. Research along this line begins to answer questions of the adequacy of the FFM to represent what is salient to children about their self-representations as well as those of others.

CONCLUSION

An Agreeableness dimension has emerged across languages, methods, raters, and ages of individuals being described. The essence of Agreeableness (or Disagreeableness)—the behaviors, states, traits, motives, and styles displayed by individuals—have intrigued teachers, parents, raters, children, spouses, peers, and strangers. This is not surprising: Agreeableness determines the quality of social interaction. We suspect that children's levels of Agreeableness affect their social interactions through a pattern of behavioral styles; a child's Agreeableness is very salient for parents. When these categories can be measured by an instrument appropriate for children, we predict that an agreeable–disagreeable factor will emerge across all countries. We predict that children will vary widely on Manageability (a facet of Agreeableness) from extremely manageable to extremely unmanageable. With a continuous dimension of Manageability or Agreeableness in general, normal-range phenomena might be distinguished from abnormal. For example, McCrae (1994) carefully illustrated the symptoms of and problems with being extreme on the adult Agreeableness factor. He stated that high Agreeableness includes such characteristics as gullibility, inability to stand up to others, excessive generosity to the detriment of self, and being easily taken advantage of. Low Agreeableness scores might be characterized by an inability to trust friends and family and quarrelsome, manipulative, rude, and alienating behaviors. As Agreeableness descriptors accounted for a large percentage of parental descriptors across age and country, we anticipate that the factor will emerge strongly as instruments are developed in each country. We expect some descriptors that we code as low Agreeableness to correlate positively with descriptors coded as low in Emotional Stability (e.g., stubborn, irritable, argumentative, easily upset), which will form a Manageability factor. Descriptors coded as high Agreeableness are expected to correlate with Sociability (a facet of Extraversion) items (e.g., kind, friendly, helpful, outgoing). Thus our coding system might not be preserved in its current form, but we hope that the emerging factor structures will allow us to explore the relation between Agreeableness and adaptive functioning in childhood.

REFERENCES

Ahadi, S. A., & Rothbart, M. K. (1994). Temperament, development and the Big Five. In C. H. Halverson, Jr., G. A. Kohnstamm, & R. P. Martin (Eds.), *The developing structure of temperament and personality from infancy to adulthood* (pp. 189–208). Hillsdale, NJ: Lawrence Erlbaum Associates.

Baldwin, A. L., Baldwin, C., & Cole, R. E. (1990). Stress-resistant families and stress-resistant children. In J. Rolf, A. S. Masten, D. Cicchetti, K. H. Nuechterlein, & S. Weintraub (Eds.), *Risk and protective factors in the development of psychopathology* (pp. 257–280). Cambridge, England: Cambridge University Press.

Bates, J. E. (1986). Measurement of temperament. In R. Plomin & J. Dunn (Eds.), *The study of temperament: Changes, continuities and challenges* (pp. 1–11). Hillsdale, NJ: Lawrence Erlbaum Associates.

Bates, J. E., & Wachs, T. D. (Eds.). (1994). *Temperament: Individual differences at the interface of biology and behavior.* Washington, DC: American Psychological Association Press.

Bjorklund, D. F., & Harnishfeger, K. K. (1995). The role of inhibition mechanisms in the evolution of human cognition. In F. N. Dempster & C. H. Brainerd (Eds.), *New perspectives on interference and inhibition in cognition* (pp. 141–173). New York: Academic Press.

Bjorklund, D. F., & Kipp, K. (1996). Parental investment theory and gender differences in the evolution of inhibition mechanisms. *Psychological Bulletin, 120,* 163–188.

Block, J. (1961). *The Q-Sort method in personality assessment and psychiatric research.* Palo Alto, CA: Consulting Psychologists Press.

Borgatta, E. F. (1964). The structure of personality characteristics. *Behavioral Science, 9,* 8–17.

Buss, D. M. (1992). Manipulation in close relationships: Five personality factors in interfactional context. *Journal of Personality, 60,* 477–499.

Campbell, S. B. (1991). *Behavior problems in preschool children: Clinical and developmental issues.* New York: Guilford Press.

Caspi, A., Elder, G. H., & Bem, D. J. (1987). Moving against the world: Life-course patterns of explosive children. *Developmental Psychology, 23,* 308–313.

Cattell, R. B. (1945). The description of personality: Principles and findings in a factor analysis. *American Journal of Psychology, 58,* 69–90.

Conley, J. J. (1985). Longitudinal stability of personality traits: A multitrait–multimethod–multioccasion analysis. *Journal of Personality and Social Psychology, 49,* 1266–1282.

Cosmides, L. (1989). The logic of social exchange: Has natural selection shaped how humans reason? Studies with the Wason selection task. *Cognition, 31,* 187–276.

Costa, P. T., Jr., McCrae, R. R., & Dye, D. A. (1991). Facet scales for Agreeableness and Conscientiousness: A revision of the NEO Personality Inventory. *Personality and Individual Differences, 12,* 887–898.

De Raad, B., Mulder, E., Kloosterman, K., & Hofstee, W. K. (1988). Personality-descriptive verbs. *European Journal of Personality, 2,* 81–96.

Digman, J. M. (1989). Five robust trait dimensions: Development, stability, and utility. *Journal of Personality, 57*, 195–214.

Digman, J. M. (1990). Personality structure: Emergence of the five-factor model. *Annual Review of Psychology, 41*, 417–440.

Digman, J. M., & Inouye, J. (1986). Further specification of the five robust factors of personality. *Journal of Personality and Social Psychology, 50*, 116–123.

Digman, J. M., & Takemoto-Chock, N. K. (1981). Factors in the natural language of personality: Re-analysis, comparison, and interpretation of six major studies. *Multivariate Behavioral Research, 16*, 255–273.

Donahue, E. M. (1994). Do children use the Big Five, too? Content and structural form in personality description. *Journal of Personality, 62*, 45–66.

Eysenck, H. J. (1994). The Big five or giant three: Criteria for a paradigm. In C. H. Halverson, Jr., G. A. Kohnstamm, & R. P. Martin (Eds.), *The developing structure of temperament and personality from infancy to adulthood* (pp. 37–51). Hillsdale, NJ: Lawrence Erlbaum Associates.

Fiske, D. W. (1949). Consistency of the factorial structures of personality ratings from different sources. *Journal of Abnormal and Social Psychology, 44*, 329–344.

Goldberg, L. R. (1981). Language and individual differences: The search for universals in personality lexicons. In L. Wheeler (Ed.), *Review of personality and social psychology* (Vol. 1; pp. 203–234). Hillsdale, NJ: Lawrence Erlbaum Associates.

Goldberg, L. R. (1990). An alternative "Description of Personality": The Big-Five Factor structure. *Journal of Personality and Social Psychology, 59*, 1216–1229.

Goldberg, L. R., & Rosolack, T. K. (1994). The big five factor structure as an integrative framework: An empirical comparison with Eysenck's P-E-N model. In C. H. Halverson, Jr., G. A. Kohnstamm, & R. P. Martin (Eds.), *The developing structure of temperament and personality from infancy to adulthood* (pp. 37–51). Hillsdale, NJ: Lawrence Erlbaum Associates.

Goldsmith, H. H., Buss, A., Plomin, R., Rothbart, M. K., Thomas, A., Chess, S., Hinde, R. A., & McCall, R. B. (1987). What is temperament? Four approaches. *Child Development, 58*, 505–529.

Graziano, W. G. (1994). The development of agreeableness as a dimension of personality. In C. H. Halverson, Jr., G. A. Kohnstamm, & R. P. Martin (Eds.), *The developing structure of temperament and personality from infancy to adulthood* (pp. 339–354). Hillsdale, NJ: Lawrence Erlbaum Associates.

Graziano, W. G., & Eisenberg, N. H. (1997). Agreeableness: A dimension of personality. In R. Hogan, J. Johnson, & S. Briggs (Eds.), *Handbook of personality psychology* (pp. 795–825). Orlando, FL: Academic Press.

Graziano, W. G., & Ward, D. (1992). Probing the Big Five in adolescence: Personality and adjustment during a developmental transition. *Journal of Personality, 60*, 425–439.

Hogan, R. (1983). A socioanalytic theory of personality. In M. M. Page (Ed.), *Nebraska Symposium on Motivation, 1982: Personality—Current theory and research*. Lincoln: University of Nebraska Press.

Hogan, R. (1986). *Hogan Personality Inventory manual*. Minneapolis, MN: National Computer Center.

John, O. P. (1990). The "Big Five" factor taxonomy: Dimensions of personality in the natural language and in questionnaires. In L. A. Pervin (Ed.), *Handbook of personality: Theory and research* (pp. 66–100). New York: Guilford Press.

Johnson, J. A., & Ostendorf, F. (1993). Clarification of the five-factor model with the Abridged Big Five Dimensional Circumplex. *Journal of Personality and Social Psychology, 65*, 563–576.

Kagan, J. (1961). Child's symbolic conceptualization of parents. *Child Development, 32*, 625–626.

Kagan, J., & Lemkin, J. (1963). The child's differential perception of parental attributes. *Journal of Abnormal and Social Psychology, 61*, 440–447.

Killeen, M. R., Ayoub, C., & Frame, C. (1993, November). *Stability of self-esteem: An individual growth modeling approach.* Paper presented at the meeting of the Society for Education and Research in Psychiatric Nursing, Chicago, IL.

Kohn, M. L. (1977). *Class and conformity* (2nd ed.). Chicago: University of Chicago Press.

Lanthier, R. P. (1993). *The Big five dimensions of personality in middle childhood and adolescence.* Unpublished doctoral dissertation, University of Denver, Denver, CO.

Leary, T. (1957). *Interpersonal diagnosis of personality.* New York: Ronald Press.

Lively, W. J., & Bromley, D. B. (1973). *Person perception in childhood and adolescence.* London: Wiley.

Loeber, R. (1990). Development and risk factors of juvenile antisocial behavior and delinquency. *Clinical Psychology Review, 10*, 1–41.

McCrae, R. R. (1994). A reformulation of Axis II: Personality and personality-related problems. In P. T. Costa & T. A. Widger (Eds.), *Personality disorders and the Five-Factor Model of personality* (pp. 303–309). Washington, DC: American Psychological Association Press.

McCrae, R. R., & Costa, P. T. (1987). Validation of the five-factor model across instruments and observers. *Journal of Personality and Social Psychology, 52*, 81–90.

McCrae, R. R., & Costa, P. T. (1989). Reinterpreting the Myers–Briggs Type Indicator from the Five-Factor model of personality. *Journal of Personality, 57*, 17–40.

McCrae, R. R., Costa, P. T., Jr., & Busch, C. M. (1986). Evaluating comprehensiveness in personality systems: The California Q-Set and the five-factor model. *Journal of Personality, 54*, 430–446.

McCrae, R. R., & John, O. P. (1992). An Introduction to the Five-Factor Model and its applications. *Journal of Personality, 60*, 175–215.

McGee, R., Partridge, F., Williams, S., & Silva, P. A. (1991). A twelve-year follow-up of preschool hyperactive children. *Journal of the American Academy of Child and Adolescent Psychiatry, 30*, 224–232.

Mead, M. (1972). *Blackberry winter: My earlier years.* New York: Simon & Schuster.

Mervielde, I. (1994). A Five-Factor Model classification of teachers' constructs on individual differences among children ages 4 to 12. In C. H. Halverson, Jr., G. A. Kohnstamm, & R. P. Martin (Eds.), *The developing structure of temperament and personality from infancy to adulthood* (pp. 37–51). Hillsdale, NJ: Lawrence Erlbaum Associates.

Myers, I. B., & McCaulley, M. H. (1985). *Manual: A guide to the development and use of the Myers–Briggs Type Indicator.* Palo Alto, CA: Consulting Psychologists Press.

Norman, W. T. (1963). Toward an adequate taxonomy of personality attributes: Replicated factor structure in peer nomination personality ratings. *Journal of Abnormal and Social Psychology, 66*, 574–583.

Offord, D. R., Boyle, M. H., Racine, Y. A., & Fleming, J. E. (1992). Outcome, prognosis, and risk in a longitudinal follow-up study. *Journal of the American Academy of Child and Adolescent Psychiatry, 31*, 916–923.

Peevers, B. H., & Secord, P. F. (1973). Developmental changes in attribution of descriptive concepts to persons. *Journal of Personality and Social Psychology, 27*, 120–128.

Prentice, D. H. (1990). Familiarity and differences in self and other representations. *Journal of Personality and Social Psychology, 59*, 369–383.

Quay, H., & Peterson, D. (1961). *Behavior problem checklist for children 2–5.* Unpublished manuscript.

Rothbart, M. K., Derryberry, D., & Posner, M. J. (1994). A psychobiological approach to the development of temperament. In J. E. Bates & T. D. Wachs (Eds.), *Temperament: Individual differences at the interface of biology and behavior* (pp. 83–116). Washington, DC: American Psychological Association Press.

Rutter, M. (1985). Resilience in the face of adversity: Protective factors and resistance to psychiatric disorder. *British Journal of Psychiatry, 147*, 598–611.

Rutter, M. (1987). Temperament, personality, and personality disorder. *British Journal of Psychiatry, 150*, 443–458.

Thomas, A., Chess, S., & Birch, H. G. (1968). *Temperament and behavior disorders in children.* New York: New York University Press.

Triandis, H. C. (Ed.). (1972). *The analysis of subjective culture.* New York: Wiley-Interscience.

Tupes, E. C., & Christal, R. C. (1961). *Recurrent personality factors based on trait ratings* (Tech. Rep. No. ASD-TR-61-97). Lackland Air Force Base, TX: U.S. Air Force.

Van Lieshout, C. F. M., & Haselager, G. J. T. (1994). The big five personality factors in Q-sort descriptions of children and adolescents. In C. H. Halverson, Jr., G. A. Kohnstamm, & R. P. Martin (Eds.), *The developing structure of temperament and personality from infancy to adulthood* (pp. 293–318). Hillsdale, NJ: Lawrence Erlbaum Associates.

Victor, J. B. (1994). The Five-Factor Model applied to individual differences in school behavior. In C. H. Halverson, Jr., G. A. Kohnstamm, & R. P. Martin (Eds.), *The developing structure of temperament and personality from infancy to adulthood* (pp. 37–51). Hillsdale, NJ: Lawrence Erlbaum Associates.

Wiggins, J. S. (1991). Agency and communion as conceptual coordinates for the understanding and measurement of interpersonal behavior. In D. Cicchetti & W. Grove (Eds.), *Thinking critically in psychology: Essays in honor of Paul E. Meehl* (pp. 89–113). New York: Cambridge Unversity Press.

Wylie, R. C. (1990). Mothers' attributions to their young children: The verbal environment as a resource for children's self-concept acquisition. *Journal of Personality, 58*, 421–441.

Yarrow, M. R., & Campbell, J. D. (1963). Person perception in children. *Merrill–Palmer Quarterly, 9*, 57–72.

A Developmental Integration of Conscientiousness From Childhood to Adulthood

Geldolph A. Kohnstamm
Leiden University

Yuching Zhang
Chinese Academy of Sciences

Anne-Marie Slotboom
Leiden University

Eric Elphick
Leiden University

Most modern concepts in psychology have roots in the past. Where and when can we locate the beginnings of psychological interest in the cluster of meanings associated with the Big Five factor of Conscientiousness? Without being comprehensive, we can cite the phrenologists of the 19th century who drew pictures of the brain with separate locations for such faculties as Cautiousness, Acquisitiveness, Constructiveness, Firmness, and Conscientiousness. Next, we recall Freud's conception of the anal character as an early formulation of Conscientiousness (Freud, 1908/1941, 1908/1977). To quote from the English translation by Strachey:

> The people I am about to describe are noteworthy for a regular combination of the three following characteristics. They are especially *orderly, parsimonious* and *obstinate*. Each of these words actually covers a small group or series of interrelated character-traits. "Orderly" covers the notion of bodily cleanliness, as well as of conscientiousness in carrying out small duties, and trustworthiness. Its opposite would be "untidy" and "neglectful." (Freud, 1908/1977, p. 209)

The editor of the 1977 Pelican edition, Angela Richards, added a footnote to explain her choice of the word "orderly" to translate Freud's original *ordentlich*: "The original meaning of the word (*ordentlich*) is 'orderly'; but it has become greatly extended in use. It can be the equivalent of such English terms as 'correct,' 'tidy,' 'cleanly,' 'trustworthy,' as well as 'regular,' 'decent,' and 'proper,' in the more colloquial senses of those words" (Freud, 1908/1977, p. 209, footnote).

Freud asserted that parsimony and obstinacy were linked with each other more closely than they were with orderliness. The first two traits were also more fundamental elements of the character complex: "Yet it seems to me incontestable that all three in some way belong together" (Freud, 1908/1941, 1908/1977, p. 210). Freud described the appearance of this character in early childhood:

> . . . they [the patients] took a comparatively long time to overcome their infantile fecal incontinence. . . . As infants, they seem to have belonged to the class who refuse to empty their bowels when they are put on the pot, because they derive a subsidiary pleasure from defecating. . . . From these indications we infer that such people are born with a sexual constitution in which the erotogenicity of the anal zone is exceptionally strong. (Freud, 1908/1941, 1977, p. 210)

Freud used the German word *Gewissenhaftigkeit* for this set of traits, a synonym of the English word Conscientiousness; he saw this trait as primarily inborn and not acquired (e.g., as a result of a type of toilet training).

Freud's description of typical orderly people and their anal fixations might explain why so little attention was initially paid to this personality trait. "Many psychologists called this *compulsiveness* and could not imagine it as a worthwhile trait to possess, least of all to investigate. Others saw it as an exceedingly minor virtue of shopkeepers" (Digman, personal communication, May 1995). In Freud's later writings, the development of the superego to resolve the oedipal conflict with the father became the major source of individual differences in Conscientiousness. The inborn orderliness of the anal character became incorporated in a broader striving to come up to the expectations of the father and other authority figures.

A first *empirical* proof of the importance of this trait came with the work of Cattell (1945), who reduced the 4,500 traits from Allport and Odbert's list of trait adjectives to 35 "primary source" traits. His famous personality instrument, the 16 PF (Cattell, Eber, & Tatsuoka, 1980), revealed a second-order source trait labeled Strength of Inner Controls. The first-order trait loading highest on this factor was named G or Superego Strength. Cattell (1973) mentioned Florence Nightingale and Abraham Lincoln as good examples of personalities high on trait G, a factor that "seems to carry all the signs of strength in the superego as described by psychoanalytic theory: Persistence, conscientiousness, and so on" (Cartwright, 1979, p. 382).

The prominent position of Conscientiousness as one of the Big Five was assured by the work of Fiske (1949) and Tupes and Christal (1961/1992). Tupes and Christal found "five relatively strong and recurrent factors and nothing more of any consequence" (p. 14). They labeled their third factor Dependability, including the scales Conscientious, Responsible, and Orderly. It took another 20 years for Digman and Takemoto-Chock (1981) to demonstrate the existence of the same five factors in teacher ratings of first- and second-grade school children on the Cattell Scales. These authors proposed the label of Will to Achieve as more appropriate than that of Conscientiousness, after Webb (1915), who suggested that Will (w) was a factor to be distinguished from General Intelligence (g) in predicting school achievement.

As can be seen from this discussion, there are a number of variations in the meanings subsumed under the broad trait of Conscientiousness. Next we summarize some of the major interpretatons of the construct.

MODERN INTERPRETATIONS
OF CONSCIENTIOUSNESS

Goldberg

Goldberg (1992) developed a set of 100 unipolar markers, 20 marking each of the Big Five Factors. These 100 markers have proved to be univocal factor definers in a variety of samples of self- and peer descriptions and are now known as the Goldberg markers. In Table 4.1 the markers for Factor III are based on self-ratings of 503 U.S. college students.

McCrae and Costa

McCrae and Costa have developed a slightly different interpretation of this factor. In the Revised NEO Personality Inventory (NEO-PI-R; Costa & McCrae, 1994), the facet scales composing Conscientiousness are labeled as Achievement Striving, Self-Discipline, Competence, Dutifulness, Deliberation, and Order. These investigators emphasized ambition and hard work, which were not strongly represented in Goldberg's markers. Goldberg's Factor III appears more restricted in meaning than is the McCrae and Costa construct, which seems to put higher value on the striving for achievement than on the degree of orderliness (see also McCrae & Costa, 1990, pp. 42–45).

TABLE 4.1
Goldberg's Markers for Factor III, Conscientiousness,
and Varimax-Rotated Factor Loadings

III+		III−	
Organized	.77	Disorganized	−.76
Neat	.67	Careless	−.61
Systematic	.63	Unsystematic	−.60
Efficient	.62	Inefficient	−.60
Thorough	.58	Sloppy	−.57
Practical	.54	Haphazard	−.53
Prompt	.50	Inconsistent	−.50
Careful	.47	Impractical	−.49
Steady	.44	Negligent	−.49
Conscientious	.30	Undependable	−.45

Note. Adapted from "The Big Five Factor Structure as an Integrative Framework: An Empirical Comparison With Eysenck's P-E-N Model," by L. R. Goldberg and T. K. Rosolack (1994), in C. F. Halverson, G. A. Kohnstamm, & R. P. Martin (Eds.), *The developing structure of temperament and personality from infancy to adulthood* (p. 32). Hillsdale, NJ: Lawrence Erlbaum Associates.

Ostendorf and Angleitner

Another illustration from the rapidly growing research literature comes from Ostendorf and Angleitner's work with German parents. Table 4.2 summarizes that work (Ostendorf & Angleitner, 1993).

Some of the highest loading adjectives in this large-scale German study, *arbeitsam* (hard working), *fleissig* (industrious), *emsig* (diligent), *strebsam* (ambitious), *arbeitsscheu* (lazy), are not represented in Goldberg's markers (Table 4.1) and seem to define the German factor of Conscientiousness more in accordance with the conception of McCrae and Costa. This impression is confirmed by another study in which 300 German adults were asked to fill out the German versions of several questionnaires, including the Personality Research Form and the NEO Personality Inventory (NEO PI), by Costa and McCrae. From their results, the authors concluded that Digman's Will to Achieve was a better label for their third factor than was Conscientiousness (Ostendorf & Angleitner, 1993).

This short excursion into the operationalizations of Conscientiousness in adult personality psychology shows that there is yet no consensus about the central meaning of this factor in adulthood. Is being conscientious mainly being organized and neat, as Goldberg asserted, or is it primarily being industrious and diligent, as McCrae and Costa and Angleitner and Ostendorf saw it? Such disagreement might be the result of slightly different rotations of axes in the factor analyses done by individual

TABLE 4.2
Results of German Study by Ostendorf and Angleitner (1993)

German Original	English Translation	PR	SR
1. *Arbeitsam*	Hardworking	.72	.68
2. *Fleissig*	Diligent	.71	.68
3. *Pflichtbewusst*	Conscientious	.74	.64
4. *Emsig*	Busy	.64	.64
5. *Strebsam*	Ambitious and industrious	.66	.64
6. *Pflichteifrig*	Zealous	.72	.62
7. *Pflichttreu*	Dutiful	.67	.60
8. *Zielbewusst*	Goal directed	.57	.59
9. *Ordentlich*	Neat and tidy	.67	.57
10. *Tüchtig*	Efficient	.67	.57
11. *Konsequent*	Logically consistent	.44	.56
12. *Verantwortungsbewusst*	Responsible	.60	.53
13. *Zielstrebig*	Determined	.54	.52
14. *Selbstdiszipliniert*	Self-disciplined	.53	.51
15. *Ordnungsliebend*	Orderly	.63	.51
16. *Zielsicher*	Decisive	.56	.51
17. *Verlässlich*	Reliable	.46	.49
18. *Tolpatschig*	Awkward, clumsy	−.51	−.47
19. *Unbeständig*	Erratic, inconsistent	−.49	−.55
20. *Arbeitsscheu*	Lazy	−.63	−.58

Note. PR = averaged peer rating (3 per subject): $N = 511$; SR = self-ratings: $N = 511$. The scales are ranked according to their factor loadings in the self-ratings. Variables with highest loadings on Factor III (Conscientiousness). Factor loadings from five varimax-rotated principal components in samples of peer and self-ratings. Some of the translations changed by the present authors.

investigators, but it might also be that investigators are more or less inclusive in ascribing meaning to this factor.

CONSCIENTIOUSNESS IN CHILDHOOD

It is relatively easy to *speculate* about which traits of children and adolescents are the precursors of facets of adult Conscientiousness. Analogies in child and adolescent behavior can easily be found for the various facets of the trait. We review the factor analytic studies of child and adolescent temperament and personality to see whether factors analogous to one or more key facets of adult Conscientiousness have emerged. We focus on two different periods: infancy and childhood up to early adolescence. For each period we ask: What traits seem to be plausible antecedents of the

Five-Factor Model (FFM) factor of Conscientiousness? While questioning, we remain mindful of the disagreement among FFM researchers about the core meaning of this factor. We do not pretend to be exhaustive in discussing the studies selected for this short review.

Infancy

Rothbart's Focus on Effortful Control.   Rothbart and Posner (1985) have proposed individual temperamental differences in Effortful Control among infants, differences reflecting individual differences in attentional self-regulation:

> Operationally, Effortful Control is reflected in individual differences in the ability to voluntarily sustain focus on a task, to voluntarily shift attention from one task to another, to voluntarily initiate action, and to voluntarily inhibit action. Although the maturation of this system undergoes rapid growth during the last half of the infant's first year, this system appears to continue to mature throughout at least the preschool period. (Ahadi & Rothbart, 1994, p. 196)

Rothbart and associates saw Effortful Control as a superordinate system of self-regulation, modulating the behavioral tendencies of approach-withdrawal, expressions of anxiety (and of anger, distress), and attentional processes. In their theorizing, all "decisions" that seem to begin or stop an activity are dependent on Effortful Control. Discussing the possible relation between Effortful Control and the adult personality trait of Conscientiousness, Ahadi and Rothbart (1994) suggested that the self-regulative aspects of the factor of Conscientiousness might be developmentally based on early expressions of individual differences in Effortful Control. Such a hypothesis, supported by an authoritative psychobiological theory, awaits testing in longitudinal studies. Do infants who can focus their attention for long periods grow up to be first more conscientious pupils and later more conscientious workers?

In our opinion, the low stability coefficients usually obtained in longitudinal studies of infant temperament offer little hope of finding a strong infancy–adulthood link in future studies, but more refined operationalizations may disclose links yet to be found. Even so, important facets of FFM Conscientiousness such as being industrious, ambitious, and hard-working (next to being organized and orderly) are not easily recognizable in Rothbart's theory of the early expressions of the self-regulative system. Further, Ahadi and Rothbart's (1994) suggestion that "one's ability to control attention facilitates internalization of social values" and that "inability to control attention may lead to the more disorganized, inconsistent, and nonconformist characterization of individuals low on Conscientiousness" (p. 200) focuses on *controls* and the regulation and direction of energy, not on the *differences* in available energy that might contribute to adult traits like being hardworking and industrious. The problem might lie with the broadness of the concept of Conscientiousness, combining as it does differences in the *energy available* to the individual, the *will* to use this energy, and the *controls* to use the energy in efficient and positively valued ways.

The Thomas–Chess Nine-Dimensional Model. Martin, Wisenbaker, and Huttunen (1994) reviewed 12 studies in which parents or teachers rated children on questionnaires tapping the nine dimensions of temperament proposed by Thomas and Chess (e.g., Thomas & Chess, 1977). Only those studies that analyzed item intercorrelations (as opposed to scale intercorrelations) were included. Four studies that factor analyzed parental ratings of *infants* were selected. In two of these four studies, both done in Sweden, a factor labeled Attentiveness was found; in the third study, done in Australia, a very small ninth factor labeled Persistence was found. No factor that could be seen as analogous resulted from the fourth, Finnish, infant study.

Martin, Wisenbaker, and Huttunen (1994) interpreted the Swedish infant Attentiveness factor as possibly related to task persistence factors found in parent and teacher ratings of children at later ages. One of the authors of the Swedish studies, Hagekull (1994), proposed, however, that infant Attentiveness might instead predict Emotional Stability. She proposed that her infant factor of Manageability was the infant precursor of Conscientiousness as this infant factor predicted scores on an Impulsivity factor in early childhood (Hagekull, 1994).

In light of this short review, specialists in infant temperament studies appear creative in proposing possible links between infant characteristics and later Conscientiousness. Differences in infant Effortful Control, Attention Regulation, Attentiveness, and Manageability were all seen as potentially important antecedents for later individual differences in Conscientiousness. Without longitudinal data, however, none of these speculations can be preferred over another.

Childhood and Early Adolescence

The Thomas–Chess Nine-Dimensional Model. A Task Persistence factor that combines items tapping Attention Span and Distractibility was prominent in most if not all item-based factor analytic studies of the questionnaires derived from the Thomas–Chess nine-dimensional model. Martin, Wisenbaker, and Huttunen (1994) stated that this factor becomes increasingly well organized as ratings of children go from the preschool period through adolescence. Further, Task Persistence is one of the dominant factors in ratings provided by teachers. These authors warned, however, against simplistic interpretations:

> The consistency with which this factor is obtained belies the complexity of the behavioral phenomena being rated. In infancy, the core items are related to the ability to notice variation in the environment, based on reaction to this variation. Attention is obviously involved in this process. Some items tap continuity of attention. At the preschool level, items assessing ability to control motoric activity, and to continue a frustrating learning experience, begin to appear. In later childhood and adolescence, the emphasis is on attention span. The most central behavior assessed by these items at all ages is continuity of activities related to learning or productive activity. (p. 166)

At the scale level, a .3 to .4 correlation between parental ratings on the scales of Persistence and Distractibility and teacher ratings of achievement in school subjects is typically found (see, e.g., Guerin, Gottfried, Oliver, & Thomas, 1994, using the Middle Childhood Temperament Questionnaire of Hegvik, McDevitt, & Carey, 1982). McClowry, Hegvik, and Teglasi (1993) factor analyzed this questionnaire at the item level. In two samples, a total of 868 children were rated by their mothers. Four reliable factors were labeled as Task Persistence, Negative Reactivity, Approach-Withdrawal, and Activity. The first factor was composed of items that mainly tapped a child's difficulty in completing assignments (homework, household chores, etc.) or projects (drawings, models, etc.).

Teacher Ratings of Schoolchildren. Earlier, we discussed the first study revealing the FFM structure in teacher ratings of schoolchildren (Digman & Takemoto-Chock, 1981; see also Digman, 1990, and Digman & Inouye, 1986). In much earlier studies by Cattell and Gruen (1953), with 11-year-olds, and by Cattell and Coan (1957), with first and second graders, a factor labeled Superego Strength was found underlying teachers' ratings of their pupils. This result was replicated by Digman (1963) using teacher ratings of 102 first- and second-grade children of the University of Hawaii Laboratory School. A first factor was found in the 38 items from the Cattell–Coan list of traits, a factor that Digman also labeled as Superego Strength. The five highest loading items (> .40) were:

> Neat, tidy, orderly versus untidy, careless with respect to appearance of self and belongings (.65).
> Responsible versus irresponsible, frivolous (.50).
> Stable of interests, attitudes, and opinions versus changeable in interests, attitudes and opinions (.44).

Careful with property of others versus careless, destructive of property of others (.41).

Persevering, determined versus quitting, fickle (.40). (Digman, 1963, pp. 49–50)

In his later studies, Digman began using single adjectives instead of the complex bipolar Cattell scales (see the preceding examples), although these adjectives were still derived from the Cattell scales. In 1986, Digman and Inouye published a study of teacher ratings for a group of sixth-grade Hawaiian children that "provided a beautiful confirmation of the essential wisdom of the five-factor model" (Digman, 1994, p. 372). A third factor that emerged was labeled Will to Achieve, with high positive (> .60) loadings of the adjectives careful (work), neat, persevering, and planful, and high negative loadings of eccentric, careless (property), and irresponsible. This result was replicated by Victor (1994), who used the same instrument to rate 180 fifth- and sixth-grade children in a rural county in Virginia.

Keogh, Pullis, and Cadwell (1982) found a strong factor labeled Task Orientation in a short form of the Thomas and Chess (1977) Teacher Temperament Questionnaire. This factor was composed of items originally intended to measure the Thomas–Chess dimensions of Persistence, Distractibility, and Activity. In the studies by Keogh and associates, this factor has consistently been the most powerful contributor to teachers' use of surveillance in all classroom situations (Keogh, 1989).

In Martin's studies with the Temperament Assessment Battery for Children (MTAB; Martin, 1988), a three-factor solution resulted in factors labeled as Emotionality, Persistence, and Sociability. Persistence (actually Task Persistence) was a combination of scales measuring being nondistractible (in attention directed at tasks), not running around, and not showing other manifestations of gross motor activity (in the classroom) and being persistent in completing tasks. The combination of these three scales was again labeled Task Orientation (Martin, Olejnik, & Gaddis, 1994) and proved to be a better predictor of school grades in reading and math than was intelligence quotient.

A similar factor of Task Orientation in teacher ratings of schoolchildren has been found in many other studies. For example, in the Dutch questionnaire SCHOBL (Bleichrodt, Resing, & Zaal, 1994), a strong factor of Task Orientation (*Werkhouding*) resulted from factoring items that were collected by interviewing teachers on pupils' individual differences in classroom behavior. The authors described a child who scored high on Task Orientation as one who can concentrate for a long time on his or her work, who has a consistent quality and speed of working, who is dedicated to the work, and who works neatly. This description is in opposition to that of a child who is distractible, uninterested, and careless, who is inconsistent in quality and speed of output, and who often has to be warned by the teacher.

Another large-scale Dutch study, by Kalverboer and his associates (Kalverboer, Pluister, & Visser, in press), was also based on an exhaustive inventory of observed classroom behaviors. In this respect, both studies differed from the ones we have reviewed (including the MTAB), which were exclusively based on the original Thomas–Chess framework and on the selection of behavioral indices. Kalverboer factor analyzed the teacher ratings of 1,381 pupils on 30 scales of three items each. He found a large first factor (explaining 37% of the variance) that he labeled as Task Orientation behavior. Ten scales loaded above .60 on this factor: Conscientious (− .88), distractible (.86), calm (−.80), irregular in quality of output (.77), hyperactive (.76), difficulty with writing (.75), careless (.74), dreamy (.69), obedient (−.67) and talkative (.64). Kohnstamm (1992), using the same instrument, replicated this result in an independent study with 290 pupils between 6 and 9 years old, rated by teachers of 290 different schools, spread all over the Netherlands.

Mervielde, Buyst, and De Fruyt (1995) had teachers rate their pupils on five bipolar scales for each of the FFM selected from the list of Goldberg's markers (in Flemish–Dutch translation; Mervielde, 1992). The Conscientiousness markers were (in Dutch translations): inaccurate–accurate, negligent–conscientious, neglectful–thorough, careless–careful, and lazy–industrious. Factor analyses at different age levels revealed that the Conscientiousness markers and the Openness to Experience and Intelligence markers often blended into one common factor. The Openness to Experience and Intelligence bipolar markers were unintelligent–intelligent, unsensible–sensible, unimaginative–imaginative, uncreative–creative, uninterested–eager to learn. In the teacher ratings of pupils aged 4 to 6 and 10 to 12, most of these markers merged into one factor. In the teacher ratings of children aged 6 to 8 and 8 to 10, however, two clearly distinct factors emerged, with only one Openness to Experience and Intelligence marker (uninterested–eager to learn) loading higher on the factor of Conscientiousness. This blend of FFM Dimensions III and V in the perceptions and ratings of the teachers was also found when schoolchildren rated their peers (Mervielde & De Fruyt, 1992).

Parents and Teachers Sorting the California Child Q Set (CCQ). In two studies, one done in Pittsburgh, Pennsylvania, and the other in Nijmegen, Netherlands, data obtained with the CCQ (J. H. Block & J. Block, 1980) were reanalyzed to see whether the FFM structure was recoverable, just as McCrae, Costa, and Busch (1986) had done for the adult version of this instrument, the California Adult Question (CAQ) set. John, Caspi, Robins, Moffitt, and Stouthamer-Loeber (1994) reported results of Q-sets provided by mothers of 350 ethnically diverse boys between 12 and 13 years old, living in a Pittsburgh inner city area (see also Robins, John, & Caspi, 1994). A "common language" version of the CCQ was used, adapted for use by laypersons. In a principal components analysis of the Pittsburgh CCQ data, involving all 100 CCQ items, seven interpretable factors emerged, the second of which strongly resembled Conscientiousness. The four highest loading items on this factor are shown in Table 4.3 (data obtained from O. P. John). In the Netherlands, van Lieshout and Haselager (1994) reported the CCQ descriptions of children and adolescents from six different studies. The CCQ cards were sorted for a total of 720 subjects, ranging in age from 3 to 16 years. The studies differed in who sorted the CCQ cards: parents, teachers, or adolescents (self- and peer ratings). A Dutch translation of the original CCQ items was used and not the "common language" version as in the study just reviewed. Factor analysis was performed on the total group and on subgroups. In the total group, a third factor labeled Conscientiousness was found. This factor was relatively small when compared with the first two, labeled as Agreeableness and Emotional Stability (Agreeableness was also the first factor in the Pittsburgh data). In Table 4.3, the Dutch factor loadings for the four highest loading CCQ items in the study by John are presented for comparison purposes.

There is some irony in the fact that Block, a devoted skeptic about the validity of the FFM (Block, 1995), has had his Q-set instrument analyzed for FFM content and FFM structure. Block and Block developed their CAQ and CCQ instruments to measure the theoretical constructs of Ego Control and Ego Resiliency. These constructs were conceptualized as dynamic individ-

TABLE 4.3
Highest Loading (> .50) Items Selected From California Child Question (CCQ) Set to Measure FFM Conscientiousness in Early Adolescence

CCQ Item	Factor Loadings: Pittsburgh	Factor Loadings: Nijmegen
41. He is determined in what he does; he does not give up easily.	.55	.73
47. He has high standards for himself. He needs to do very well in the things he does.	.52	.68
66. He pays attention well and can concentrate on things.	.61	.70
99. He thinks about his actions and behaviors; he uses his head before doing or saying something.	.53	.51

Note. Loadings in first column are on a second factor resulting from PCA of intercorrelations of 100 CCQ items by John et al. (data obtained from O. P. John). Loadings in the second column are on a third factor in a Dutch study by van Lieshout and Haselager (1994).

ual differences with variables that have powerful organizing effects on behavior across time and contexts (J. H. Block & J. Block, 1980). Robins et al. (1994) discussed the possible relations among these two constructs, as operationalized in the CAQ and CCQ; the FFM-related factors appeared to be accounting for 30% to 50% of the variance. They computed the usual scores for Ego Control and Ego Resiliency and found that Ego Undercontrol correlated positively (.51) with FFM Extraversion and negatively with both Agreeableness (–.62) and Conscientiousness (–.60). Ego Resiliency correlated positively with Conscientiousness (.76), Agreeableness (.62), and Extraversion (.38) and negatively with Emotional Stability (–.68). It is clear from these findings that Ego Resiliency and Ego Control are constructs of even broader scope than is the FFM.

Several conclusions can be drawn from these studies. First, all studies done with children, either with ratings by parents or by teachers, found a factor similar to McCrae and Costa's conception of Conscientiousness. Second, this factor could be more properly labeled Will to Achieve or Task Orientation to avoid the moral connotations as well as the psychoanalytic implications of Freud's theory of the superego. Third, this factor is clearly producible when the personality characteristics of children of *school age* are being rated—by parents and by teachers—but there are as yet insufficient data about the usefulness of such a construct for infants and toddlers. Ahadi and Rothbart's (1994) hypothesis that in infancy individual differences in Effortful Control are probably related to later individual differences in Conscientiousness seems plausible. Effortful Control, however, has been conceptualized as a superordinate temperament system, possibly influencing a wide array of behaviors, more than those behaviors that are typical for school-age manifestations of Conscientiousness.

Parental Descriptions of Child Conscientiousness. In Table 1.1 the three subcategories of our rationally constructed category of childhood Conscientiousness were presented, with examples of descriptors coded in each subcategory. In Table 4.4 the proportions of descriptors coded in this category are shown. The average proportions in the Total row range from 7.3% to 19.4%. The Chinese sample stands out from all the others in frequency of descriptors coded in this category. In Fig. 4.1 results of analysis of variance show that the Chinese average was significantly higher than all other sample means (Scheffé Multiple Range test after arcsine transformation for proportions: $F = 54.9$; $p < .000$; effect size, $\eta^2 = 12\%$). Also, the Greek average was significantly higher than those from the U.S., Polish, and Dutch parents ($p < .01$), but in the Greek case, the effect size was small. Among the five other samples no significant differences were found in the use of this category of descriptors.

TABLE 4.4
Average Proportions of Descriptors in Three Subcategories of
Main Category III, Conscientiousness (All Age Groups Combined)

		Belgium	Netherlands	Germany	Greece	China	Poland	U.S.A.
					Percentage			
A.	Carefulness	4.5	3.2	3.7	3.1	7.1	3.5	2.8
B.	Faithfulness	0.4	0.3	0.7	0.2	0.2	0.5	0.1
C.	Diligence	3.0	3.2	3.9	7.4	12.2	4.1	4.4
	Total III	7.9	6.8	8.3	10.8	19.4	8.1	7.3

In chapter 7, it is shown that there were clear increases in the proportions coded in this category with increases in the age of the children being described (from 3 to 9 years). This general age trend in the salience of Conscientiousness might be due in part to the age that children begin formal schooling. Clearly, parents rarely described preschool children as conscientious, but when the children began school, conscientiousness-related terms were used increasingly by parents.

Facets of Conscientiousness. For the three facets of Carefulness, Faithfulness, and Diligence-Perseverance, descriptors coded in the second facet, Faithfulness, were mentioned rarely (below 1% across all age levels and samples). No further analysis of this subcategory was done. The Chinese parents on average gave significantly more descriptors coded as Carefulness than did parents of all other samples ($ps < .05$; largest effect size: China-U.S.A. = 7.6%).

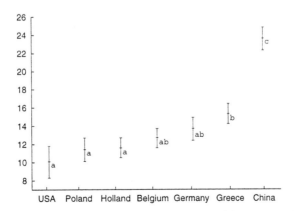

FIG. 4.1. Arcsine transformed means and 95% confidence intervals for Category III, Conscientiousness. *Note.* a, b, ab, etc. = Means of samples sharing a common letter are *not* significantly different from one another according to post hoc Scheffé tests.

For Diligence, both Chinese and Greek parents gave more descriptors coded in this subcategory than did parents in the five other samples. (All comparisons $p < .01$; largest effect size: China-U.S.A. = 14.2%.) Among these five, no differences were significant. The difference between Chinese and Greek parents was also significant ($p < .01$), with the Chinese being higher.

Descriptors Coded as High or Low. Parents' descriptions could be coded as either high or low in the coding scheme. In Table 1.1, examples were given of descriptors of both kinds. In Table 4.5 and Fig. 4.2, the average proportions of descriptors are shown as coded on the high or low side of the hypothetical dimensions. Parents not giving descriptors coded in this category were excluded from this analysis, a strategy that considerably reduced the number of parents. Analysis of variance showed that Chinese parents used significantly fewer high-end descriptors than did the parents in all other samples. Conversely, Chinese parents gave significantly more low-end descriptors. Although more than half of U.S. parents gave no descriptors coded as Conscientiousness, those who did showed the reverse pattern from the Chinese. Their average proportion of high-end descriptors was significantly higher than in all other samples. Among the other five samples no significant differences were found.

For the two subcategories of Carefulness and Diligence, the results were similar to those of the total category. Chinese parents used significantly more low-end descriptors than did all other samples coded in Carefulness and Diligence (with the exception of Poland for Diligence). Polish parents also gave many low-end descriptors in this subcategory (not significantly different from Chinese and significantly more than U.S. parents).

The relatively high proportions of Conscientiousness descriptors in the Greek and Chinese samples, as shown in Table 4.4, clearly have different meanings. In the Greek sample, the majority of such descriptors were on the high end while in the Chinese sample, they were on the low end of the dimension. Parents who described their children in terms coded on

TABLE 4.5
Average Proportions of Descriptors Coded
as III, Conscientiousness, High and Low

	Belgium	Netherlands	Germany	Greece	China	Poland	U.S.A.
N	274	204	180	316	339	176	86
Mean high–low	58–42	63–37	62–38	65–35	40–60	57–43	83–17

Note. Only parents giving at least one descriptor coded in this category were used in this analysis.

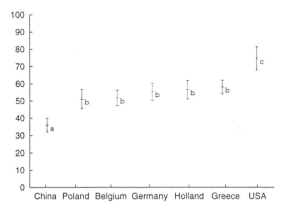

FIG. 4.2. Mean proportions coded as III high after arcsine transformation, with 95% confidence intervals. *Note.* a, b, ab, etc. = Means of samples sharing a common letter are *not* significantly different from one another according to post hoc Scheffé tests. Only parents that gave at least one descriptor coded in this category are included in the analysis.

the low end were mostly critical in their perceptions and apparently wanted their children to do better. A particular culture or society might be in a stage of socioeconomic and political development that influences parents to accentuate the shortcomings in their children's behavior, especially in regard to schoolwork. Apart from the fact that the Chinese culture by tradition is very achievement oriented, the present societal circumstances ensure that Chinese parents exert extra pressure on an (only) child to perform well in school. Another possibility for explaining the differences in high and low proportions between the samples is that children in different countries do actually behave differently. Chinese children might behave more carelessly than, say, Dutch children. This explanation seems less plausible than one couched in terms of cultural and societal values, interests, and ambitions. For example, the high standard of living of Dutch families contrasts sharply with Chinese families. Dutch parents can afford the luxury of being satisfied with a child, even if that child receives only average grades in school. In contrast, Chinese parents know that only when their child performs better than most other children do will the child have a chance to escape from the hardship of ordinary living circumstances and help the parents to escape as well.

The relatively high proportions of descriptors coded as Conscientiousness in the Chinese sample is in accordance with findings of other studies comparing Western and Asian attitudes of education and childrearing. Several studies have shown that Chinese parents, like parents in some other Asian countries, stress achievement motivation more than U.S. parents do and also that they are more critical. In a study of childrearing attitudes and practices in Hong Kong, with fathers and grandfathers as subjects, Ho and Kang (1984) found that "the most frequently mentioned personal characteristics expected of the child when grown up were those concerned with competence and achievement, followed by those concerned with moral character, sociability and controlled temperament" (p. 25). Generalizing, Ho and Kang (1984) stated: "It is generally recognized that modern Chinese parents place great emphasis on the achievement of their children" (p. 1006).

In a study comparing mathematics achievement of children in Beijing and Chicago, Stevenson and colleagues (1990) found: "Most American parents were satisfied and few expressed dissatisfaction. Chinese parents were much more critical. Less than half of the Chinese parents were satisfied with their child's academic performance, and at least one out of five was dissatisfied" (p. 1063).

Okagaki and Sternberg (1993) studied the beliefs that parents of six different cultural backgrounds expressed about childrearing, conceptions of intelligence, and school goals. All the parents had children in first or second grade and thus were more or less comparable to the parents of the 6-year-old children in our own study. Just as Stevenson and colleagues found for mothers in Japan and Taiwan (Stevenson & Lee, 1990; Stevenson, Lee, & Stigler, 1986), for the Filipino and Vietnamese parents in this study, the drive to do well—motivation—was most important to parents' conceptions of intelligence. "To be intelligent is to work hard at achieving one's goals":

> The primary difference between American-born parents and immigrant parents was that American-born parents believed that it is more important to teach academic thinking skills, such as how to ask questions and how to be creative, than it is to teach children to print and write neatly. In contrast, all of the immigrant parents rated learning to do work neatly and orderly as being at least as important as, if not more important than, learning basic facts, developing problem-solving skills, and developing creativity. (Okagaki & Sternberg, 1993, p. 47)

In these studies, the two facets of Conscientiousness, Diligence and Orderliness, were both stressed as differing in importance for Asian immigrant and U.S.-born parents, a finding consistent with those in our free-description data. In our interviews, Chinese parents mentioned characteristics coded in the two Conscientiousness subcategories of Diligence and Carefulness much more than did U.S. parents. In contrast, U.S. parents stressed the characteristics coded in the category of Intellect-Openness (see chapter 6). Congruent with the results found by Stevenson et al. (1990) in the Beijing–Chicago study mentioned earlier, the Chinese parents in our study expressed much more critical concern about the shortcomings of their children in matters of Carefulness and Diligence than did the U.S. parents in our study (see Table 4.5 & Fig. 4.2). Such concordances between our data and those of other studies lend support to the validity of the cross-sample similarities *and* differences reported in this book.

More data using samples from five Chinese cities are presently being collected by Zhang, and the results from another Asian sample of parents are still to be published. In a meeting of our group in Athens, Georgia, in 1996, the first results from a South Korean sample of parents were presented (Sung, Havill, & Halverson, 1996). The proportion of Conscientiousness descriptors was as high as in the Chinese sample and more than twice as large as in the Western samples. A major difference between the Chinese and South Korean Conscientiousness descriptors, however, was that Chinese parents used predominantly low-end descriptors whereas South Korean parents used predominantly high-end descriptors. This distinction could mean that South Koreans have more confidence in their children's success in school. Whether this is a valid distinction between Chinese and South Korean parents' perceptions and evaluations awaits further study with more diverse samples composed of comparable groups of parents. The findings reported in this chapter are consonant with findings in Chinese adult personality psychology. Bond (1991), an experienced and keen observer of Chinese students, noticed that Chinese students in general behave more conscientiously than American students, at least in regard to academics. When asked to rate themselves on facets of NEO-PI Conscientiousness, however, Chinese students scored merely average on Order, Dutifulness, Achievement-Striving, Self-Discipline and Deliberation, and distinctly low on Competence (McCrae, Costa, & Yik, 1996). To explain this contradiction between observed behaviors and self-ratings, McCrae et al. suggested "a real insecurity about personal effectiveness which may be a response to heavy social pressures to succeed" (p. 203).

CONCLUSION

We return to the different distinctions made by the proponents of the two leading approaches to the adult Big Five factor of Conscientiousness, that of Goldberg on being organized and neat and that of McCrae and Costa on being industrious and diligent. Our data indicated that in most samples, parents, when describing their children, paid about equal attention to both facets (Table 4.4).

In most samples, the total attention paid to this category of behavior did not exceed 10%, with the exception of the Chinese sample. As is described in chapter 7, the attention that parents paid to descriptors coded in this category was very low for children of age 3 and sharply rose with children's age.

The proportion of low-end descriptors given by parents in the Chinese sample was exceptionally high for the facet of Carefulness and relatively high for the facet of Diligence-Perseverance. This finding is congruent with the literature comparing differing Asian and U.S. emphases on educational values and childrearing beliefs. From our data it can be inferred that parents in European countries hold views midway between those of the U.S. and Chinese positions.

REFERENCES

Ahadi, S., & Rothbart, M. K. (1994). Temperament, development, and the Big Five. In C. F. Halverson, Jr., G. A. Kohnstamm, & R. P. Martin (Eds.), *The neuropsychology of individual differences: A developmental perspective* (pp. 93–123). New York: Plenum.

Bleichrodt, N., Resing, W. C. M., & Zaal, J. N. (1994). *Beoordeling van schoolgedrag: SCHOBL-R* [Evaluation of classroom behavior: SCHOBL-R]. Lisse, Netherlands: Swets Test Services.

Block, J. (1995). A contrarian view of the five-factor approach to personality description. *Psychological Bulletin, 117,* 187–215.

Block, J., & Block, J. H. (1980). *The California Child Q-set.* Palo Alto, CA: Consulting Psychologists Press. (Original work published 1969)

Bond, M. H. (1991). *Beyond the Chinese face: Insights from psychology.* Hong Kong: Oxford University Press.

Cartwright, D. S. (1979). *Theories and models of personality.* Dubuque, IA: Brown.

Cattell, R. B. (1945). The description of personality: Principles and findings in a factor analysis. *American Journal of Psychology, 58,* 69–90.

Cattell, R. B. (1973). *Personality and mood by questionnaire.* San Francisco: Jossey-Bass.

Cattell, R. B., & Coan, R. A. (1957). Child personality structure as revealed in teachers' ratings. *Journal of Clinical Psychology, 13,* 315–327.

Cattell, R. B., Eber, H. W., & Tatsuoka, M. M. (1980). *Handbook for the sixteen personality factor questionnaire (16 PF).* Champaign, IL: Institute for Personality and Ability Testing.

Cattell, R. B., & Gruen, W. (1953). The personality factor structure of 11-year-old children in terms of behavior rating data. *Journal of Clinical Psychology, 9,* 256–266.

Costa, P. T., & McCrae, R. R. (1994). Stability and change in personality from adolescence through adulthood. In C. F. Halverson, Jr., G. A. Kohnstamm, & R. P. Martin (Eds.), *The developing structure of temperament and personality from infancy to adulthood* (pp. 139–150). Hillsdale, NJ: Lawrence Erlbaum Associates.

Digman, J. M. (1963). Principal dimensions of child personality as inferred from teachers' judgments. *Child Development, 34,* 43–60.

Digman, J. M. (1990). Personality structure: Emergence of the five-factor model. *Annual Review of Psychology, 41,* 417–440.

Digman, J. M. (1994). Child personality and temperament: Does the five-factor model embrace both domains? In C. F. Halverson, Jr., G. A. Kohnstamm, & R. P. Martin (Eds.), *The developing structure of temperament and personality from infancy to adulthood* (pp. 323–338). Hillsdale, NJ: Lawrence Erlbaum Associates.

Digman, J. M., & Inouye, J. (1986). Further specifications of the five robust factors of personality. *Journal of Personality and Social Psychology, 50,* 116–123.

Digman, J. M., & Takemoto-Chock, N. K. (1981). Factors in the natural language of personality: Re-analysis, comparison and interpretation of six major studies. *Multivariate Behavioral Research, 16*, 149–170.

Fiske, D. W. (1949). Consistency of the factorial structures of personality ratings from different sources. *Journal of Abnormal and Social Psychology, 44*, 329–344.

Freud, S. (1941). Charakter und Analerotik [Character and anal eroticism]. *Gesammelte Werke 7* (pp. 205–209). London: Imago. (Original work published 1908)

Freud, S. (1977). *Character and anal erotism* (A. Richards, Ed. & Trans.). London: Pelican Books. (Original work published 1908)

Goldberg, L. R. (1992). The development of markers of the Big Five factor structure. *Psychological Assessment, 4*, 26–42.

Guerin, D. W., Gottfried, A. W., Oliver, P. M., & Thomas, C. W. (1994). Temperament and school functioning during early adolescence. *Journal of Early Adolescence, 14*, 200–225.

Hagekull, B. (1994). Infant temperament and early childhood functioning: Possible relations to the five-factor model. In C. F. Halverson, Jr., G. A. Kohnstamm, & R. P. Martin (Eds.), *The developing structure of temperament and personality from infancy to adulthood* (pp. 227–240). Hillsdale, NJ: Lawrence Erlbaum Associates.

Hegvik, R. L., McDevitt, S. C., & Carey, W. B. (1982). Middle Childhood Temperament Questionnaire. *Developmental and Behavioral Pediatrics, 4*, 197–200.

Ho, D. Y. F., & Kang, T. K. (1984). Intergenerational comparisons of child-rearing attitudes and practices in Hong Kong. *Developmental Psychology, 20*, 1004–1006.

John, O. P., Caspi, A., Robins, R. W., Moffitt, T. E., & Stouthamer-Loeber, M. (1994). The "Little-five": Exploring the homological network of the Five-factor model in adolescent boys. *Child Development, 65*, 160–178.

Kalverboer, A. F., Pluister, C., & Visser, J. (in press). *Handleiding bij de GGBS* [Manual for the GGBS]. Lisse, Netherlands: Swets & Zeitlinger.

Keogh, B. K. (1989). Applying temperament research to school. In G. A. Kohnstamm, J. E. Bates, & M. K. Rothbart (Eds.), *Temperament in childhood*. Chichester, England: Wiley.

Keogh, B. K., Pullis, M., & Cadwell, J. (1982). A short form of the Teacher Temperament Questionnaire. *Journal of Educational Measurement, 29*, 323–329.

Kohnstamm, G. A. (1992). Factoren in gedragsbeoordelingen van leerlingen [Factors in ratings of pupil behavior]. *Pedagogische Studiën, 69*, 12–22.

Martin, R. P. (1988). *The temperament assessment battery for children*. Brandon, VT: Clinical Psychology.

Martin, R. P., Olejnik, S., & Gaddis, L. (1994). Is temperament an important contributor to schooling outcomes in elementary school? Modeling effects of temperament and scholastic ability on academic achievement. In W. B. Carey & S. C. McDevit (Eds.), *Prevention and early intervention, a Festschrift for Stella Chess and Alexander Thomas* (pp. 59–68). New York: Brunner/Mazel.

Martin, R. P., Wisenbaker, J., & Huttunen, M. (1994). Review of factor analytic studies of temperament measures based on the Thomas–Chess structural model: Implications for the Big Five. In C. F. Halverson, Jr., G. A. Kohnstamm, & R. P. Martin (Eds.), *The developing structure of temperament and personality from infancy to adulthood* (pp. 157–172). Hillsdale, NJ: Lawrence Erlbaum Associates.

McClowry, S. G., Hegvik, R. L., & Teglasi, H. (1993). An examination of the construct validity of the Middle Childhood Temperament Questionnaire. *Merrill–Palmer Quarterly, 39*, 279–293.

McCrae, R. R., & Costa, P. T. (1990). *Personality in adulthood*. New York: Guilford Press.

McCrae, R. R., Costa, P. T., & Busch, C. M. (1986). Evaluating comprehensiveness in personality systems: The California Q-set and the Five-factor model. *Journal of Personality, 54*, 430–446.

McCrae, R. R., Costa, P. T., & Yik, M. S. M. (1996). Universal aspects of Chinese personality structure. In M. H. Bond (Ed.), *The Handbook of Chinese Psychology*. Hong Kong: Oxford University Press.

Mervielde, I. (1992). The B5BBS-25: A Flemish set of bipolar markers for the "Big-Five" personality factors. *Psychologia Belgica, 32*, 195–210.

Mervielde, I., Buyst, V., & De Fruyt, F. (1995). The validity of the Big Five as a model for teachers' ratings of individual differences in children aged 4 to 12. *Personality and Individual Differences, 18*, 1827–1836.

Mervielde, I., & De Fruyt, F. (1992). *The "Big-Five" personality factors as a model for the structure and development of peer nominations* (Reports in Psychology 3). Ghent, Belgium: University of Ghent.

Okagaki, L., & Sternberg, R. J. (1993). Parental beliefs and children's school performance. *Child Development, 64*, 36–56.

Ostendorf, F., & Angleitner, A. (1993, July). *A German replication study of the Five-Factor Model based on a comprehensive taxonomy of personality descriptive adjectives*. Paper presented at the sixth meeting of the International Society for the Study of Individual Differences, Baltimore, MD.

Robins, R. W., John, O. P., & Caspi, A. (1994). Major dimensions of personality in early adolescence: The Big Five and beyond. In C. F. Halverson, Jr., G. A. Kohnstamm, & R. P. Martin (Eds.), *The developing structure of temperament and personality from infancy to adulthood* (pp. 267–291). Hillsdale, NJ: Lawrence Erlbaum Associates.

Rothbart, M. K., & Posner, M. (1985). Temperament and the development of self-regulation. In L. C. Hartlage & C. F. Telzrow (Eds.), *The neuropsychology of individual differences: A developmental perspective* (pp. 93–123). New York: Plenum.

Stevenson, H. W., Lee, S. Y., Chen, C., Lummis, M., Stigler, J. W., Fan, L., & Ge, F. (1990). Mathematics achievement of children in China and the United States. *Child Development, 61*, 1053–1066.

Stevenson, H. W., Lee, S. Y., & Stigler, J. W. (1986). Mathematics achievement of Chinese, Japanese, and American children. *Science, 231*, 693–699.

Stevenson, H. W., & Lee, S. (1990). Contexts of achievement. *Monographs of the Society for Research in Child Development, 55*, no. 221, 1–2.

Sung, S., Havill, V., & Halverson, C. F., Jr. (1996, April). *Descriptions of child personality by South Korean parents*. Paper presented at fifth meeting of International Consortium, University of Georgia, Athens, GA.

Thomas, A., & Chess, S. (1977). *Temperament and development*. New York: Brunner/Mazel.

Tupes, E. C., & Christal, R. E. (1992). Recurrent personality factors based on trait ratings. *Journal of Personality, 60*, 225–251. (Original work published 1961)

Van Lieshout, C. F. M., & Haselager, G. J. T. (1994). The Big Five personality factors in Q-sort descriptions of children and adolescents. In C. F. Halverson, Jr., G. A. Kohnstamm, & R. P. Martin (Eds.), *The developing structure of temperament and personality from infancy to adulthood* (pp. 293–318). Hillsdale, NJ: Lawrence Erlbaum Associates.

Victor, J. B. (1994). The five-factor model applied to individual differences in school behaviour. In C. F. Halverson, Jr., G. A. Kohnstamm, & R. P. Martin (Eds.), *The developing structure of temperament and personality from infancy to adulthood* (pp. 323–338). Hillsdale, NJ: Lawrence Erlbaum Associates.

Webb, E. (1915). Character and Intelligence. *British Journal of Psychology Monograph Series, 1*, 3.

5

Emotional Stability:
Developmental Perspectives
From Childhood to Adulthood

Alois Angleitner
University of Bielefeld

Geldolph A. Kohnstamm
University of Leiden

Anne-Marie Slotboom
University of Leiden

Elias Besevegis
University of Athens

Emotional stability (neuroticism) is a broad dimension of normal personality characterized by confidence and poise at the high end and by a propensity to experience chronic negative emotions at the low end (dysphoria). The construct is one of the most widely used and important dimensions of adult personality and plays a central role in virtually every scheme of personality and in most explanations of both normal and abnormal behavior. As we summarize here, there are many instruments designed to measure emotional stability and neuroticism, each measuring a variety of negative affective experiences (Watson & Clark, 1984). As we also detail, the history of the construct as it applies to children is less clear and more complex than it is in the literature dealing with adults. Neuroticism can be mapped onto childhood negative affectivity fairly readily (Rothbart, Posner, & Hershey, 1995), but little work of a developmental nature has been done. We begin with a brief history of the construct.

BURT'S GENERAL EMOTIONALITY

In 1915, Burt published a factor analysis based on data collected in Liverpool (1911), from 172 "normal" children aged 9 to 12 and 157 "normal" adults. These people were rated for their positions on 12 "primary emotions" (joy, sex, sociability, assertiveness, anger, curiosity, disgust, sorrow, fear, submissiveness, tenderness, and comfort) that Burt had adapted from McDougall. Burt assumed that these primary emotions were the major constituents of the emotional domain (contrasted with the intelligence domain). Curiously, he saw no need to distinguish between major traits for children and for adults (which might explain why in his studies children below the age of puberty were assessed for their susceptibility to sexual feelings).

In 1948, Burt reported the results of factor analyses of data collected over the course of 20 years from 483 normal boys and girls attending ordinary elementary schools in London. The majority of the children were between 9 and 13 years of age. The assessments of primary emotions were based on teacher ratings. Burt believed that three orthogonal factors could explain most of the variance in the 12 traits: a general Emotionality factor (37% of the variance); a bipolar factor distinguishing "sthenic" (or extraverted) from "asthenic" (or introverted) emotions (13%); and another bipolar factor distinguishing euphoric (or pleasurable) from dysphoric (or unpleasurable) emotions (5.4%). Analyses like these took enormous effort, because all correlations and all factor loadings had to be computed without calculators or computers; results that today are obtained in minutes took months of computation (and might have contained many errors).

Burt also collected data from "psychoneurotic" children. Factoring the ratings of these children, he again obtained a first factor of General Emotionality, which in this instance accounted for less of the total variance (22% vs. 37%). His explanation for this phenomenon was that by selecting psychoneurotic cases he had been sampling from the upper end of the scale of emotional instability, with the effect of reducing the variance in this General Emotionality factor.

EYSENCK'S NEUROTICISM

In 1947, H. J. Eysenck postulated the independence of the two personality dimensions of Extraversion-Introversion (E) and Neuroticism-Emotional Stability (N). Eysenck (1967) later proposed a model containing a third major dimension: Psychoticism-Superego Control (P). H. J. and S. B. G. Eysenck also adapted all their questionnaires to measure N and E for children, beginning with the Maudsley Personality Inventory (MPI; H. J. Eysenck, 1959), which was later adapted into the junior versions of the Eysenck Personality Inventory (EPI; S. B. G. Eysenck, 1965) and Eysenck Personality Questionnaire (EPQ; H. J. Eysenck & S. B. G. Eysenck, 1975). The Eysencks obviously never doubted the validity of their model for classifying individual personality differences in childhood (e.g., S. B. G. Eysenck & H. J. Eysenck, 1980). Factoring the data obtained with different samples of children on these questionnaires, rated by parents and teachers alike, repeatedly reproduced the Eysenck adult three-factor structure. As for E and N, the Eysencks asserted "that these two factors contribute more to a description of personality than any other set of two factors outside the cognitive field" (Eysenck & Eysenck, 1975, p. 7). Whereas H. J. Eysenck (e.g., 1994) saw his E and N as more or less identical with two of the Big Five, he criticized the adherents of the Five-Factor Model (FFM) for not believing that Conscientiousness and Agreeableness were actually facets of the higher order factor P.

After having given a brief account of the typical extravert and the typical introvert, H. J. Eysenck and S. B. G. Eysenck (1975) stated that no such account was required for N,

> as our description would be very similar to those given by countless other writers since Woodworth published his Personal Data Sheet and Taylor her Manifest Anxiety Scale. However, for the sake of completeness we may describe the typical high N scorer as being an anxious, worrying individual, moody and frequently depressed. He is likely to sleep badly, and to suffer from various psychosomatic disorders. He is overly emotional, reacting too strongly to all sorts of stimuli, and finds it difficult to get back on an even keel after each emotionally arousing experience. His strong emotional re-actions interfere with his proper adjustment, making him react in irrational, sometimes rigid ways. When combined with extraversion, such an individ-ual is likely to be touchy and restless, to become excitable and even aggres-sive. If the high N individual has to be described in one word, one might say that he was a *worrier*; his main characteristic is a constant preoccupation with things that might go wrong, and a strong emotional reaction of anxiety to these thoughts. The stable individual, on the other hand, tends to respond emotionally only slowly and generally weakly, and to return to baseline quickly after emotional arousal; he is usually calm, even-tempered, con-trolled and unworried. (pp. 9–10)

ADULT CONTENT AND SCOPE OF EMOTIONAL STABILITY-NEUROTICISM

Tupes and Christal (1961/1992), in a classic study of the FFM, found six bipolar adjectives from Cattell's 35-variable list (Cattell, 1947) to be mark-ers for the N domain. These authors labeled them as the six markers of Emotional Stability: neurotic versus not so; worrying, anxious versus placid; easily upset versus poised, tough; hypochondriacal versus not so; emotional versus calm; changeable versus emotionally stable.

Cattell's final selection of 35 personality traits was not intended to be an exhaustive compilation of the full domain of personality-relevant adjectives in English. His initial list, from which the 35 were derived by various steps of categorizing and selection, included many terms that Cattell took from technical, psychological descriptions, many of which concerned psychopathology (Cattell, 1946). This historical event has led to a modern overrepresentation of terms describing Emotional Stability (Peabody & Goldberg, 1989).

Based on the earlier work of Allport and Odbert (1936) and Cattell (1946), Norman (1963, 1967) began to analyze peer nomination ratings on large pools of representative English personality terms. Norman (1967) categorized 1,431 trait-descriptive adjectives into 75 categories. This categorization was based on Norman's own judgments on meaning similarity. After first sorting the adjectives into the positive and negative factor poles of the FFM, Norman further differentiated his categorizations. In Table 5.1 we list the categories for Emotionality with examples of marker adjectives as well as the number of terms in each category (taken from Goldberg, 1990, p. 1219). A total of 93 terms for the positive pole of this domain and 115 terms for the negative pole was selected as representative for all the English-language adjectives that indicated adult emotionality. The 208 Emotionality terms made up only 12% of the 1,431 trait-descriptive adjectives. This relatively small percentage is interesting with regard

TABLE 5.1
Categories in Norman's Taxonomy for Emotionality Domain

Factor Pole	Examples	Number of Terms
IV+		
Durability	Tough, rugged, unflinching	11
Poise	Worry-free, calm, stable, sedate, peaceful	23
Self-Reliance	Confident, independent, resourceful	11
Callousness	Ruthless, insensitive, cold, stern	17
Candor	Frank, blunt, explicit, curt, terse	31
IV−		
Self-Pity	Touchy, careworn, whiny, oversensitive	14
Anxiety	Fearful, nervous, fussy, unstable	30
Insecurity	Unconfident, self-critical, unpoised	17
Timidity	Cowardly, timid, unventurous, wary	14
Passivity	Docile, dependent, submissive, pliant	22
Immaturity	Naive, gullible, superstitious, childlike	18

Note. Terms from an inventory of 1,710 trait-descriptive adjectives. From "An Alternative 'Description of Personality' . . . ," by L. R. Goldberg (1990), *Journal of Personality and Social Psychology, 59,* 1219. Copyright © 1990 by the American Psychological Association. Reprinted by permission.

to our own results in categorizing behavioral descriptions of children as presented at the end of this chapter.

In factor analytic studies using Norman's 75 categories as well as 57 bipolar scales selected by Peabody from a representative pool of 571 terms (Peabody, 1987), Peabody and Goldberg (1989; Goldberg, 1990) clearly replicated the Big Five. In terms of variance explained, however, three of these (II, III, and I, in that order) were much larger than the remaining two, Intellect and Emotional Stability. In several different factor methods, Emotional Stability explained between only 2% and 8% of the variance (Peabody & Goldberg, 1989). This small amount of variance was partly a consequence of Peabody's (1987) selection, where only 7% of all adjectives could be rationally categorized as representative for this domain.

Even though there is some inequality in size of the five adjective domains taken from dictionaries, Goldberg (1992) proposed 10 bipolar-adjective scales measuring each of the five domains of the FFM. In Table 5.2, we list these adjective scales for Emotional Stability. Based on self-descriptions and descriptions of liked peers, Goldberg also developed 100 unipolar adjectives measuring the five factors (20 for each factor) for Emotional Stability. There were six adjectives indicative of the positive factor pole: Unenvious, Unemotional, Relaxed, Imperturbable, Unexcitable, and Undemanding; and 14 adjectives indicative of the negative pole: Anxious, Moody, Temperamental, Envious, Emotional, Irritable, Fretful, Jealous, Touchy, Nervous, Unsecure, Fearful, Self-Pitying, and High-Strung.

Personality researchers are always confronted with the problem that varimax-rotated factors tend to intercorrelate substantially with other rotated factors. De Raad, Hendriks, and Hofstee (1992, 1994) started with this finding and developed their Abridged Big Five Circumplex Model (AB5C). The model represents all possible pairs of the Big Five factor poles and defines facets by the two highest loadings of the trait variables in 10 two-dimensional circumplexes. The model clearly has different numbers of trait terms in each of the AB5C quadrants. As with the selections previously mentioned, the number of trait terms found for

TABLE 5.2
Goldberg's Bipolar Marker Scales for Emotional Stability

Angry–calm	Discontented–contented
Tense–relaxed	Insecure–secure
Nervous–at ease	Emotional–unemotional
Envious–not envious	Guilt ridden–guilt free
Unstable–stable	Moody–steady

Note. From "The Development of Markers of the Big Five Factor Structure," by L. R. Goldberg (1992), Psychological Assessment, 4, p. 31. Copyright © 1992 by the American Psychological Association. Reprinted with permission.

Emotional Stability was smaller in contrast to Extraversion or Agreeable-ness. Factor-pure adjectives for the negative pole of Emotional Stability were the following (translated from Dutch): Panicky, Emotional, Oversen-sitive, Hypersensitive, Jumpy, and Sentimental (De Raad, Hendriks, & Hofstee, 1994, p. 103). The factor-pure adjectives for the corresponding positive pole of Emotional Stability were Sober, Unperturbable, Unshak-able, and Cold.

This research group has stressed that most of the markers developed for Emotional Stability show substantial loadings on other factors of the FFM. For instance, the adjectives Insecure and Nervous relate also to the nega-tive pole of Extraversion, the adjectives Touchy and Irritable to the nega-tive pole of Agreeableness, and the adjective Fearful with the negative pole of the fifth factor. Trait ratings of the Dutch students produced only three marker adjectives for Emotional Stability, Steady, Stable, and Calm. All three showed substantial secondary loadings from Extraversion. When Dutch nouns and verbs were used instead of adjectives, no factor equiva-lent to N was found (De Raad, 1992).

Starting with a German trait taxonomy, Angleitner, Ostendorf, and John (1990) had large samples of adults rate 430 unipolar-trait adjectives in both self- and peer-rating formats. Ostendorf (1990) and, in a replication study, Ostendorf and Angleitner (1993) found a clear five-factor structure. The Emotional Stability factor in the replication study is illustrated by a sample of 20 highest loading adjectives in Table 5.3.

In the Ostendorf study (1990), out of 430 personality adjectives, Emo-tional Stability was defined by 27 adjectives for self-ratings, 29 for peer ratings, and 22 for both. This number was small, about 6 to 7% of all adjectives, and was about the same percentage as Peabody's English results. When the criterion was set higher, with the highest loading with IV in both peer *and* self-ratings, the percentage dropped to 5. Emotional Stability appears to explain only about half the variance explained by the four other factors in the German studies because everyday German contains relatively few adjectives that can serve as clear markers for Emotional Stability.

In an Italian trait-taxonomy study, Caprara and Perugini (1994) could not produce clear Agreeableness and Emotional Stability factors, even though the remaining three factors of the FFM were clearly replicable. Two factors, however, labeled Quietness and Selfishness, correlated (.55 and .57, respectively) with the Emotional Stability scale of the Italian version of the NEO-Personality Inventory (NEO-PI).

For Hungarian traits, Szirmák and De Raad (1994) reported that a factor analysis of 561 adjectives replicated four of the Big Five, with the exception of an Intellect or Openness factor. The factor-pure terms for the Hungarian factor of Emotional Stability were, in translated form, Nerves of Steel, Talented (!), Superstitious, Crybaby, Excitable, Complaining, and Vulnerable.

TABLE 5.3
Adjectives With Highest Loadings in Emotional Stability,
From List of 430 Trait-Descriptive Adjectives in
Replication Study of Ostendorf and Angleitner (1993)

German	Translation	PR	SR
1. Sensibel	Sensitive	−.61*	−.57*
2. Zartbesaitet	Highly sensitive	−.57*	−.54*
3. Empfindsam	Sensitive, sentimental	−.62*	−.53*
4. Gefühlsbetont	Emotional	−.58*	−.51*
5. Feinfühlig	Sensitive, tactful	−.50	−.51*
6. Empfindlich	Touchy, oversensitive	−.58*	−.49*
7. Unempfindlich	Insensitive	.55*	.49*
8. Verletzbar	Vulnerable	−.57*	−.48*
9. Gefühlsarm	Unemotional, unfeeling	.47*	.48*
10. Dickfellig	Thick-skinned	.52*	.46*
11. Kaltschnäuzig	Cold, unfeeling, callous	.37	.45*
12. Weich	Soft	−.54*	−.44*
13. Dickhäutig	Thick-skinned	.55*	.43*
14. Emotional	Emotional	−.50*	−.43*
15. Warmherzig	Warmhearted	−.30	−.43
16. Kaltherzig	Coldhearted	.33	.43*
17. Poetisch	Poetic	−.50*	−.41*
18. Zartfühlend	Sensitive, delicate	−.49	−.41*
19. Berechnend	Calculating	.32	.40*
20. Abgebrüht	Hardened, cool	.42*	.39*

Note. PR = Peer ratings (three subjects averaged, N = 511). SR = Self-ratings, N = 511.
* = Highest loading on Factor IV (Emotional Stability). Scales are ranked according to their factor loadings in the self-ratings.

The first results of trait-taxonomy studies based on the Czech and Polish languages have also been reported. Both taxonomy studies used procedures identical to the ones developed and used by the German team. Hrebickova, Ostendorf, and Angleitner (1995) and Szarota and Ostendorf (1995) clearly replicated the Big Five. In both studies an Emotional Stability factor appeared.

What is clear from these studies conducted in the lexical tradition is that N is found when representative selections of adjectives are made. The proportion of adjectives that loads primarily on N is, however, relatively small. The variance explained by N is also relatively modest when compared to the important position that N occupies in psychopathology and psychotherapy, in the thinking of Eysenck, and in the work of Burt and McDougall as well as many others. Evidently, the centrality of N in explanations of psychopathology is not matched by its representation in the lexicon.

THE FFM BY McCRAE AND COSTA

Each of the five broad factors can be conceptualized as containing some narrower factors of intercorrelated traits, or facets. In the view of Costa and McCrae:

> The general tendency to experience negative affects such as: fear, sadness, embarrassment, anger, guilt and disgust is the core of the N-domain. However, N includes more than susceptibility to psychological distress. Perhaps because disruptive emotions interfere with adaptation, men and women high in N are also prone to have irrational ideas, to be less able to control their impulses and to cope more poorly than others with stress. (Costa & McCrae, 1992, p. 15)

Table 5.4 presents the six facets of N, according to Costa and McCrae.

The facet scales of their questionnaire, the NEO-PI-R, showed good reliabilities and structural equivalences. The factor structures were also replicated in a German translation of the NEO-PI-R (Ostendorf & Angleitner, 1994) with the exception of the N5 facet of Impulsiveness, which in the German study showed a slightly higher association with the Extraversion domain (loadings of .39 vs. .49 in the self-ratings and .32 vs. .50, respectively, in the peer ratings).

TABLE 5.4
Neuroticism Facets in NEO PI-R and
Short Description of High and Low Scorers

Neuroticism Facets	High Scorers	Low Scorers
N 1: Anxiety	Apprehensive, fearful, prone to worry, nervous, tense, jittery	Calm, relaxed
N 2: Angry Hostility	Tendency to experience anger, frustration, and bitterness	Easygoing, slow to anger
N 3: Depression	Feelings of guilt, sadness, hopelessness, loneliness	Tendency not to experience such emotions
N 4: Self-Consciousness	Shame, embarrassment, shyness, social anxiety	Tendency not to experience such emotions
N 5: Impulsiveness	Inability to control cravings and urges	Resistance to temptations
N 6: Vulnerability	Unable to cope with stress, dependent, hopeless, panicked when facing emergency	Capable of handling themselves in difficult situations

Note. From *Revised NEO Personality Inventory (NEO-PI-R) and NEO Five-Factor Inventory (NEO-FFI) Professional Manual* (p. 16), by P. T. Costa Jr. and R. R. McCrae (1992), Odessa, FL: Psychological Assessment Resources. Copyright © 1992 by Psychological Assessment Resources. Reprinted with permission.

EMOTIONAL STABILITY OR NEGATIVE AFFECT IN CHILDHOOD

In addition to the studies by the Eysencks previously mentioned, numerous other studies done with children have found a factor similar to the Eysencks' N. Because of space constraints, we review only two studies that used instruments not designed to obtain the Big Five factors.

Factoring Child Descriptions on California Child Q-Set (CCQ)

As described in the preceding chapter, two research teams, one in the Netherlands, the other in the United States, factor analyzed the scores on the 100 items of the CCQ (Block & Block, 1980) to see which of the Big Five were represented in this instrument. In the Netherlands, with over six different samples of children and adolescents, a clear Emotional Stability or Affect factor was found summarizing the covariance of 16 items (Van Lieshout & Haselager, 1994). In all samples, this factor was the second largest after the first factor, Agreeableness. Of the 16 items shown in Table 5.5, 11 (69%) are phrased in negative terms.

TABLE 5.5
Items Defining Emotional Stability in Dutch Version of the CCQ

Factor 2: Emotional Stability	
Self-reliant, confident	64
Fearful, anxious	−.63
Tends to go to pieces under stress	−.61
Tends to brood and ruminate or worry	−.59
Anxious in unpredictable situations	−.58
Self-assertive	−.57
Calm and relaxed, easygoing	.53
Appears to feel unworthy	−.47
Inhibited and constricted	−.47
Has a readiness to feel guilty	−.46
Shows bodily symptoms from stress	−.45
Indecisive, vacillating	−.42
Recoups after stressful experiences	.41
Seeks to be independent	.40
Cries easily	−.40
Immobilized under stress	−.39

Note. From "The Big Five Personality Factors . . . ," by C. F. M. Van Lieshout & G. J. T. Haselager (1994), in C. F. Halverson Jr., G. A. Kohnstamm, and R. P. Martin (Eds.), *The Developing Structure of Temperament and Personality From Infancy to Adulthood* (p. 300). Hillsdale, NJ: Lawrence Erlbaum Associates. Copyright © 1994 by Lawrence Erlbaum Associates.

In the U.S. study by John, Caspi, Robins, Moffit, and Stouthamer-Loeber (1994; see also Robins, John, & Caspi, 1994), 350 boys between 12 and 13 years old were described by their mothers using a common-language version of the CCQ. Compared with the Dutch studies previously cited, a smaller Emotional Stability factor was found (Factor IV), "primarily defined by anxiety, nervous worry, guilt feelings, and low-esteem, representing a more limited range of negative affects than typically found on the Neuroticism factor in adulthood" (Robins et al., 1994, pp. 278–279). A fifth factor suggestive of N was also found as "defined by negative affect expressed in immature and age-inappropriate behaviors (such as whining, crying and tantrums), being overly sensitive to teasing, and irritable" (Robins et al., 1994, p. 279).

Factoring Items From Questionnaires Based on the Nine Dimensions of Thomas and Chess

In their overview of item-based factor analytic studies of data collected with the Thomas, Chess, and Korn questionnaires, or instruments based largely on these questionnaires, Martin, Wisenbaker, and Huttunen (1994) concluded:

> [These studies] show ample evidence that a factor that taps variation in the tendency to express negative emotional reactions can be obtained from infancy through adolescence, whether assessed via parental, self, or teacher ratings. This factor is composed of items focused on the negative quality of the emotional reaction, the intensity of negative emotional reaction, and the persistence of the negative reaction. (p. 165)

The authors claimed similarity between factors found with Thomas–Chess questionnaires for infants and preschool children in Finland, Sweden, Australia, and the United States, although they were differentially labeled by their authors as Manageability, Negative Emotionality, and Irritability. For school-age children, factors were given labels such as Negative Re-activity, Reactivity, and Mood. The focus on negative reactions to frustration that makes children difficult to manage was strongly represented in factors in parent ratings on the Thomas–Chess questionnaires for infants and preschool children. These factors appeared different from the core of the Emotional Stability factor derived from the CCQ, as indicated in Table 5.5. In the CCQ analyses, N was defined as being fearful, anxious, brittle, and demonstrating a lack of self-confidence. The temperament factor appeared to consist mainly of reacting with loud protest, crying, and misbehavior to undesired events.

In the Dutch CCQ study, items such as obedient, compliant, and over-reacts to minor frustrations loaded primarily on the Agreeableness factor (.54 and –.52, respectively) and not on the Emotional Stability factor (–.08

and −.21). In the U.S. CCQ study, an Irritability factor was found to have high loadings on items other than those in the Emotional Stability factor. The authors of the present volume categorized aggressive behavior and other unpleasant forms of opposition to parental management as low Agreeableness and reactions of crying and outbursts of anger as low Emotional Stability. Our coding procedures used in the present study did not allow classifying a descriptor in *two or more* categories. In the next phase of this study, however, the results of factor analysis on item inter-correlations will show how negative emotions and oppositional behavior load on broad-based factors.

The difference between the core meaning of the Thomas–Chess factor and the CCQ factor resembles the distinction between the two inde-pendent dimensions found in the self-ratings of Filipino university stu-dents on 288 items developed by indigenous methods (Church & Katig-bak, 1989; Katigbak, Church, & Akamine, 1996). These two dimensions were labeled as Emotional Control (able to control one's emotional reac-tions to events, not easily irritated or angered) and Affective Well-Being (feels happy, content, and satisfied as opposed to lonely, worried, or confused). In a joint factor analysis of (translated) NEO-PI scales and the indigenous Philippine scales, the two Philippine factors correlated best with NEO-PI Neuroticism (the pattern of secondary loadings was, how-ever, quite different for the two dimensions).

The Philippine distinction is one between outbursts of observable behav-iors and longer lasting inner feelings, between externalizing behavior problems and internalizing emotional problems. This venerable empirical distinction (Quay, 1968) was also represented in the two independent higher order factors derived from the Child Behavior Check List (CBCL; Achenbach & Edelbrock, 1981, 1983). McCrae and John stated succinctly that "N represents individual differences in the tendency to experience distress, and in the cognitive and behavioral styles that follow from this tendency" (McCrae & John, 1992, p. 195). Frequent outbursts of negative emotions have regularly been seen in children not known by their parents as typical worriers. The externalizing child is different from the internaliz-ing one, although both types probably have their temperamental origins in early Negative Affect or Negative Emotionality (Tellegen, 1985; Watson & Clark, 1992).

EMOTIONALITY IN THE THEORY
OF TEMPERAMENT BY BUSS AND PLOMIN

Buss and Plomin proposed that infant distress gradually differentiates into two factors, fear and anger. These two emotions compose the trait of emotionality. To measure anger in adults, Buss (1988) recommended using the irritability scale of the Hostility Inventory (Buss & Durkee, 1957): For example, I lose my temper quickly but get over it quickly. In the EAS Survey for children, however, the five emotionality items (Child cries easily; Child tends to be somewhat emotional; Child often fusses and cries; Child gets upset easily; Child reacts intensely when upset) are neither good representations of fear nor of anger. All five items could be coded in our subcategory dealing with Emotional Reactivity. In an earlier version of this questionnaire, the Emotionality Activity Sociability Impulsivity (EASI; Buss & Plomin, 1975), the items Child is easily frightened and Child has a quick temper (anger) were included in the Emotionality scale.

Negative and Positive Emotionality

Since the early 1980s, Tellegen and Watson have demonstrated that negative and positive emotionality (synonyms: mood, affect) are not opposites, (i.e., negatively correlated), but rather independent constructs (see, e.g., Watson & Tellegen, 1985):

> These two factors have been characterized as descriptively bipolar but affectively unipolar dimensions, to emphasize that only the high end of each dimension represents a state of emotional arousal (or high affect), whereas the low end of each factor is most clearly and strongly defined by terms reflecting a relative absence of affective involvement (e.g. *calm* and *relaxed* for Negative Affect, *dull* and *sluggish* for Positive Affect). (Watson & Tellegen, 1985, p. 221)

Studies relating measures of Negative and Positive Affect with scales for FFM Neuroticism and Extraversion have consistently found that measures of Negative Affect are substantially correlated with Neuroticism but are generally unrelated to Extraversion, whereas Positive Affect scales are significantly related to Extraversion, but not to Neuroticism (Watson & Clark, 1992):

> The clarity and robustness of this pattern has led Tellegen . . . to argue that the Neuroticism and Extraversion dimensions should be relabeled "Negative Emotionality" and "Positive Emotionality" respectively. In Tellegen's view, Neuroticism and Extraversion represent basic dimensions of emotional temperament that broadly reflect individual differences in the propensity to experience negative and positive affect, respectively. (p. 445)

This conception of negative and positive emotionality as two independent dimensions might aid us in characterizing antecedents of the Big Five in childhood. Our coding scheme was not developed to code free descriptions with this distinction in mind. Factor analysis of items developed from parental descriptors will reveal, however, whether there are *two* clusters of characteristics that can be labeled as negative and positive emotionality or better as Emotional Stability and Extraversion.

EMOTIONAL STABILITY IN PARENTAL FREE
DESCRIPTIONS OF CHILDREN'S CHARACTERISTICS

In our coding scheme, Emotional Stability has three facets: Emotional Reactivity, Self-Confidence, and Anxiety-Fearfulness. Overall, the proportions of parental free descriptions coded in this category ranged between 7.1% (China) and 9.9% (Netherlands) (see Table 5.6 and Fig. 5.1). Although analysis of variance showed a significant main effect (Scheffé test after arcsine transformation, $F = 7.96$; $p < .000$), the effect sizes were small, not exceeding 1.9%. The mean proportions for the total category were remarkably similar over all the countries sampled.

How do we evaluate the relative low percentage of Emotional Stability descriptors? First, the low percentage might have been due in part to some descriptors that could have been coded N but were placed in other categories of our coding scheme. Also, in the studies reported in this volume, frequency counts were made of sorted elements in free personality descriptions of children by their parents. As these children were for the most part normal, we should not expect to find high frequencies of descriptors indicating emotional instability. Further, as we discussed earlier, we categorized aggressive behavior and other forms of opposition

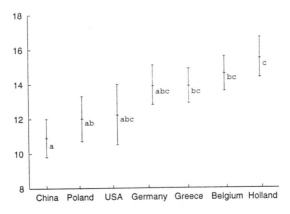

FIG. 5.1. Arcsine transformed means and 95% confidence intervals for Category IV, Emotional Stability. *Note.* a, ab, etc. = Means of samples sharing a common letter are *not* significantly different from one another according to post hoc Scheffé tests.

to parental management in Agreeableness. It may be that descriptors placed in VI, Independence (e.g., too dependent on mother), VII, Mature for Age (e.g., emotionally immature), and VIII, Illness, Handicaps (e.g., allergy problems) might have been categorized under N in other studies (as has been the case in many studies on neurotic behavior in adults). Even if we added some of these descriptions coded in these other categories to Emotional Stability, we still would not have more than 12% or 13% coded as N. Our results are also in line with studies using adjectives from dictionaries. As we discussed earlier, English-language studies found somewhere between 7% (Peabody) and 12% (Norman) of personality adjectives descriptive of Neuroticism-Emotional Stability. Although parental free descriptions of children were only loosely related to dictionary lists of adult personality words, very similar proportions of dictionary adjectives and parental descriptions of Emotional Stability were found.

Facets of Emotional Stability

The three facets in this dimension received different proportions of descriptors. These proportions are presented in Table 5.6. Clearly the first facet, Emotional Reactivity, received most descriptors. Over the seven countries very similar results were obtained. The Chinese parents were significantly lower than were all Western samples. Among the six Western samples, none of the differences was significant. Because of the magnitude of the Chinese proportion, there was a significant main effect for country ($F = 18.01$; $p < .000$, with an effect size, $\eta^2 = .043\%$).

Descriptors Coded High and Low. In Table 5.7, the average proportions of high versus low descriptors are presented. In comparison with all other categories of our coding scheme, the vast majority of parental descriptors were coded low (73.4%). Whenever parents mentioned behavioral characteristics concerning Emotional Stability, it was most often the unstable, reactive, negative emotional behavior patterns (neuroticism) that were used, rather than the stable, confident, behavioral characteristics of Emotional Stability. To return to our earlier discussion on the difference between negative and positive emotionality, it is clear that our category is mostly about negative affect terms. This finding is consistent with the frequency of terms in the adult lexicon for IV. Few words connote emotional stability; conversely, many more connote neuroticism.

Analysis of variance on these average proportions showed a significant overall between-groups effect (Scheffé test after arcsine transformation; $F = 8.0$; $p < .000$) with an effect size of 3%. Polish parents said least about characteristics that could be coded on the positive side of this dimension,

TABLE 5.6

Average Proportions of Descriptors in Three Subcategories of
Main Category IV, Emotional Stability (All Age Groups Together)

	Belgium	Netherlands	Germany	Greece	China	Poland	U.S.A.
				Percentage			
A. Emotional Reactivity	6.5	6.7	5.6	6.5	3.4	6.6	6.1
B. Self-Confidence	2.1	2.5	1.4	1.0	3.0	1.1	1.7
C. Anxiety	0.7	0.6	1.0	1.1	0.7	0.7	0.8
Total IV	9.2	9.9	8.0	8.7	7.1	8.4	8.6

TABLE 5.7
Average Proportions of Descriptors Coded
as IV, Emotional Stability, High and Low

	Belgium	Netherlands	Germany	Greece	China	Poland	U.S.A.
N	301	242	194	323	206	178	107
Mean high and low	22–78	31–69	34–66	22–78	38–62	17–83	24–76

Note. Only parents giving at least one descriptor coded in this category participated in this analysis.

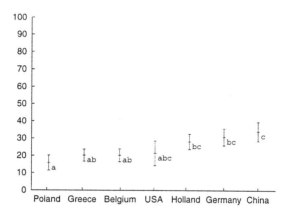

FIG. 5.2. Mean proportions coded as IV high after arcsine transformation, with 95% confidence intervals. *Note.* a, ab, etc. = Means of samples sharing a common letter are *not* significantly different from one another according to post hoc Scheffé tests. Only parents that gave at least one descriptor coded in this category are included in the analysis.

and Chinese most; but only a few of the pair-wise sample comparisons were significant, and most effect sizes were small. The largest difference—between China and Poland—had an effect size of 6.5% (see Fig. 5.2).

CONCLUSION

Across all our samples, less than 10% of parental descriptors were categorized in Emotional Stability. This proportion might have been lowered somewhat because other categories could have been categorized as typical for N. Most descriptors were also on the low end of the dimension, a finding agreeing with childhood temperament literature in which negatively valued constructs such as Emotional Reactivity and Negative Mood are used. Similarly, in adult Big Five personality psychology, the majority of adjectives that load on this factor are located at the negative pole.

In contrast to what we might expect from parents seeking help for their children in child-guidance clinics, most of our parents were not concerned about negative emotionality, anxiety, or self-confidence in their children. Most parents evidently assumed that they had good-functioning and emotionally stable children. We suspect that what is taken for granted is less likely to be mentioned during the interviews; this possibility might be a consequence of the methods used in this project. Many other characteristics of children could have been taken for granted and consequently were less likely to be mentioned at the time of the interview. It would be wrong to equate what is tacitly taken for granted with what is unimportant.

Some characteristics of children are thought of as typical and expectable. For example, most children are assumed to be generally healthy, self-confident, without fears, and usually happy. When these typical, expectable characteristics are absent, they are likely to be mentioned more frequently. This same reasoning may apply to categories in adult studies. In English and many other languages, far fewer words denote emotional stability than denote neuroticism and poor functioning. The importance of the low end, Neuroticism, cannot be underestimated. Neuroticism is associated with various measures of illness and with psychological processes linked to dysphoria and poor functioning. When adults or children are characterized by low-end Neuroticism terms, the consensus is that many important adaptive processes might be compromised. Despite the small size of the lexicon and the relatively small size of factors describing N, we suspect that longitudinal work linking negative emotionality in childhood with differences in N in adulthood will benefit researchers and practitioners by helping people understand how N can mediate many effects of personality on both physical and mental health.

REFERENCES

Achenbach, T. M., & Edelbrock, C. S. (1981). Behavioral problems and competencies reported by parents of normal and disturbed children aged four through sixteen. *Monographs of the Society for Research in Child Development, 46*(1, Serial No. 188).

Achenbach, T. M., & Edelbrock, C. S. (1983). *Manual for the Child Behavior Checklist and Revised Child Behavior Profile*. Burlington: University of Vermont, Department of Psychiatry.

Allport, G. W., & Odbert, H. S. (1936). Trait-names: A psycho-lexical study. *Psychological Monographs, 47*(1, Whole No. 211).

Angleitner, A., Ostendorf, F., & John, O. (1990). Towards a taxonomy of personality descriptors in German: A psycholexical study. *European Journal of Personality, 4*, 89–118.

Block, J., & Block, J. H. (1980). *The California Child Q-set*. Palo Alto, CA: Consulting Psychologists Press. (Original work published 1969)

Burt, C. (1915). The general and specific factors underlying the primary emotions. *British Associations Annual Reports, 84*, 694–696.

Burt, C. (1948). The factorial study of temperament traits. *British Journal of Psychology: Statistical Section, 1*, 178–203.

Buss, A. H. (1988). *Personality: Evolutionary heritage and human distinctiveness*. Hillsdale, NJ: Lawrence Erlbaum Associates.

Buss, A. H., & Durkee, A. (1957). An inventory for assessing different kinds of hostility. *Journal of Consulting Psychology, 21,* 343–349.

Buss, A. H., & Plomin, R. A. (1975). *A temperament theory of personality development.* New York: Wiley-Interscience.

Caprara, G. V., & Perugini, M. (1994). Personality described by adjectives: Generalizability of the Big Five to the Italian lexical context. *European Journal of Personality, 8,* 357–369.

Cattell, R. B. (1946). *The description and measurement of personality.* Yonkers, NY: World Book Company.

Cattell, R. B. (1947). Confirmation and clarification of primary personality factors. *Psychometrika, 12,* 197–220.

Church, A. T., & Katigbak, M. S. (1989). Internal, external and self-reward structure of personality in non-Western culture: An investigation of cross-language and cross-cultural generalizability. *Journal of Personality and Social Psychology, 57,* 857–872.

Costa, P. T., Jr., & McCrae, R. R. (1992). *Revised NEO Personality Inventory (NEO-PI-R) and NEO Five-Factor Inventory (NEO-FFI) professional manual.* Odessa, FL: Psychological Assessment Resources.

De Raad, B. (1992). The replicability of the Big Five personality dimensions in three word-classes of the Dutch language. *European Journal of Personality, 6,* 15–29.

De Raad, B., Hendriks, A. A. J., & Hofstee, W. K. B. (1992). Towards a refined structure of personality traits. *European Journal of Personality, 6,* 301–319.

De Raad, B., Hendriks, A. A. J., & Hofstee, W. K. B. (1994). The Big Five: A tip of the iceberg of individual differences. In C. F. Halverson Jr., G. A. Kohnstamm, & R. P. Martin, *The developing structure of temperament and personality from infancy to adulthood* (pp. 91–110). Hillsdale, NJ: Lawrence Erlbaum Associates.

Eysenck, H. J. (1959). *The manual of the Maudsley Personality Inventory.* London: University of London Press.

Eysenck, H. J. (1967). *The biological basis of personality.* Springfield, IL: Charles C. Thomas.

Eysenck, H. J. (1994). The Big Five or Giant Three: Criteria for a paradigm. In C. F. Halverson Jr., G. A. Kohnstamm, & R. P. Martin (Eds.), *The developing structure of temperament and personality from infancy to adulthood* (pp. 37–52). Hillsdale, NJ: Lawrence Erlbaum Associates.

Eysenck, H. J., & Eysenck, S. B. G. (1975). *Manual of the Eysenck Personality Questionnaire.* Loughton, Essex, England: Hodder & Stoughton.

Eysenck, S. B. G. (1965). *Manual of the Junior Eysenck Personality Inventory.* London: Hodder & Stoughton.

Eysenck, S. B. G., & Eysenck, H. J. (1980). Impulsiveness and venturesomeness in children. *Personality and Individual Differences, 1,* 73–78.

Goldberg, L. R. (1990). An alternative "description of personality": The Big-Five factor structure. *Journal of Personality and Social Psychology, 59,* 1216–1229.

Goldberg, L. R. (1992). The development of markers of the Big Five factor structure. *Psychological Assessment, 4,* 26–42.

Hrebickova, M., Ostendorf, F., & Angleitner, A. (1995, July). *Basic dimensions of personality description in the Czech language.* Poster presented at the seventh meeting of the International Society of Individual Differences, Warsaw, Poland.

John, O. P., Caspi, A., Robins, R. W., Moffitt, T. E., & Stouthamer-Loeber, M. (1994). The "little five": Exploring the nomological network of the five-factor model of personality in adolescent boys. *Child Development, 65,* 160–178.

Katigbak, M. S., Church, A. T., & Akamine, T. X. (1996). Cross-cultural generalizability of personality dimensions: Relating indigenous and imported dimensions in two cultures. *Journal of Personality and Social Psychology, 70,* 99–114.

Martin, R. P., Wisenbaker, J., & Huttunen, M. (1994). Review of factor analytic studies of temperament measures based on the Thomas–Chess structural model: Implications for the Big Five. In C. F. Halverson Jr., G. A. Kohnstamm, & R. P. Martin (Eds.), *The developing structure of temperament and personality from infancy to adulthood* (pp. 157–172). Hillsdale, NJ: Lawrence Erlbaum Associates.

McCrae, R. R., & John, O. P. (1992). An introduction to the five-factor model and its applications. *Journal of Personality, 60,* 175–215.

Norman, W. T. (1963). Toward an adequate taxonomy of personality attributes: Replicated factor structure in peer nomination personality ratings. *Journal of Personality of Abnormal and Social Psychology, 66,* 574–583.

Norman, W. T. (1967). *2800 personality trait descriptors: Normative operating characteristics for a university population.* Ann Arbor: Department of Psychology, University of Michigan.

Ostendorf, F. (1990). *Sprache und Persönlichkeitsstruktur: Zur Validität des Fünf-Faktoren-Modells der Persönlichkeit* [Language and personality structure: On the structural validity of the Five-Factor model of personality]. Regensburg: Roderer.

Ostendorf, F., & Angleitner, A. (1993, July). *A German replication study of the five-factor model based on a comprehensive taxonomy of personality descriptive adjectives.* Paper presented at the sixth meeting of the International Society for the Study of Individual Differences, Baltimore, MD.

Ostendorf, F., & Angleitner, A. (1994). *Psychometric properties of the German translation of the NEO Personality Inventory (NEO-PI-R).* Unpublished manuscript, University of Bielefeld, Germany.

Peabody, D. (1987). Selecting representative trait-adjectives. *Journal of Personality and Social Psychology, 52,* 59–71.

Peabody, D., & Goldberg, L. R. (1989). Some determinants of factor structures from personality-trait descriptors. *Journal of Personality and Social Psychology, 57,* 552–567.

Quay, H. C. (Ed.). (1968). *Children's behavior disorders.* London: Van Nostrand.

Robins, R. W., John, O. P., & Caspi, A. (1994). Major dimensions of personality in early adolescence: The big five and beyond. In C. F. Halverson Jr., G. A. Kohnstamm, & R. P. Martin (Eds.), *The developing structure of temperament and personality from infancy to adulthood* (pp. 267–292). Hillsdale, NJ: Lawrence Erlbaum Associates.

Rothbart, M. K., Posner, M. I., & Hershey, K. L. (1995). Temperament, attention, and developmental psychology. In D. Cicchetti & D. J. Cohen (Eds.), *Developmental psychopathology: Vol. 1, Theory and methods* (pp. 315–342). New York: Wiley.

Szarota, P., & Ostendorf, F. (1995). *Taxonomy and structure of Polish personality-relevant adjectives.* Unpublished manuscript, University of Bielefeld, Germany.

Szirmák, Z., & De Raad, B. (1994). Taxonomy and structure of Hungarian personality traits. *European Journal of Personality, 8,* 95–117.

Tellegen, A. (1985). Structures of mood and personality and their relevance to assessing anxiety, with an emphasis on self-report. In A. H. Tuma & J. D. Maser (Eds.), *Anxiety and Anxiety Disorders* (pp. 681–706). Hillsdale, NJ: Lawrence Erlbaum Associates.

Tupes, E. C., & Christal, R. C. (1992). Recurrent personality factors based on trait ratings. *Journal of Personality, 60,* 225–251. (Work originally published 1961)

Van Lieshout, C. F. M., & Haselager, G. J. T. (1994). The Big Five personality factors in Q-sort descriptions of children and adolescents. In C. F. Halverson Jr., G. A. Kohnstamm, & R. P. Martin (Eds.), *The developing structure of temperament and personality from infancy to adulthood* (pp. 293–318). Hillsdale, NJ: Lawrence Erlbaum Associates.

Watson, D., & Clark, L. A. (1984). Negative affectivity: The disposition to experience aversive emotional states. *Psychological Bulletin, 96,* 465–490.

Watson, D., & Clark, L. A. (1992). On traits and temperament: General and specific factors of emotional experience and their relation to the five-factor model. *Journal of Personality, 60,* 441–475.

Watson, D., & Tellegen, A. (1985). Toward a consensual structure of mood. *Psychological Bulletin, 98,* 219–235.

6

Linking Openness and Intellect in Childhood and Adulthood

Ivan Mervielde
University of Ghent

Filip De Fruyt
University of Ghent

Slawomir Jarmuz
University of Wroclaw

To understand why Openness and Intellect retains a double label, a short history of the dimension is helpful. We review three strands of research that have kept researchers from reaching a consensus on the meaning of the construct.

THE LEXICAL TRADITION

Allport and Odbert's (1936) compilation and categorization of nearly 18,000 person descriptive terms still provides the basis for the lexical approach to personality assessment. Only about 25% of that list, the "real," stable personality traits, were used by Cattell (1943) to define the "trait sphere." Terms referring to temporary states, social roles as well as highly evaluative terms, were excluded from further analyses. Norman (1967) grouped 18,125 descriptive terms into his domains of personality containing 15 categories. The first three categories, "Stable 'Biophysical' Traits," accounted for 15% of the terms and were further reduced to 1,431 (8%) to construct a hierarchical classification system. The German lexical study (Angleitner, Ostendorf, & John, 1990; Ostendorf, 1990) was based on an initial set of 5,092 terms, but only 430 terms finally qualified as *Dispositionen*. A similar reduction took place for the construction of the Dutch Abridged Big Five Circumplex Model (AB5C) taxonomy, beginning with 8,690 terms culled from the dictionary by Brokken (1978) and ending with

551 AB5C adjectives (Hofstee & De Raad, 1991). The major reason for significantly reducing the number of terms was to guarantee that they reflected stable traits and to avoid ambiguous and evaluative words. Further, this emphasis on stable traits has led most lexical researchers to limit the person-descriptive terms only to trait adjectives and to exclude nouns and verbs. One effect of this strategy has been that less stable indicators of personality such as interests, values, and various attitudes have been underrepresented in measures of the Big Five. This reduction is unlikely to affect the content of the other Big Five factors that explain most of the variance, but it is perhaps not so surprising that the Openness-Intellect factor's content has been less stable because of differences in the way the universe of trait-descriptive terms has been typically defined and sampled.

ABILITIES

A second major issue in describing the domain of personality traits is to decide on the role of abilities in such descriptions. Angleitner, Ostendorf, and John (1990) considered *Fähigkeiten, Begabungen, und Talente* (skills, abilities, and talents) as composing a major subcategory of *Dispositionen*, with 125 (of 430) terms in the subcategory. Brokken's (1978) Dutch criteria, however, excluded most ability-related terms. Major personality theorists such as H. J. Eysenck (1971, 1994) and Zuckerman (1991) have consistently argued for excluding ability-related traits like intelligence from the personality domain and have instead measured them with traditional intelligence tests.

Other theorists, however, have included abilities. For example, Rorer (1990) defined personality as including intellectual abilities, aptitudes, attitudes, interests, as well as behavioral and personality traits. Brand (1994a, 1994b) made the case for not only including g (general intelligence) as an important part of personality, but also for including general intelligence as the core of a taxonomy for individual differences because: "In any random sample of important human outcomes, g would account for more variance than most of psychology's other variables put together" (Brand, 1994b, p. 301). The issue of the relations between intelligence and personality, as well as their conceptual integration or distinction, is far from resolved (see, for example, Ackerman & Goff, 1994; Goff & Ackerman, 1992). The ongoing discussion about the best label for the fifth personality factor (De Raad & Van Heck, 1994) is to some extent part of a broader issue of the relation between personality and intelligence (Saklofske & Zeidner, 1995). The decision to include ability-related terms either by providing a separate category for them or by screening dictionary terms with an appropriate filter can shift the evidence from Intellect to Openness and back again as the most suitable label for this construct.

BEHAVIORAL ITEMS

A third development contributing to the lack of consensus about Openness-Intellect is the extension of the lexical model to include content covered by traditional personality questionnaires. Although some personality questionnaires such as the Adjective Checklist (Gough & Heilbrun, 1983), use trait adjectives to assess personality, most traditional personality questionnaires consist of many items that refer to concrete behavior, with only a few items phrased as trait adjectives. The clinical origins of many personality questionnaires is also revealed in their emphasis on behavioral items as reliable indicators of various personality disorders. The lexical approach, based as it is on the analysis of the structure of trait adjectives, had to demonstrate that the Big Five covered a significant part of the variance captured by traditional personality questionnaires to become acceptable to the vast majority of clinical psychologists. The validity of Cattell's Sixteen Personality Factor Questionnaire (16PF), a personality questionnaire based on the Allport and Odbert taxonomy (Cattell, Eber, & Tatsuoka, 1970), was repeatedly questioned because the 16-factor structure promoted by Cattell turned out to be unreliable and virtually unreplicable.

With the benefit of hindsight, the challenge and opportunity to demonstrate that the Big Five represented the core content of personality questionnaires was taken up by Costa and McCrae. In the mid-1970s, they constructed the NEO, a three-factor questionnaire measuring Neuroticism, Extraversion, and Openness. The first two factors were analogous to those of the well-known personality EPQ questionnaire. The third factor was added based on a cluster analysis of Cattell's 16PF (Costa & McCrae, 1976), which revealed a loose cluster of items from scales such as Experimenting and Imaginative. Costa and McCrae conceptualized it as Experiential Style and broadened its scope by relating it to Coan's Experience Inventory (Coan, 1972). A joint factor analysis of the 16PF and the Experience Inventory yielded a clean Openness factor with the following six Openness facets: Fantasy, Aesthetics, Feelings, Actions, Ideas, and Values (Costa & McCrae, 1985; McCrae & Costa, 1997).

Goldberg's taxonomic research (e.g., Goldberg, 1992) in the lexical Big Five tradition led to an inclusion of two additional scales measuring Conscientiousness and Agreeableness as part of the NEO Personality Inventory/NEO Five-Factor Inventory (NEO-PI/NEO-FFI; Costa & McCrae, 1989). This model has been commonly referred to as the Five-Factor Model (FFM) to contrast it with conceptions of the Big Five emerging from the lexical research tradition. Four of the five factors included in both models are similar, in terms of both labels and factors derived from empirical research (Goldberg, 1989; McCrae, 1990; but see chapter 4, this volume, for discrepancies in the content of the Conscientiousness factor in both models). The fifth factor, however, has turned into a sort of "scientific embarrassment" (Goldberg, 1994), with two major interpretations, one stemming from the lexical research (Culture and Intellect) and the other from Costa and McCrae's emphasis on Openness and the divergent results of lexical studies in Hungarian, Dutch, and Italian (Ostendorf & Angleitner, 1994a).

CHANGING INTERPRETATIONS
OF THE FIFTH FACTOR

Cattell's Legacy

The first major lexical research program, and indeed the blueprint for the lexical approach, was spelled out by R. B. Cattell (1943, 1945, 1946). His list of 171 variables constituting the complete "personality sphere" (Cattell, 1946, p. 219) included abilities, intelligence, and special abilities such as mathematical, musical, mechanical, logical, visual, and verbal. Further, variables 88 to 97 were defined as special interests such as artistic, economic, music, political, religious, and theoretical. For Cattell, both general intelligence and special abilities and interests were part and parcel of personality. Moreover, they were not culled from the dictionary:

> The list of personality traits was finally brought to 171 items through the addition of two kinds of personality variables not enjoying such precise representation in the dictionary material as in the psychological literature, namely: (1) interests and (2) abilities. . . . The decision to add these interest and ability categories to the personality items was made on the clinical evidence that special abilities, and to some extent general intelligence, are likely to be related to, and perhaps therefore determining or determined by, dynamic and constitutional personality traits. (Cattell, 1943, pp. 492–493)

Several of these interest and ability categories were typical markers for the various present-day interpretations of the fifth factor (Table 6.1). Further reduction of the trait sphere to 35 variables deleted most of the variables listed in Table 6.1 or combined them into one group. Much of what is currently thought to be typical for the Openness-Intellect factor seemed to be lost in the final stages of Cattell's attempts to reduce the

TABLE 6.1
Cattell's Variables Related to Different
Interpretations of Openness-Intellect

Intellect	Culture	Openness
Abilities: Intelligence	Eloquent–inarticulate	Imaginative–dull
Special abilities: Mathematical,	Sophisticated–	Curious–uninquiring
mechanical, logical, reason-	simple-hearted	Imitative–nonimitative
ing, spatial, visual, verbal	Interest: Wide, narrow	Original–banal
Analytical	Interest, special:	Interest, special:
Clever	Music, political	Aesthetic, artistic
Clear-thinking–incoherent		Opinionated–tolerant
Intuitive–logical		Fantasizing

number of variables to make a manually computed factor analysis feasible. Two of Cattell's (Cattell, 1945, p. 89) twelve questionnaire factors, Factor B (General Mental Capacity) and I (Sensitive, Imaginative, and Neurotic), can be related to the current interpretations of Openness-Intellect.

Recurrent and Orthogonal Factors

Cattell's factors turned out to be very difficult to replicate because as Fiske stated: "Cattell uses unusually low loadings to help him identify his rotated factors. . . . The author does not share his confidence in the significance of low loadings" (Fiske, 1949, p. 342). Fiske (1949), Tupes and Christal (1961, 1992), and later on Norman (1963) looked for recurrent factors in different data sets. They used Cattell's established clusters or subsets to look for orthogonal and recurrent factors across different samples. Table 6.2 lists the factor labels and the adjective marker variables for their "fifth" factors (Openness-Intellect). These pioneers of the Big Five emphasized the culture label and interpretation for this factor. Goldberg (1989, 1992) collected and structured various adjective clusters based on Norman's (1967) hierarchical classification. His list of bipolar marker variables covered all three major interpretations, but because of the high loadings for the intellect markers, he labeled his fifth factor Intellect.

The Questionnaire Approach

The Openness facets of the revised NEO (Costa & McCrae, 1992) correlated with various trait adjectives. Imaginative was, however, the most prominent and consistent correlate across the six Openness facets. Saucier (1992,

TABLE 6.2
Adjective Markers and Labels for Various
Fifth Factors of Openness-Intellect

Study	Label	Adjective Marker Variables
Fiske (1949)	Inquiring Intellect	Broad interests, independent minded, imaginative
Tupes & Christal (1961)	Culture	Artistic, cultured, imaginative, polished
Norman (1963)	Culture	Artistically sensitive–Artistically insensitive Intellectual–Unreflective, narrow Polished, refined–Crude, boorish Imaginative–Simple, direct
Goldberg (1992)	Intellect	Intelligent–Unintelligent Perceptive–Imperceptive Analytical–Unanalytical Reflective–Unreflective Curious–Uninquisitive Imaginative–Unimaginative Creative–Uncreative Cultured–Uncultured Refined–Unrefined Sophisticated–Unsophisticated
Costa & McCrae (1992)	Openness to Fantasy	Dreamy, imaginative, humorous, mischievous, idealistic, artistic, complicated
	Aesthetics	Imaginative, artistic, original, enthusiastic, inventive, idealistic, versatile
	Feelings	Excitable, spontaneous, insightful, imaginative, affectionate, talkative, outgoing
	Actions	Interests wide, imaginative, adventurous, optimistic, mild, talkative, versatile
	Ideas	Idealistic, interests wide, inventive, curious, original, imaginative, insightful
	Values	Conservative, unconventional, cautious, flirtatious

Note. Adjectives from the Adjective Check List (Gough & Heilbrun, 1983) correlated with the NEO facets, presented in descending order of absolute magnitude. From NEO-PI-R Professional Manual (p. 49), by P. T. Costa, Jr., and R. R. McCrae (1992), Odessa, FL: Psychological Assessment Resources. Copyright © 1992 by Psychological Assessment Resources. Reprinted with permission.

1994) concluded that Imagination would be a more appropriate label for the Openness-Intellect factor. A special issue of the *European Journal of Personality* (De Raad & Van Heck, 1994) documented, however, that a consensus on the label for the construct had not yet been reached. On the contrary, Johnson (1994) argued for Creative Mentality as the best label, but Ostendorf and Angleitner (1994b) continued to see Intellect as the core feature of the factor. Moreover, the Openness factor of the NEO-PI-R is differentially loaded by its six facets. De Fruyt (1996, p. 72) showed that for both the American and the Dutch–Flemish versions of this instrument the Ideas and Aesthetics facets constituted the core of the factor, in that they had high primary and no important secondary loadings. Openness to Feelings, however, was a blend of Openness and both Extraversion and Neuroticism.

In an attempt to link temperament and personality research, Angleitner and Ostendorf (1994) factor analyzed 29 temperament scales derived from the Revised short form of the Strelau Temperament Inventory (STI-RS: Strelau, Angleitner, Bantelmann, & Ruch, 1990), the Sensation-Seeking Scales (SSS: Zuckerman, 1979), the EASI-Temperament Survey (EASI: Buss & Plomin, 1984), and the Revised Dimensions of Temperament Survey (DOTS-R: Windle & Lerner, 1986). They identified an Openness component that explained 11.4% of the variance, defined primarily by the SSS, a finding suggesting a more restricted interpretation, much like the NEO-PI-R openness facet of Actions. Other temperament scales with primary loadings on this Openness factor showed considerable secondary and tertiary loadings.

INFANCY AND CHILDHOOD

Developmental psychologists have often relied on teachers and parents as the main source of information about children's behavior and development. Personality and temperament assessment has typically been based on standardized procedures such as questionnaires and Q sorts designed to collect information about a child's social and emotional behavior (Carey & McDevitt, 1978; S. B. G. Eysenck, 1965; Kohnstamm, Bates, & Rothbart, 1989; Thomas & Chess, 1977). For instance, the classic Thomas and Chess temperament scales employed a nine-dimensional structure, whereas the Eysencks' PEN model (H. J. Eysenck & M. W. Eysenck, 1985) defined three factors.

Temperament Literature

Several empirical studies reviewed by Martin, Wisenbaker, and Huttunen (1994) showed that the proposed nine-factor structure for the Thomas and Chess scales cannot be recovered from factoring at the item level. A review of 12 large-sample factor analyses of parents' and teachers' temperament ratings showed evidence for seven factors, although there was more support for some factors than for others. Based on this meta-analysis, Martin et al. (1994) concluded that seven factors—Activity Level, Negative Emotionality, Task Persistence, Adaptability, Inhibition, Biological Rhythmicity, and Threshold—accounted for the variance in the Thomas and Chess item pool. They hypothesized developmental connections between these factors and the first four of the adult Big Five. They concluded that temperamental factors of childhood are probably not related to Openness to Experience, but suggested that the adult factor is probably best predicted from childhood intellectual ability.

Ahadi and Rothbart (1994) mapped infant and child temperamental systems of approach and anxiety onto the adult Big Five personality structure and hypothesized about the role of attentional self-regulation as a mechanism underlying or moderating Extraversion, Neuroticism, Agreeableness, and Conscientiousness. They did not, however, attempt to relate temperament factors to Openness or Intellect. Hagekull (1994) also related Buss and Plomin's EASI dimensions of childhood functioning to the Big Five dimensions. The results from all temperament studies were convergent and showed that no investigator had conceptualized any clear precursors of adult Openness or Intellect in studies with infants and children.

Traits such as creativity and fantasy have been considered markers of the Openness factor (Costa & McCrae, 1992). The literature on childhood fantasy has been mainly psychoanalytically oriented; although there is a considerable literature on the structure and measurement of creativity in childhood (e.g., Khatena, 1982; Torrance, 1966), this trait has been largely neglected in the temperament literature. Zarnegar, Hocevar, and Michael (1988) investigated the relations between creativity and intelligence in large samples of fourth to sixth graders and concluded that creativity scores were independent of measured intelligence for this age group. These findings agree with adult studies and suggest only moderate correlations between Openness and Intelligence (Costa & McCrae, 1992). Paguio and Hollet (1991) investigated temperament and creativity in a small sample of preschool children, using Torrance Tests of Creative Thinking and Martin's Temperament Assessment Battery (MTAB: Martin, 1988). Creativity was significantly related to adaptability and sociability, but only for girls. There were no significant relations with other MTAB dimensions.

Personality Ratings of Children

Digman and Takemoto-Chock (1981) provided the first evidence about the validity of the FFM theory as a model for individual differences among elementary school-age children. Subsequently, Digman and Inouye (1986) recovered the five-factor structure from Hawaiian teachers' nominations of sixth-grade children on 43 scales. The scales primarily loading the fifth factor in descending order were Knowledgeable (.99), Perceptive (.87),

Imaginative (.86), Verbal (.84), Original (.83), Curious (.78), Adaptable (.55), Sensible (.50), Socially Confident (.50), Rigid (−.43), and Aesthetically Sensitive (.34) (Digman & Inouye, 1986, p. 119). Digman and Inouye suggested the label of Inquiring Intellect for this factor because it also appeared to include items referring to Openness to Experience.

Mervielde, Buyst, and De Fruyt (1995) confirmed and extended the evidence for the usefulness of the Big Five model in representing individual differences among children aged 4 to 12 years. A sample of 2,240 children was rated by teachers on a set of 25 bipolar scales marking the five factors of Extraversion, Agreeableness, Conscientiousness, Emotional Stability, and Intellect-Openness. Principal component analysis of ratings of kindergarten children (aged 4 to 6) revealed four of the five factors. The complete five-factor structure emerged from the ratings of primary school children. Conscientiousness accounted for a greater part of the variance than is usually observed in self-ratings of adults. To clarify the meaning of the fifth factor, a six-factor solution was obtained for three primary school-age levels. As a result, the fifth factor bifurcated into two components: one marked by Openness scales and the other marked by Intellect rating scales. Table 6.3 shows that the fifth and sixth factors correlated primarily with the fifth factor from the five-factor solution, but the pattern of correlations changed with increasing age.

For younger children, the fifth factor was highly correlated with Intellect and to a lesser extent with Openness. For the oldest children, this pattern was reversed. The group aged 8 to 10 showed intermediate correlations with both components. This pattern suggested the growing importance of the Openness scales as part of the fifth factor. Openness and Intellect had a differential pattern of correlations with some of the other factors as well. Openness was positively related to Agreeableness, whereas Intellect was negatively related to the same factor. Intellect, on the other hand, correlated with Conscientiousness, while Openness tended

TABLE 6.3

Correlations of Intellect and Openness Factor Scores (Six-Factor Solution) With Fifth-Factor Scores of a Five-Factor Solution for Three Age Groups

	Fifth Factor of Five-Factor Solution		
Six-Factor Solution	Aged 6–8 yr (N = 560)	Aged 8–10 yr (N = 600)	Aged 10–12 yr (N = 520)
Intellect	0.90**	0.73**	0.27**
Openness	0.43**	0.68**	0.96**

Note. From "The Validity of the Big-Five . . . ," by I. Mervielde, V. Buyst, and F. De Fruyt, 1995, *Personality and Individual Differences, 18*, p. 531. Copyright © 1995 by Elsevier Science Ltd. Reprinted with permission.

**$p < .001$.

TABLE 6.4
Correlations of Intellect and Openness Factor Scores
With Grade Point Average for Three Age Groups

	Aged 6–8 yr (N = 560)	Aged 8–10 yr (N = 600)	Aged 10–12 yr (N = 520)
Intellect	0.52**	0.51**	0.40**
Openness	0.07	0.13*	0.21**

Note. From "The Validity of the Big-Five . . . ," by I. Mervielde, V. Buyst, and F. De Fruyt, 1995, *Personality and Individual Differences, 18*, p. 531. Copyright © 1995 by Elsevier Science Ltd. Reprinted with permission.
*p < .01. **p < .001.

to be inversely related to this factor. This study also illustrated that Intellect and Openness were differentially related to grade point average (GPA) from 8 years onward as reported in Table 6.4. The role of Openness grew increasingly important with increasing age, while the importance of Intellect declined with age. Victor (1994) and Graziano and Ward (1992) also provided evidence for the validity of the Intellect-Openness dimension as a predictor of school or academic achievement.

Digman and Shmelyov (1996) have demonstrated the validity of the FFM in representing the structure of temperament and personality ratings provided by Russian teachers rating 8- to 10-year-old children. An analysis of a set of 21 combined temperament and personality scales revealed five factors, including one factor loading scale such as Original (.80), Perceptive (.74), Knowledgeable (.71), Adaptable (.71), Curious (.67), Imaginative (.61), Dependent (–.58), and Rigid (–.58). Digman and Shmelyov labeled this factor Intellect, but Openness to Experience seems an equally appropriate label for this dimension.

Personality Q Sorts

Using an existing set of Dutch California Child Q-set descriptors (CCQ: Block & Block, 1980; Nijmegen CCQ: van Lieshout et al. 1986), van Lieshout and Haselager (1994) examined whether the FFM could account for the structure of parents' and teachers' ratings of a large sample of Dutch children and adolescents. A principal component analysis showed seven factors, explaining 40.5% of the variance. Besides the adult Big Five dimensions, two additional factors referring to Motor Activity and Dependency could be identified. The fourth factor combined items referring to Openness to new ideas, fantasy, and creativity as well as physical attractiveness. Surprisingly, the item Daydreaming, which was a marker for Openness in the NEO-PI-R, had no substantive loading on the CCQ Openness component and instead loaded negatively on Conscientiousness and Motor Activity. Separate principal component analyses for different subsamples demonstrated that Openness based on parental ratings was composed of a broad range of items, including references to social and relational skills.

John, Caspi, Robins, Moffitt, and Stouthamer-Loeber (1994) and Robins, John, and Caspi (1994) confirmed the findings of van Lieshout and Hase-lager (1994) in a study with caregiver common-language CCQ (Caspi et al., 1992). Ratings of a sample of 350 ethnically diverse Pittsburgh, Penn-sylvania, boys between 12 and 13 years old yielded a seven-factor solution that was very similar to the components reported by van Lieshout and Haselager (1994). John and colleagues extended the former findings by showing significant relations to constructs used in research on personality development and by providing evidence for the validity of the CCQ Big Five dimensions for predicting important real-world criteria such as psychopathology, delinquency, school performance, and intelligence (Robins et al., 1994).

Peer Nominations

The common denominator in the studies reviewed thus far is that children were rated by adults (teachers or parents); therefore, the emergence of the FFM could still possibly be attributed to the cognitive structure of the adult perceivers. If the Big Five are basic categories for ordering person perception and personality, then they should also guide children's person perception at some point in their development. Finding out whether children's perceptions of personality develop toward the five-factor adult structure is not only relevant from a developmental point of view, but could also provide knowledge of the origins of the FFM and its gener-alizability across the lifespan (see also chapter 3, this volume, for data on children's free descriptions; see also Donahue, 1994).

De Fruyt and Mervielde (1992) and Mervielde and De Fruyt (1992) assessed the validity and usefulness of the five-factor theory of personality as a model for children's peer nominations. Eighty-nine groups of 10 schoolchildren, attending the same class and aged 9 to 12 years, nominated the child that was the most or the least typical on each of 25 bipolar trait pairs that covered the Big Five personality factors. Factor analysis of summed peer nominations for the total sample showed that nominations on the positive trait poles were represented by four factors: Extraversion, Agreeableness, Emotional Stability, and a combined Intellect-Conscien-tiousness factor. The analysis of negative trait poles indicated that Agree-ableness and Emotional Stability combined into one factor, resulting in a three-factor solution: Agreeableness-Emotional Stability, Intellect-Consci-entiousness, and Introversion. For both positive and negative nomination scales, children did not distinguish Conscientious from Intellectual peers. Moreover, principal component analysis for each of the four age groups showed that the three-factor structure, obtained for negative nominations, could be differentiated into four factors from 11 years onward, but Conscientiousness and Intellect still remained as a unitary factor. The factor loadings for both positive and negative nomination scales for the combined Intellect-Conscientiousness factor are reported in Table 6.5.

Several explanations for this lack of differentiation between Conscientiousness and Intellect can be suggested. First, the behavioral repertoire of children aged 9 to 12 years might not yet include those behaviors that are necessary to make the distinction. This explanation is, however, contradicted by studies showing that teachers can make independent ratings of Intellect and Conscientiousness. For example, Digman and Inouye (1986) illustrated that sixth-grade teachers easily made this distinction. Mervielde, Buyst, and De Fruyt (1995) showed that although kindergarten teachers did not make independent judgments of Conscientiousness and Intellect, teachers' ratings of Intellect and Conscientiousness were independent beginning in the first grade.

Second, making the distinction between Conscientiousness and Intellect appears not functional for children at this age, while for teachers, differentiating between children with good grades that are due to effort and children who are intellectually talented may be important in predicting future educational success. Research on the development of causal attribution schemata has suggested that for younger children, judgments of effort and ability covary, but for older children, both causes compensate for each other (Barker & Graham, 1987; Kun, 1977; Meyer, 1992). Kun

TABLE 6.5
Factor Loadings of Peer Nomination Scales on Combined
Intellect–Conscientiousness Factor ($N = 890$)

Positive Scales	Loading[a]	Negative Scales	Loading[a]
Smartest	.91	Most stupid	.86
Most intelligent	.90	Least intelligent	.83
Hardest working	.90	Laziest	.80
Most eager to learn	.83	Least interested in school	.79
Most interested in school	.83	Most forgetful	.76
Most attentive	.81	Least eager to learn	.75
Least forgetful	.77	Least attentive	.73
Most careful	.56	Least careful	.70
Least sloppy	.53	Most sloppy	.66

Note. From The "Big Five Personality Factors as a Model . . . by I. Mervielde and F. De Fruyt, 1992, Ghent, Belgium: University of Ghent. Copyright © 1992 by the University of Ghent. Reprinted with permission.
[a]Only loadings > .50 are reported.

(1977) labeled this judgmental heuristic the "halo schema." *Effort* and *ability* are prototypical concepts respectively for the traits of Conscientiousness and Intellect. The observed covariation of the nominations reflecting both traits is consonant with experimental research on the development of effort and ability attributions.

FREE DESCRIPTIONS OF CHILDREN'S CHARACTERISTICS

Our collaborative research group subdivided the Openness-Intellect category into facets to accommodate both Intellect and Openness. Also, in keeping with Cattell's conceptualization of personality (1946), a third facet capturing the range and type of interests of the child was included. The type and range of preferences might be a good indicator of Openness at younger age levels, whereas fantasy and creativity might become more salient later in development.

The distribution of the free personality descriptors across the first five categories of the lexicon showed that between 11 and 21% of the descriptors were assigned to Openness-Intellect (Table 6.6). A comparison among the different countries showed that Openness-Intellect received more descriptors than did the categories referring to Conscientiousness and Emotional Stability (except for the Chinese data; see chapter 1, Table 1.5). The results summarized in Fig. 6.1 demonstrate that parents in Germany and the United States used significantly more descriptors referring to Openness-Intellect when describing their children.

We performed ANOVAs across countries on the three facets for the Openness-Intellect dimension. Results are depicted in Figs. 6.2, 6.3, and 6.4. For the Openness facet, there were three groupings of countries (Fig. 6.2). At the high end were China and Germany, and at the low end were

TABLE 6.6
Average Proportions of Descriptors in Three Subcategories of Main
Category V, Openness-Intellect (All Age Groups Combined)

		Belgium	Netherlands	Germany	Greece	China	Poland	U.S.A.
A.	Openness to Experience	3.7	3.8	4.2	3.0	5.9	2.0	5.4
B.	Interests	6.4	5.1	10.0	3.0	4.3	4.4	8.1
C.	Intelligence, Reasoning	2.5	3.3	3.4	5.1	3.9	5.1	7.7
	Total V	12.6	12.2	17.6	11.1	14.0	11.5	21.2

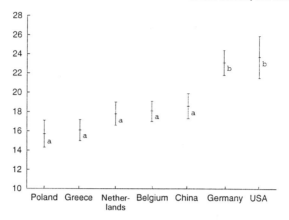

FIG. 6.1. Arcsine transformed means and 95% confidence intervals for Category V, Openness to Experience. *Note.* a, ab, etc. = Means of samples sharing a common letter are *not* significantly different from one another according to post hoc Scheffé tests.

Greece and Poland. In the middle, overlapping both ends of the distribution, were the United States, Netherlands, and Belgium.

For the Interests facet, Germany was clearly higher than all the other countries (Fig. 6.3). Greece and Poland were at the low end of this facet, along with China. Chinese parents found Openness to be most salient and Interests much less salient in describing their children.

For the Intellect facet, the United States was high along with Greece and Poland, while Belgium anchored the low end of the Intellect distribution (Fig. 6.4). For Intellect, there was much overlap in the distribution,

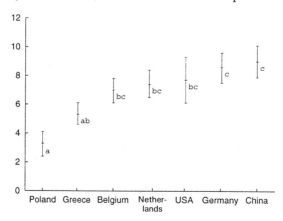

FIG. 6.2. Arcsine transformed means and 95% confidence intervals for Category Va, Openness. *Note.* a, ab, etc. = Means of samples sharing a common letter are *not* significantly different from one another according to post hoc Scheffé tests.

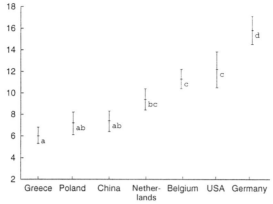

FIG. 6.3. Arcsine transformed means and 95% confidence intervals for Category Vb, Interests. *Note.* a, ab, etc. = Means of samples sharing a common letter are *not* significantly different from one another according to post hoc Scheffé tests.

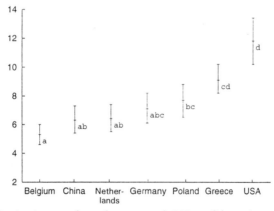

FIG. 6.4. Arcsine transformed means and 95% confidence intervals for Category Vc, Intelligence. *Note.* a, ab, etc. = Means of samples sharing a common letter are *not* significantly different from one another according to post hoc Scheffé tests.

and the differences among countries were generally small, although the United States, Greece, and Poland were clearly different from Belgium in the use of the Intellect descriptors.

The average proportions of descriptors assigned to the high and low ends of Category V for parents giving at least one descriptor coded in this category (Table 6.7) illustrate that the majority of the descriptors were consistently assigned to the high-end subcategory. A visual representation of the between-country differences for parents providing at least one descriptor for this category is presented in Fig. 6.5 (high end).

TABLE 6.7
Average Proportions of Descriptors Assigned to
High and Low Ends of Openness–Intellect Category

	Belgium	Netherlands	Germany	Greece	China	Poland	U.S.A.
N	341	260	229	338	299	236	152
Mean high and low	95–5	92–8	88–12	93–7	86–14	91–9	99–1

Note. Only parents who gave at least one descriptor in this category were included in this analysis.

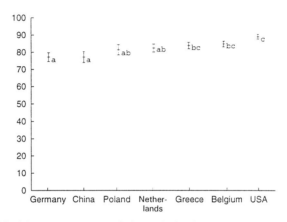

FIG. 6.5. Mean proportions coded as V high after arcsine transformation, with 95% confidence intervals. *Note.* a, ab, etc. = Means of samples sharing a common letter are *not* significantly different from one another according to post hoc Scheffé tests. Only parents who gave at least one descriptor coded in this category are included in the analysis.

CONCLUSIONS

The three major interpretations for the fifth factor—Culture, Intellect, and Openness—were not equally salient as dimensions of individual differences among children. Culture, referring to the outcome of education and perhaps also to socioeconomic and cultural environment, is not very promising as a dimension of individual differences, especially for younger children.

The temperament literature infrequently refers to any of the three variants of Openness-Intellect. To the extent that Intellect can be regarded as a correlate of intellectual ability, individual differences in intelligence and information processing capacity might be considered as early indicators of Intellect.

Recall that kindergarten teachers rating children aged 4 to 6 years were unable to differentiate Intellect and Openness from Conscientiousness, and research based on teacher ratings of primary school children provided clear evidence for Intellect as well as for Openness as dimensions of personality. The factor most resembling the adult Openness in these studies usually contained items that were a mixture of Intellect and Openness markers (Digman & Inouye, 1986; Digman & Shmelyov, 1996; Mervielde et al., 1995). Extraction of six factors sometimes bifurcated the factor into separate Intellect and Openness components. The meaning of the fifth factor apparently shifted from primarily Intellect in younger children to essentially Openness for children aged 10 to 12 years. Intellect ratings, and to a lesser extent individual differences in Openness, have been found to be significant and independent predictors of GPA for children aged 6 to 12 years.

A broader set of 7 dimensions, including the Big Five, has emerged from studies based on the CCQ (John et al., 1994; van Lieshout & Haselager, 1994) and has confirmed the predictive validity of teacher ratings (John et al., 1994). This research illustrates that Openness-Intellect of the Big Five independently predicts GPA and teacher reports of performance in reading, writing, spelling, and mathematics as well as measured intelligence.

The development of peer perception and, in particular, the validity of the Big Five as a framework for the dimensions of peer perception might be an interesting topic for future research on the development of person perception. Our research, based on an extension of the classic peer nomination methodology, showed that elementary school children did not distinguish Conscientiousness indicators from Intellect-Openness markers. Whether this was due to the particular selection of scales is a topic for future research. Although the final aim of this project is the construction of childhood personality questionnaires to be used by parents or teachers, the free-description item pool might also be an interesting starting point to construct self- or peer rating personality scales for children. The availability of such a scale would certainly advance research on peer perception and might show a more differentiated structure than demonstrated thus far.

The distribution of the free descriptors across the categories of the personality lexicon illustrated that between 11% and 21% of the parental free descriptors could be classified as indices of Openness-Intellect, a finding that underscores the saliency of this domain in infancy and childhood. These findings are in strong contrast with the absence of markers or precursors of the fifth factor in the traditional temperament literature and assessment instruments, such as the DOTS-R and the Thomas and Chess questionnaires. Parents, however, often referred to indicators of

Openness-Intellect when freely describing children's personalities. Moreover, the free-description results were convergent *across different language groups*, regardless of minor differences in sampling procedures.

The changing faces of Openness-Intellect have been well represented in the lexicon used to code parental personality descriptions. The proportions of descriptors assigned to the three facets of Openness-Intellect illustrate that parents referred both to Openness and Intellect as well as interests when they were asked to describe their children's personalities. The parental free descriptions were similar to Cattell's first representation of the "personality sphere," including general intelligence, special abilities, and interests. The operationalization of the parental conceptualization of childhood personality should include items referring to these different facets of Openness-Intellect.

The evidence for the usefulness and predictive validity of Openness-Intellect as a dimension of child personality is certainly encouraging. Both the Intellect and the Openness interpretations are emerging as relevant dimensions from factor analyses of teacher ratings and CCQ sorts. The fifth factor has not, however, been as yet established as an independent and developmentally salient dimension of children's peer perception.

REFERENCES

Ackerman, P. L., & Goff, M. (1994). Typical intellectual engagement and personality: Reply to Rocklin 1994. *Journal of Educational Psychology, 86,* 150–153.

Ahadi, S. A., & Rothbart, M. K. (1994). Temperament, development and the Big Five. In C. F. Halverson Jr., G. A. Kohnstamm, & R. P. Martin (Eds.), *The developing structure of temperament and personality from infancy to adulthood* (pp. 189–207). Hillsdale, NJ: Lawrence Erlbaum Associates.

Allport, G. W., & Odbert, H. S. (1936). Trait-names: A psycho-lexical study. *Psychological Monographs, 47*(1, Whole No. 211).

Angleitner, A., & Ostendorf, F. (1994). Temperament and the Big Five factors of personality. In C. F. Halverson Jr., G. A. Kohnstamm, & R. P. Martin (Eds.), *The developing structure of temperament and personality from infancy to adulthood* (pp. 69–90). Hillsdale, NJ: Lawrence Erlbaum Associates.

Angleitner, A., Ostendorf, F., & John, O. (1990). Towards a taxonomy of personality descriptors in German: A psycho-lexical study. *European Journal of Personality, 4,* 89–118.

Barker, G., & Graham, S. (1987). Developmental study of praise and blame as attributional cues. *Journal of Educational Psychology, 79,* 62–66.

Block, J. H., & Block, J. (1980). The role of ego-control and ego-resiliency in the organization of behavior. In W. A. Collins (Ed.), *Development of cognition, affect, and social relations* (Minnesota symposia on child psychology, 13; pp. 39–101). Hillsdale, NJ: Lawrence Erlbaum Associates.

Brand, C. (1994a). How many dimensions of personality?—The "Big 5," the "Gigantic 3" or the "Comprehensive 6"? *Psychological Belgica, 34,* 257–273.

Brand, C. (1994b). Open to experience—closed to intelligence: Why the "Big Five" are really the "Comprehensive Six." *European Journal of Personality, 8,* 299–310.

Brokken, F. B. (1978). *The language of personality.* Unpublished dissertation, University of Groningen, Groningen, Netherlands.

Buss, A. H., & Plomin, R. (1984). *Temperament: Early developing personality traits.* Hillsdale, NJ: Lawrence Erlbaum Associates.

Carey, W. B., & McDevitt, S. C. (1978). Revision of the infant temperament questionnaire. *Pediatrics, 61,* 735–739.

Caspi, A., Block, J., Block, J. H., Klopp, B., Lynam, D., Moffitt, T. E., & Stouthamer-Loeber, M. (1992). A "common language" version of the California Q-set for personality assessment. *Psychological Assessment, 4,* 512–523.

Cattell, R. B. (1943). The description of personality: Basic traits resolved into clusters. *Journal of Abnormal and Social Psychology, 38,* 476–506.

Cattell, R. B. (1945). The description of personality: Principles and findings in a factor analysis. *American Journal of Psychology, 58,* 69–90.

Cattell, R. B. (1946). *Description and measurement of personality.* Yonkers on Hudson, NY: World Book Company.

Catell, R. B., Eber, H. W., & Tatsuoka, M. M. (1970). *The Handbook for the Sixteen Personality Factor Questionnaire.* Champaign, IL: Institute for Personality and Ability Testing.

Coan, R. A. (1972). Measurable components of openness to experience. *Journal of Consulting and Clinical Psychology, 39,* 346.

Costa, P. T., Jr., & McCrae, R. R. (1976). Age differences in personality structure: A cluster analytic approach. *Journal of Gerontology, 31,* 564–570.

Costa, P. T., Jr., & McCrae, R. R. (1985). *The NEO Personality Inventory manual.* Odessa, FL: Psychological Assessment Resources.

Costa, P. T., Jr., & McCrae, R. R. (1989). *The NEO-PI/NEO-FFI manual supplement.* Odessa, Fl: Psychological Assessment Resources.

Costa, P. T., Jr., & McCrae, R. R. (1992). *NEO-PI-R. professional manual.* Odessa, FL: Psychological Assessment Resources.

De Fruyt, F. (1996). *Personality and vocational interests: Relationship between the Five-Factor Model of personality and Holland's RIASEC typology.* Unpublished doctoral dissertation, University of Ghent, Belgium.

De Fruyt, F., & Mervielde, I. (1992). The "Big-Five" in children's sociometric judgements [Abstract]. *International Journal of Psychology, 27,* 353.

De Raad, B., & Van Heck, G. (Eds.). (1994). The fifth of the Big Five [Special Issue]. *European Journal of Personality, 8,* 225–356.

Digman, J. M., & Inouye, J. (1986). Further specification of the five robust factors of personality. *Journal of Personality and Social Psychology, 50,* 116–123.

Digman, J. M., & Shmelyov, A. G. (1996). The structure of temperament and personality in Russian children. *Journal of Personality and Social Psychology, 71,* 341–351.

Digman, J. M., & Takemoto-Chock, N. K. (1981). Factors in the natural language of personality: Re-analysis, comparison, and interpretation of six major studies. *Multivariate Behavioral Research, 16,* 149–170.

Donahue, E. M. (1994). Do children use the Big Five too? Content and structural form in personality description. *Journal of Personality, 62,* 45–66.

Eysenck, H. J. (1971). Relation between intelligence and personality. *Perceptual and Motor Skills, 32,* 637–638.

Eysenck, H. J. (1994). The importance of theory in the taxonomy of personality. In B. De Raad, W. K. B. Hofstee, & G. L. Van Heck (Eds.), *Personality psychology in Europe* (Vol. 5; pp. 7–12). Tilburg, Netherlands: Tilburg University Press.

Eysenck, H. J., & Eysenck, M. W. (1985). *Personality and individual differences: A natural science approach.* New York: Plenum Press.

Eysenck, S. B. G. (1965). *Manual of the Junior Eysenck Personality Inventory*. London: University of London Press.

Fiske, D. W. (1949). Consistency of the factorial structures of personality ratings from different sources. *Journal of Abnormal and Social Psychology, 44,* 329–344.

Goff, M., & Ackerman, P. J. (1992). Personality–intelligence relations: Assessment of typical intellectual engagement. *Journal of Educational Psychology, 84,* 537–552.

Goldberg, L. R. (1989, June). *Standard markers of the Big Five factor structure.* Paper presented at the First International Workshop on Personality Language, Groningen, Netherlands.

Goldberg, L. R. (1992). The development of markers of the Big-Five factor structure. *Psychological Assessment, 4,* 26–42.

Goldberg, L. R. (1994). Resolving a scientific embarrassment: A comment on the articles in this special issue [Special issue]. *European Journal of Personality, 8,* 351–356.

Gough, H. G., & Heilbrun, A. B., Jr. (1983). *Adjective Check List manual.* Palo Alto, CA: Consulting Psychologists Press.

Graziano, W. G., & Ward, D. (1992). Probing the Big Five in adolescence: Personality and adjustment during a developmental transition. *Journal of Personality, 60,* 425–440.

Hagekull, B. (1994). Infant temperament and early childhood functioning: Possible relations to the Five-Factor model. In C. F. Halverson Jr., G. A. Kohnstamm, & R. P. Martin (Eds.), *The developing structure of temperament and personality from infancy to adulthood* (pp. 227–240). Hillsdale, NJ: Lawrence Erlbaum Associates.

Hofstee, W. K. B., & de Raad, B. (1991). Persoonlijkheidsstructuur: De AB5C-taxonomie van Nederlandse eigenschapstermen [Personality structure: The AB5C-taxonomy of Dutch trait terms]. *Nederlands Tijdschrift Psychologie, 46,* 262–274.

John, O. P., Caspi, A., Robins, R. W., Moffitt, T. E., & Stouthamer-Loeber, M. (1994). The "Little Five": Exploring the nomological network of the Five-Factor Model of personality in adolescent boys. *Child Development, 65,* 160–178.

Johnson, J. A. (1994). Clarification of factor five with the help of the AB5C Model. *European Journal of Personality, 8,* 311–334.

Khatena, J. (1982). Myth: Creativity is too difficult to measure—Response. *Gifted Child Quarterly, 26*(1), 21–23.

Kohnstamm, G. A., Bates, J. E., & Rothbart, M. K. (1989). *Temperament in childhood.* Chichester, England: John Wiley & Sons.

Kun, A. (1977). Development of the magnitude-covariation and compensation schemata in ability and effort attributions of performance. *Child Development, 48,* 862–873.

Martin, R. P. (1988). *The Temperament Assessment Battery for Children.* Brandon, VT: Clinical Psychology Publishing Company.

Martin, R. P., Wisenbaker, J., & Huttunen, M. (1994). Review of factor analytic studies of temperament measures based on the Thomas–Chess structural model: Implications for the Big Five. In C. F. Halverson Jr., G. A. Kohnstamm, & R. P. Martin (Eds.), *The developing structure of temperament and personality from infancy to adulthood* (pp. 157–172). Hillsdale, NJ: Lawrence Erlbaum Associates.

McCrae, R. R. (1990). Traits and trait names: How well is Openness represented in natural languages? *European Journal of Personality, 4,* 119–129.

McCrae, R. R. & Costa, P. T., Jr. (1997). Conceptions and correlates of openness to experience. In R. Hogan, J. Johnson, & S. Briggs (Eds.). *Handbook of personality psychology* (pp. 825–847). San Diego, CA: Academic Press.

Mervielde, I., Buyst, V., & De Fruyt, F. (1995). The validity of the Big-Five as a model for teachers' ratings of individual differences among children aged 4–12 years. *Personality and Individual Differences, 18,* 1827–1836.

Mervielde, I., & De Fruyt, F. (1992). *The "Big Five" personality factors as a model for the structure and development of peer nominations* (Reports in psychology, No. 3). Ghent, Belgium: University of Ghent.

Meyer, W. (1992). Paradoxical effects of praise and criticism on perceived ability. In W. Stroebe & M. Hewstone (Eds.), *European review of social psychology* (Vol. 3; pp. 259–283). New York: John Wiley & Sons.

Norman, W. T. (1963). Toward an adequate taxonomy of personality attributes: Replicated factor structure in peer nomination personality ratings. *Journal of Abnormal and Social Psychology, 66,* 574–583.

Norman, W. T. (1967). *2.800 personality trait descriptors: Normative operating characteristics for a university population.* Ann Arbor: University of Michigan Press.

Ostendorf, F. (1990). *Sprache und Persönlichkeitstruktur: Zur Validität des Fünf-Faktoren-Modells der Persönlichkeit* [Language and personality structure: On the validity of the Five-Factor Model of Personality]. Regensburg: Roderer.

Ostendorf, F., & Angleitner, A. (1994a). The Five-Factor taxonomy: Robust dimensions of personality description. *Psychologica Belgica, 34,* 175–194.

Ostendorf, F., & Angleitner, A. (1994b). Reflections on different labels for factor V. *European Journal of Personality, 8,* 341–349.

Paguio, L. P., & Hollet, N. (1991). Temperament and creativity of preschoolers. *Journal of Social Behaviour and Personality, 6*(4), 975–982.

Robins, R. W., John, O. P., & Caspi, A. (1994). Major dimensions of personality in early adolescence: The Big Five and beyond. In C. F. Halverson Jr., G. A. Kohnstamm, & R. P. Martin (Eds.), *The developing structure of temperament and personality from infancy to adulthood* (pp. 267–291). Hillsdale, NJ: Lawrence Erlbaum Associates.

Rorer, L. G. (1990). Personality assessment: A conceptual survey. In L. A. Pervin (Ed.), *Handbook of personality: Theory and research* (pp. 693–720). New York: Guilford Press.

Saklofske, D. H., & Zeidner, M. (Eds.). (1995). *International handbook of personality and intelligence.* New York: Plenum.

Saucier, G. (1992). Openness versus intellect: Much ado about nothing? *European Journal of Personality, 6,* 381–386.

Saucier, G. (1994). Trapnell versus the lexical factor: Much ado about nothing? *European Journal of Personality, 8,* 291–298.

Strelau, J., Angleitner, A., Bantelmann, J., & Ruch, W. (1990). The Strelau Temperament Inventory-Revised (STI-R): Theoretical considerations and scale development. *European Journal of Personality, 4,* 209–235.

Thomas, A., & Chess, S. (1977). *Temperament and development.* New York: Brunner/Mazel.

Torrance, E. P. (1966). *Torrance Tests of Creative Thinking.* Lexington, MA: Personnel Press.

Tupes, E. C., & Christal, R. C. (1961). *Recurrent personality factors based on trait ratings* (Tech. Rep. No. ASD-TR-61-97). Lackland Air Force Base, TX: U.S. Air Force.

Tupes, E. C., & Christal, R. C. (1992). Recurrent personality factors based on trait ratings. *Journal of Personality, 60,* 225–251.

van Lieshout, C. F. M., & Haselager, G. J. T. (1994). The Big Five personality factors in Q-sort descriptions of children and adolescents. In C. F. Halverson Jr., G. A. Kohnstamm, & R. P. Martin (Eds.), *The developing structure of temperament and personality from infancy to adulthood* (pp. 293–318). Hillsdale, NJ: Lawrence Erlbaum Associates.

van Lieshout, C. F. M., Riksen-Walraven, J. M. A., ten Brink, P. W. M., Siebenheller, F. A., Mey, J. T. H., Koot, J. M., Janssen, A. W. H., & Cillessen, A. H. N. (1986). *Zelfstandigheidsontwikkeling in het basisonderwijs* [Development of autonomy in middle childhood]. Nijmegen, Netherlands: ITS.

Victor, J. B. (1994). The Five-Factor Model applied to individual differences in school behavior. In C. F. Halverson Jr., G. A. Kohnstamm, & R. P. Martin (Eds.), *The developing structure of temperament and personality from infancy to adulthood* (pp. 355–370). Hillsdale, NJ: Lawrence Erlbaum Associates.

Windle, M., & Lerner, R. M. (1986). Reassessing the dimensions of temperament individuality across the life span: The Revised Dimensions of Temperament Survey (DOTS-R). *Journal of Adolescent Research, 1,* 213–230.

Zarnegar, Z., Hocevar, D., & Michael, W. B. (1988). Components of original thinking in gifted children. *Educational and Psychological Measurement, 48*(1), 5–16.

Zuckerman, M. (1979). *Sensation seeking: Beyond the optimal level of arousal.* Hillsdale, NJ: Lawrence Erlbaum Associates.

Zuckerman, M. (1991). *Psychobiology of personality.* Cambridge, England: Cambridge University Press.

Developmental Changes in Personality Descriptions of Children: A Cross-National Comparison of Parental Descriptions of Children

Anne-Marie Slotboom
Leiden University

Valerie L. Havill
University of Georgia

Vassilis Pavlopoulos
University of Athens

Filip De Fruyt
University of Ghent

Researchers studying personality development have been concerned with a variety of issues, one of them being the lack of consensus about the structure of adult personality. In the adult personality domain, however, many researchers have adopted the Five-Factor Model (FFM) as a guide to the structure of personality traits (e.g., Digman, 1990; Goldberg, 1990; John, 1989; McCrae & Costa, 1985). This model of adult personality has provided a set of adult dimensions that can serve as targets of temperament and personality dimensions assessed in infancy and childhood.

The preceding chapters in this book have focused on the structure of early temperament and personality and how they might be linked to the FFM in adulthood. This framework can help us in describing the links between infancy, childhood, and adulthood personality. Although many theorists have tried to hypothetically link the different temperament constructs and the FFM (e.g., Hagekull, 1994; Martin, Wisenbaker, & Huttunen, 1994; Rothbart, 1989), so far very few studies have tried to recover the five-factor structure in personality ratings of children. The question remains whether the five factors assessed in adult personality can also be usefully applied to descriptions of children's personality. Digman and Inouye (1986) were one of the first to replicate the FFM in teacher ratings of sixth-grade children. Strong resemblance was also found between analyses of the California Child Question (CCQ) set (Block & Block, 1980) and the FFM (John, Caspi, Robins, Moffitt, & Stouthamer-Loeber, 1994; van Lieshout & Haselager, 1994). Nevertheless we still have little data about whether the five general dimensions important for describing adult personality are also salient to parents when describing individual differences in children of different ages. Is a construct such as Conscientiousness, for example, equally salient to parents of preschool children and to parents of early adolescents? The project described in this book has used a lexically based approach to study individual differences in children. A major purpose of this study was the collection of free descriptions that identified personality dimensions most salient to parents of 3- to 12-year-old children. From these descriptors, we plan to develop new individual difference measures of personality. The factor structure underlying these questionnaires can then be compared across age and country to search for continuity or change in the personality structure of children, as well as to determine cross-national comparability of factor structure.

Studying continuity and change in personality characteristics has been an important issue for many years (e.g., Bloom, 1964; Kagan, 1980; Moss & Susman, 1980). According to Asendorpf (1992), a construct shows continuity over time if it can be operationalized by the same behaviors at different times. Kagan (1980), however, was more precise. He made a distinction between *homotypic* and *heterotypic* continuity and would classify Asendorpf's conceptualization as "homotypic continuity." Kagan defined heterotypic continuity as continuity at the *construct* level, with changing indicators as children grew older, while the underlying construct remained the same. For example, Kagan and Moss (1962) showed behavioral continuity by employing a broad concept instead of a narrow range of behaviors. They demonstrated continuity over long time spans by classifying certain behaviors under a single concept of masculinity. Their analysis of masculinity revealed continuity despite phenotypic change. Both continuity and change can be described at different conceptual levels: Change can be at the mean levels of a personality attribute or in correlational patterns that imply normative developmental transformations (Moss & Susman, 1980). Before considering changes in mean levels or stability across time, it is necessary to know whether there is some invariance of the correlational structure across ages (Costa & McCrae, 1994).

Pedlow, Sanson, Prior, and Oberklaid (1993) searched for continuity of factor structures across ages and assumed heterotypic continuity across time. They used age-appropriate questionnaires to measure temperament in a longitudinal sample of 450 children from infancy to 8 years. Their study was based on the nine-dimensional framework of Thomas and Chess (1977). They used confirmatory factor analysis to test the factor structures underlying the questionnaires at different ages. In some cases, no similarity was found in phenotypic behaviors measuring a specific factor. In that case, similarity of factor meaning was decided according to conceptual relations among the factors. The researchers found that the dimensions of Approach, Irritability, Cooperation-Manageability, Inflexibility, Rhythmicity, and Persistence showed continuity from infancy to 8 years. An Approach factor was consistently present from infancy onward, although the items changed from those tapping shyness and reactions to new experiences in infancy and toddlerhood to items tapping sociability in childhood. Irritability and Cooperation-Manageability were found in both infancy and toddler periods. In childhood, aspects from both factors were combined in what they called Inflexibility. According to Pedlow et al. (1993), Inflexibility might be seen as a core aspect of difficultness, including both negative emotionality and management problems. Persistence, defined by a child's tendency to stay on task and to pay attention for long periods, showed continuity from age 3 onward. Approach and Rhythmicity were the only factors showing continuity from 6 months of age onward.

Bronson (1966) was also concerned with heterotypic continuity. She saw this continuity as the most interesting and meaningful form and stated that to regard phenotypically different behaviors measured at different age periods as equivalent, one had to have an underlying stable theoretical framework. To create such a framework, she searched for phenotypically similar behaviors in children between the ages of 5 and 16, behaviors that represented an enduring, underlying personality dimension. She used a pool of 34 different behaviors to "represent descriptive statements that interviewers felt were useful and important to make in their over-time description of the subject's development" (p. 128). She found three developmental dimensions: Withdrawal-Expressiveness, Reactivity-Placidity, and Passivity-Dominance. The first dimension seemed to reflect characteristics that we now would label as Extraversion. The second dimension reflected characteristics that would be interpreted in the FFM as a blend of Negative Emotionality and Agreeableness. Although the first two dimensions were relatively independent of each other, the Passivity–Dominance dimension overlapped with the other two dimensions. These three dimensions then summarized behaviors with high degrees of stability and were good predictors of other behaviors.

Guerin and Gottfried (1994) searched for continuity in children from ages 2 to 12 years in the nine temperament dimensions of Thomas and Chess (1977). Just as in the Pedlow et al. (1993) study, they used questionnaires based on the nine-dimensional model, although no factor analyses were performed. They did not compare ages when scales with different item content were used. Continuity was assessed by comparing means of the same cohort across time. Most developmental changes were found in the preschool period (from age 3 to age 5), with fewer changes noted in the elementary school period. From age 3 to age 5, a developmental pattern of greater biological regularity, increasing adaptability, milder intensity of reaction, and more positive mood was found. Only activity and sensitivity-reactivity showed developmental changes in both preschool and elementary school periods. With increasing age, children were seen as less active and more reactive. The researchers concluded that with increasing age, more temperament dimensions showed invariance in mean levels. In contrast to Pedlow et al. (1993), Guerin and Gottfried (1994) searched for homotypic continuity and looked for change in the importance of the same dimension at different age levels.

Most researchers interested in development in infancy and childhood have focused on measures of temperament. Research in this area has been hampered by an overwhelming number of concepts and scales (Strelau, 1991), making the accumulation of findings and the communication among researchers very difficult. Consensus about the main dimensions of adult personality, however, could enhance the search for links between both fields. Now that the FFM is an accepted model among many different researchers, an increasing number of studies have searched for relations between temperament dimensions and the FFM (see, for example, Hagekull & Bohlin, 1996; Lanthier & Bates, 1995). One of the main goals of the project described in this book is the exploration of relation between child personality and the FFM. The study described here is aimed at building a lexicon of personality descriptors provided by parents of children in four different age groups. From this lexicon, questionnaires will be developed to measure the underlying structure of parental ratings of children aged 3 to 12. To search for the main personality dimensions salient to parents of children ranging from preschool to early adolescence, it is necessary to know first *which* personality characteristics are salient to parents of children of different ages. The behavioral repertoire of children changes considerably from preschool to middle childhood. Thus, before discussing continuity or change in personality structure across ages, it is important to know the age-specific behavioral repertoire of children reported by their parents. We then can develop age-appropriate questionnaires to measure personality development in children. From a developmental perspective, we have to balance face validity and appropriateness of items at a given age with attempts to provide as much item overlap as possible across ages. The development of questionnaires guided by these two directives enables the assessment of patterns of consistency as well as patterns of change in developmental functions and individual differences (McCall, 1986).

To develop age-appropriate questionnaires, we need to know which characteristics are salient at different age periods. In this chapter, parental free descriptions of children aged 3, 6, 9, and 12 years are compared. This study was carried out in seven different countries. The participation of different countries affords us the opportunity to examine the cultural universality of major dimensions of temperament and personality in childhood as perceived by parents.

One of the main differences between this study and other studies searching for the main temperament–personality dimensions in children is that parents were provided the opportunity to decide which characteristics they thought were important when describing children of different ages. The advantage of using a free-description approach is that it permits us to study personality characteristics that are most meaningful to parents. We assumed that the traits parents mentioned depended on not only their children's actual behavior, but also parental expectations, values, and belief systems about what traits are important for children in their own culture (Kagitcibasi, 1982).

A number of studies have explored the beliefs and expectations of parents in different cultures about the development of children (Goodnow, Cashmore, Cotton, & Knight, 1984; Hess, Kashiwagi, Azuma, Price, & Dickson, 1980; Rosenthal & Bornholt, 1988). Hess et al. (1980), for example, asked mothers in the United States and Japan whether they expected each of 38 different behaviors to occur before the age of 4, at the age of 4 or 5, or after the age of 6. The most striking results were differences across cultures. Japanese mothers expected their children to show emotional maturity, self-control, and social courtesy earlier than did mothers in the United States. Mothers in the United States, however, expected their children to show verbal assertiveness and social skills with peers earlier than did Japanese mothers. Goodnow et al. (1984) have also asked about mothers' "implicit developmental timetables," in an attempt to tap mothers' beliefs about the course of development. For example, mothers were asked whether a behavior present at one age (age 6) was more likely to remain stable or to change by the time the child was age 12. They found that behaviors regarded as desirable (e.g., friendly, generous to others) were regarded as likely to be stable. Behaviors regarded as undesirable (easily upset by mistakes, cries easily) were expected to change. These results were supported by those of Gretarsson and Gelfand (1988), who reported that mothers' perceptions of their children showed positive bias. Mothers participating in their study saw their children's positive characteristics, such as "She is a helpful child," as inborn and stable over time. Negative characteristics were seen as changing over time and were more often attributed to situational influences.

The studies of Goodnow et al. (1984), Hess et al. (1980), and Rosenthal and Bornholt (1988) showed that although mothers expected certain behaviors to show up earlier than others (e.g., compliant behavior was expected at an earlier age than certain social skills such as "Sympathetic to other children"), most differences occurred between cultures. Cultural values might also influence the way parents perceived their children's temperament and personality. Many cross-cultural studies of temperament and personality in children have been based on translated U.S. questionnaires and therefore have ignored the possible influence of ideas, beliefs, and values shared by parents living in different cultures. For example, Ahadi, Rothbart, and Renmin (1993) found a strong similarity in factor structure for their Children's Behavior Questionnaire (CBQ) in the United States and the People's Republic of China. They added, however, that "even if the underlying structure of temperament were invariant across cultures, there would still be important differences in personality cross-culturally, precisely because the individual's experiences would influence the manifestation of temperamental characteristics" (Ahadi et al., 1993, p. 370).

The present study focuses on changes and similarities in personality characteristics across age as seen by parents in different countries. In this chapter, we test whether parents' free descriptions of 3- to 12-year-old children, in different languages and from different cultures, can be coded into a categorization system based partly on the FFM. Using this Big Five-related categorization system, we demonstrate similarities and differences in age-related patterns of personality descriptors used by parents in various countries. The personality descriptors came from focusing on the language used to describe children of 3, 6, 9, and 12 years of age living in seven different cultures. We view culture as a template, primarily an ideation including beliefs, attitudes, rituals, social scripts, and ideals of a population; language is the expression that arises from culture. We recognize that using language as a medium to interpret feelings, thoughts, and perceptions is far from perfect, but it is, nevertheless, the best way to find out how parents think about children's personalities. Even if we could observe behavior as an indication of personality, the behavior would be placed into cognitive–linguistic categories. Asking people to tell us how they think might be as close as we can get to the "thinking through others" suggested by Shweder (1990).

CHILDREN'S PERSONALITY CHARACTERISTICS AS SEEN BY PARENTS IN DIFFERENT COUNTRIES

Sample

The following seven countries participated in this study: Belgium, the Netherlands, Germany, Greece, China, the United States, and Poland. Mothers, and in some countries also fathers, were asked to give completely

unconstrained descriptions of their children. If fathers agreed to participate, mothers and fathers were interviewed separately. Detailed information about the collection of samples in different countries and the
procedure followed to analyze the contents of the free descriptions appears in chapter 1.

Content Analysis of Free Descriptions

Some idea of the content and organization of parental personality descriptions of children in the different countries can be gained from the
four examples we present here. These examples represent a very small
sample of the total number of interviews held but provide an impression
of the parental descriptions. Although the examples clearly illustrate
differences among individual children, they obviously cannot reveal systematic differences between age groups or between different countries.
We discuss systematic changes in descriptions between age groups and
between countries later.

> Oh boy, for some reason, the first thing that came to my mind was preco-
> cious. She's fun loving, she's intelligent and I guess loving. She's a real
> loving, sweet person, and she likes to cuddle a lot. She's real interested in
> reading and learning, and she's real inquisitive. Particularly now she's going
> into first grade, and it's a big jump. I like the fact that she's real active. It's
> hard to be bothered by her because she's such a sweet person. She's very
> willing to please. She's real good at cooperating with other kids. She plays
> well with other kids, interacts with them well. (Father of a 6-year-old Ameri-
> can girl)

> Just to start out saying that she's usually pretty laid back. She doesn't get
> in a hurry about anything. She's pretty energetic about what she wants to
> do, what she likes. She doesn't really have any sad days. I think she's really
> a happy child. She likes to read, and she loves to play outside, just with
> her brother. She's easygoing. She is just really open and honest with me
> now at 9 years old. And she's fun to have around. She's not a child that
> gets in a hurry. She's just slow, and she's a perfectionist about things.
> (Mother of a 9-year-old American girl)

> She is very eager to learn, she's good with words and language. She absorbs
> everything. But she's also rather jealous. She's not pigheaded. You can easily
> make things clear to her, and then she goes along with it. She gets on well
> with other children, but she likes to be the center of attention. She doesn't
> think there's anything wrong with that, especially at birthday parties. On
> the other hand, if she's drawing, she likes to do it on her own. Yes, she's
> very independent. (Father of a 6-year-old Dutch girl)

> He is very loyal. He feels responsible. For his brothers too, especially for
> the youngest. He organizes things for him or helps him clean up. And he's

very good with his hands. He's better with his hands than with his mind. He's also creative. But he does not like doing homework and tests. He becomes insecure and cries quickly. But if you help him and boost his confidence, then he is OK and can do it. (Mother of a 9-year-old Dutch boy)

RESULTS AND DISCUSSION

Frequency Distribution of Descriptors by Age Level

The focus of this chapter is on age-related changes in personality descriptions as given by parents living in different countries. Do parents of children ranging in age from 3 to 12 years differ in their frequency of use of descriptors classified in the various categories? To answer this question, the number of descriptive phrases used to describe a child, coded in any one (sub)category, was transformed into a proportion of the total number of descriptive phrases. Statistical analyses were performed, using the mean proportion of descriptors produced by parents. Analyses were performed on arcsine transformed proportion scores. The mean proportions shown in tables and figures are the untransformed data, so that scores can be easily interpreted. No significance tests were performed for (sub)categories accounting for less than 3% of the descriptors in all different groups (e.g., age groups, countries). As described in chapter 1, descriptors were coded either on the high or on the low end of a category. A global inspection of the data suggested different effects over age for descriptors coded at the high and the low end of each category. Therefore, it was decided to separately analyze descriptors coded at each end. First, results referring to the first five main categories are presented. Second, results referring to the eight remaining categories are presented.

Effects of country for each of the five main categories were discussed in chapters 2 through 6. Here we focus on age effects and age-by-country effects. Univariate results are separately discussed for each main category.

Extraversion

Extraversion High. A significant univariate effect of age was found on descriptors coded at the high end of Extraversion, $F(3, 2237) = 27.1, p < .001$ ($\eta^2 = .035$). Parents of 3-year-olds described their children more in terms of descriptors coded at the high end of Extraversion than did parents of 6- to 12-year-old children (ranging from 25.1% for 3-year-olds to 17.1% for 12-year-olds). Figure 7.1 shows the grand means (arcsine transformed proportion scores) for each age group, including the 95% confidence limits. There was a clear linear decrease from age 3 to age 9 and no changes from age 9 to 12.

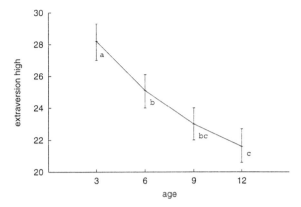

FIG. 7.1. Arcsine transformed means and 95% confidence intervals over countries for Category I, Extraversion high. (Note: Means of samples sharing a common letter are *not* significantly different from one another according to post hoc Scheffé tests.)

These Extraversion results were summed across country (see Table 7.1). In all countries, except the United States and the Netherlands, there was a significant decrease in frequency of use of high Extraversion descriptors over age (see Fig. 7.2). Personality descriptors related to the high end of Extraversion were more salient in the perceptions of parents describing younger children.

Extraversion was divided into three facets: Sociability, Dominance, and Activity. The decrease in descriptors coded at the high end of Extraversion was caused primarily by a decrease in descriptors referring to high Sociability and high Activity. Both facets were used more by parents of younger children although the effect size was very small ($\eta^2 = .019$ and .014, respectively). The proportions of descriptors related to Sociability

TABLE 7.1
Average Proportions of Descriptors in High Extraversion

	Age 3	Age 6	Age 9	Age 12	Total	η^2
Belgium	23.2_a	21.8_{ac}	16.7_b	17.2_{bc}	19.8	.04
Netherlands	22.5	20.9	19.9	17.4	20.3	.03
Germany	23.1_a	23.1_a	18.7_{ab}	17.3_b	20.9	.05
Greece	24.0_a	18.4_{ab}	17.8_{ab}	16.8_b	19.1	.02
China	22.5_a	20.4_{ab}	16.4_b	17.1_{ab}	18.4	.03
U.S.A.	26.8	26.3	24.8	20.8	24.8	.01
Poland	32.4_a	21.0_b	19.8_b	15.6_b	22.0	.08
Total	25.1_a	21.2_b	18.4_{bc}	17.1_c	20.3	.04

Note. Means sharing a common subscript are *not* significantly different from one another according to post hoc Scheffé tests ($p < .05$).

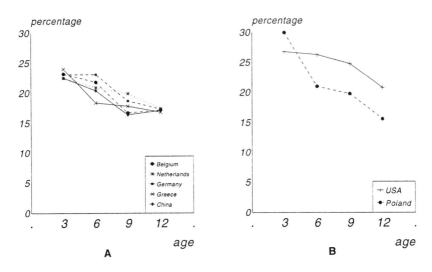

FIG. 7.2. Mean proportions of high Extraversion descriptors.

and Activity are shown separately for each country in Tables 7.2 and 7.3. A significant age effect for Sociability was found in three countries (China, the United States, and Poland). To a lesser extent, these trends were also found in the Netherlands and Germany. The largest decrease in high Sociability descriptors occurred before age 9. Perhaps Sociability is most salient to parents when exploration of the environment, including meeting new people and making contact with other children (at school), are important issues in a child's life.

TABLE 7.2
Average Proportions of Descriptors in High Sociability

	Age 3	Age 6	Age 9	Age 12	Total
Belgium	9.8	11.3	7.9	10.3	9.8
Netherlands	13.3	10.8	10.7	10.0	11.3
Germany	11.5	11.3	10.7	9.4	10.8
Greece	11.7	10.1	7.6	10.2	9.8
China	12.5_{ab}	10.4_a	6.9_b	7.5_{ab}	8.7
U.S.A.	15.1	11.7	12.9	9.9	12.4
Poland	15.9_a	8.9_b	7.2_b	5.9_b	8.7
Total	12.6_a	10.5_c	8.4_b	8.7_{cd}	10.0

Note. Means sharing a common subscript are *not* significantly different from one another according to post hoc Scheffé tests ($p < .05$).

TABLE 7.3
Average Proportions of Descriptors in High Activity

	Age 3	Age 6	Age 9	Age 12	Total
Belgium	6.6_a	5.5_a	4.0_{ab}	2.7_b	4.8
Netherlands	4.2	4.2	4.6	2.4	3.8
Germany	5.5	6.8	4.1	3.9	5.2
Greece	7.2_a	5.5_{ab}	6.3_{ab}	3.8_b	5.7
China	7.6	8.9	7.8	8.0	8.2
U.S.A.	10.1	11.8	11.0	9.8	10.7
Poland	14.0_a	11.1_{ab}	10.1_{ab}	6.9_b	10.4
Total	7.9_a	7.6_a	6.7_a	5.4_b	6.9

Note. Means sharing a common subscript are *not* significantly different from one another according to post hoc Scheffé tests ($p < .05$).

A significant decrease in Activity descriptors was found in Belgium, Greece, and Poland. Actually the frequency of use of Activity-related descriptors decreased over age in all European countries, with the most important decrease after age 9. In contrast, no age effect for Activity was found in China and the United States. Guerin and Gottfried (1994) did find, however, that with increasing age children were seen as less active. The difference in salience might or might not reflect actual change in mean level. In a comparison of 42 studies relating age to activity level, Eaton (1994) reported the presence of a curvilinear trajectory in the mean level of activity level in humans. Increasing activity was found from the very beginning of life to some time between 2 and 5 years, after which decreasing levels of motor activity were found. Although activity level is recognized as an independent dimension in different temperament models (e.g., Buss & Plomin, 1975; Thomas & Chess, 1977), most developmentalists have noticed a change from motor schemes in infancy to symbolic schemes in childhood and adolescence (Eaton, 1994). The decrease in Activity might reflect that laypersons, in this case parents, like experts in the field of developmental psychology, recognized the changing phenotype of Activity. We need to recognize, however, the disjunction between mean changes in temperament–personality measures and changes in salience. The decrease in Activity mentioned indicates that it is less salient to parents of older children. For Chinese and U.S. parents, their children's participation in sporting and athletic activities might be highly valued and very salient, a possibility that would account for no decrease in Activity mentions at age 9. In U.S. society this is exactly the age when increasing numbers of children participate in organized activities during evenings and weekends (e.g., gymnastics, soccer, baseball, martial arts, dance). Hence, parents might continue to mention how much their children practice the skills needed, their general energy level, and involvement in many different activities.

Extraversion Low. In contrast to the substantial proportion of descriptors coded at the high end of Extraversion, a relatively small proportion of descriptors was coded at the low end (overall $M = 7.2\%$). Not only were low Extraversion descriptors used less frequently by parents, but in contrast to decreasing proportions of descriptors referring to the high end of Extraversion, no important age trend was found for descriptors coded at the low end of Extraversion. Neither were there any country effects by age. Parents did not tend to employ either more or less shy, withdrawn, or passive descriptors from age 3 to age 12.

Agreeableness

Agreeableness High. When the samples were combined, a very small increase in the proportion of descriptors coded as high on the Agreeableness dimension occurred between ages 6 and 9 (increasing from 12.6% to 13.9%), stabilizing after age 9. This trend is shown in Fig. 7.3, with 95% confidence intervals plotted for each age group. Parents of 9- and 12-year-old children tended to describe their children with more Agreeableness descriptors than did parents of 3- and 6-year-olds. Yet, when each country was analyzed separately, a significant age trend was found only in the Greek and Polish samples (Fig. 7.4). A further examination of the data revealed that these slight trends were due to an increase in the use of descriptors coded in the Helpfulness facet.

Agreeableness Low. A stronger univariate age effect was found on the low end of Agreeableness, $F(3, 2237) = 20.3$, $p < .001$ ($\eta^2 = .027$). After

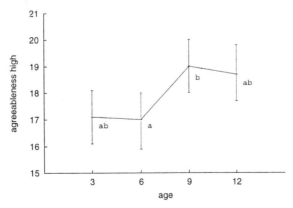

FIG. 7.3. Arcsine transformed means and 95% confidence intervals over countries for Category II, Agreeableness high. (Note: Means of samples sharing a common letter are *not* significantly different from one another according to post hoc Scheffé tests.)

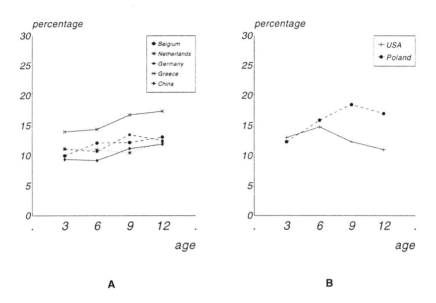

FIG. 7.4. Mean proportions of high Agreeableness descriptors.

aggregating frequencies across all countries, it was found that parents used low Agreeableness descriptors most frequently to describe 3-year-olds (10.2%), decreasing to 6.0% for 9-year-olds. Figure 7.5 shows that descriptors for 3-year-olds significantly differed from all other age groups.

Again, separate analyses were performed for each country, as seen in Fig. 7.6. This same trend was found in four of the seven countries (Belgium, Germany, Poland, and China). Parents of younger children described them more often with descriptors referring to the low end of Agreeableness than did parents of older children.

Agreeableness was divided into facets: Helpfulness, Manageability, and Honesty-Sincerity. The age trend for overall Agreeableness was due mainly to age changes in Manageability (see Table 7.4). Both at the overall level and at the within-country level, a decrease was found in the percentage of Manageability descriptors. In six of the seven countries, the strongest decrease was found between ages 3 and 6. Manageability seems to be more salient when describing younger children; parents of 3-year-olds were more likely to talk about disobedience and stubbornness than were parents of older children. Pedlow et al. (1993) showed that until the age of 4, Cooperation-Manageability was regarded as an independent factor, describing individual differences in young children. Manageability, which

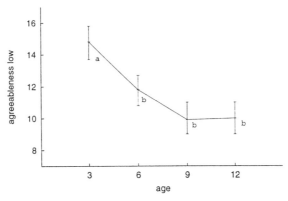

FIG. 7.5. Arcsine transformed means and 95% confidence intervals over countries for Category II, Agreeableness low. (Note: Means of samples sharing a common letter are *not* significantly different from one another according to post hoc Scheffé tests.)

can be interpreted as socially demanding behavior, seems also related to one of the most widely used concepts in the temperament literature, namely, Difficultness (Bates, 1986). Factor analyses of our newly developed questionnaires will allow for exploration of the Manageability concept in parental perceptions of young children. Although Manageability was not found in the adult FFM, this facet in the original categorization

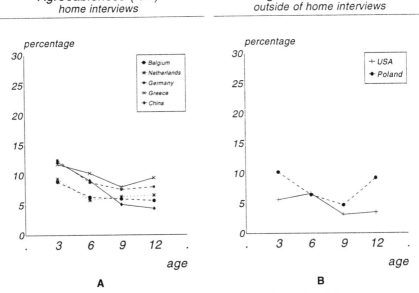

FIG. 7.6. Mean proportions of low Agreeableness descriptors.

TABLE 7.4
Average Proportions of Descriptors in Low Manageability

	Age 3	Age 6	Age 9	Age 12	Total
Belgium	6.2$_a$	3.6$_b$	3.5$_b$	3.5$_b$	4.2
Netherlands	7.4	4.7	4.1	4.3	5.3
Germany	9.8$_a$	6.5$_b$	5.3$_b$	5.1$_b$	6.9
Greece	9.0	7.8	6.1	6.7	7.4
China	10.7$_a$	5.9$_b$	3.7$_{bc}$	2.7$_c$	4.7
U.S.A.	4.8	4.8	2.0	2.2	3.6
Poland	8.3$_a$	5.5$_{ab}$	3.4$_b$	5.7$_{ab}$	5.8
Total	8.0$_a$	5.7$_b$	4.2$_{bc}$	4.4$_c$	5.5

Note. Means sharing a common subscript are *not* significantly different from one another according to post hoc Scheffé tests ($p < .05$).

system has proven to be quite useful in the identification of individual differences that were very important to parents during early childhood.

Conscientiousness

Conscientiousness High. A strong univariate effect of age was found on descriptors coded at the high end of Conscientiousness, $F(3, 2237) = 47.5$, $p < .001$ ($\eta^2 = .06$). Parents of 3-year-olds seldom used high-end Conscientiousness descriptors (2.5%). With older children, parents used the category increasingly to account for 7.3% of all descriptors. Figure 7.7 shows that the strongest increase was found between ages 3 and 6, stabilizing after age 9.

Separate ANOVAs conducted for each of the seven countries show that in five of the seven countries the overall age trend was replicated

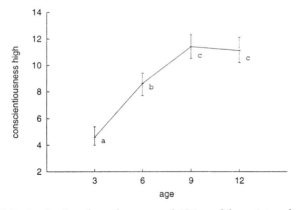

FIG. 7.7. Arcsine transformed means and 95% confidence intervals over countries for Category II, Conscientiousness high. (Note: Means of samples sharing a common letter are *not* significantly different from one another according to post hoc Scheffé tests.)

TABLE 7.5
Average Proportions of Descriptors in High Conscientiousness

	Age 3	Age 6	Age 9	Age 12	Total	η^2
Belgium	2.5$_a$	3.5$_{ab}$	6.0$_b$	6.4$_b$	4.5	.06
Netherlands	2.0$_a$	5.5$_{ab}$	5.3$_{ab}$	4.7$_b$	2.3	.05
Germany	2.7$_a$	5.4$_b$	5.4$_b$	6.8$_b$	4.9	.07
Greece	2.1$_a$	6.4$_b$	9.3$_c$	9.6$_c$	7.0	.15
China	5.7	6.7	7.0	7.9	7.1	.0
U.S.A.	3.1	6.5	7.4	6.8	5.9	.03
Poland	1.2$_a$	3.4$_a$	7.4$_b$	6.7$_b$	4.7	.13
Total	2.5$_a$	5.3$_b$	7.1$_c$	7.3$_c$	5.6	.06

Note. Means sharing a common subscript are *not* significantly different from one another according to post hoc Scheffé tests ($p < .05$).

(see Table 7.5). Only in China and the United States, was no age trend found for the high end of Conscientiousness. At the facet level, Carefulness and Diligence were used more as children's ages increased, both at global and the within-country levels. Diligence, however, showed the largest increase, ranging from 2.5% for 3-year-olds to 4.5% for 12-year-olds. Parents of school-age children talked more about their children being achievement oriented and diligent than did parents of toddlers.

Conscientiousness Low. Comparing the proportions coded as low Conscientiousness, we found age and age-by-country effects. A univariate effect of age was found, $F(3, 2237) = 82.8$, $p < .001$ ($\eta^2 = .10$). The use of low Conscientiousness descriptors increased substantially over age (ranging from 0.9% for 3-year-olds to 6.7% for 12-year-olds). Figure 7.8 shows that

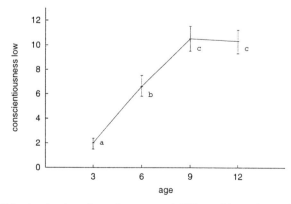

FIG. 7.8. Arcsine transformed means and 95% confidence intervals over countries for Category II, Conscientiousness low. (Note: Means of samples sharing a common letter are *not* significantly different from one another according to post hoc Scheffé tests.)

low Conscientiousness had the same age trend as did high Conscientiousness. Figure 7.9 shows the changes in each country separately. With children's increasing age, parents in all countries talked more about characteristics referring to the low end of Conscientiousness. Further, fewer descriptors were used to describe 3-year-olds in any country. After age 3, parents increasingly used more low Conscientiousness terms to describe their children. The use of this category stabilized at ages 9 and 12. At the facet level, proportions of descriptors coded in Carefulness and Diligence increased across age. As children's age increased, parents increasingly described them as lacking in carefulness and diligence (e.g., concentration problems, sloppy behavior, laziness).

Martin et al. (1994) analyzed 12 large-sample factor analytic studies of questionnaires based on the original Thomas, Chess, and Korn formulation and found a factor tapping attentiveness or "task persistence" in 11 of the 12 studies. Task persistence in children is primarily descriptive of attentive behavior shown in learning or mental skill performance. Persistence, although seen in a rudimentary form during infancy, is clearly more easily observed by parents and teachers beginning in preschool years. This factor is logically related to Conscientiousness. Costa and McCrae (1985) used words like hardworking, self-disciplined, and persevering to describe the high end of this dimension in adulthood. We now have evidence that parents use similar phrases to describe their children.

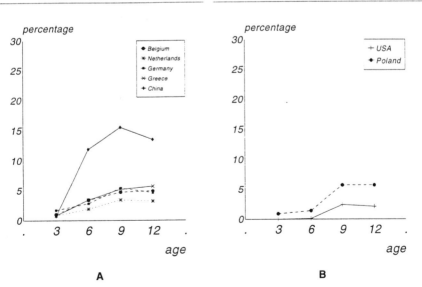

FIG. 7.9. Mean proportions of low Conscientiousness descriptors.

These characteristics became particularly salient when children reached school age.

A significant interaction effect of age by country was also found, $F = 4.0, p < .001$ ($\eta^2 = .32$). As seen in Fig. 7.12, very similar age-trend patterns were found in most countries; only China deviated from the overall pattern. In the Chinese sample, there was a sharp increase in the frequency of descriptors from age 3 (0.7%) to age 6 (11.9%). Chinese parents of 3-year-olds used about the same proportions of low Conscientiousness descriptors as did parents of 3-year-olds in other countries. From age 6, however, Chinese parents described their children with more descriptors such as "Easily distracted," "Not motivated enough," and "Indolent" than did parents in any other country.

Conscientiousness and Emotional Stability accounted for the fewest descriptors in all countries except in China. Although parents referred to Conscientiousness less often than to Extraversion or Agreeableness, the largest age effect was found for this dimension. In the age-related patterns across countries, the largest age effect was found for China, with low Conscientiousness descriptors deviating the most from the six other countries. From age 6, low Conscientiousness was increasingly salient in China, more so than in any other country. These differences between Chinese parents and parents in other countries might reflect the importance of education in China where education has always been extremely important for personal advancement (Chen & Uttal, 1988). Chinese philosophy, based on Confucian doctrine, has emphasized human malleability and the importance of effort to self-improvement (Chen & Stevenson, 1995). The differences in the Conscientiousness category might demonstrate the influence of cultural values on parental descriptions of personality. Chinese parents emphasized high achievement and reported satisfaction with their children's performance only when it was at a very high level. In contrast, U.S. parents reported satisfaction with their children's achievement at a lower level (Chen & Uttal, 1988). Further, modesty and humility are highly valued behaviors in Chinese culture; thus it might be culturally inappropriate to describe one's own child in very positive terms (Qiying Zhou, personal communication).

Emotional Stability

Emotional Stability High. For Emotional Stability, unlike the four other main dimensions, more parental descriptors were coded on the low end of the dimension than on the high end, a characteristic true for all countries and all age groups. The low end captures terms reflecting emotional *in*stability or neuroticism. Descriptors referring to the high end of Emotional Stability were infrequently mentioned by parents when describing their children's personalities (overall $M = 2.0\%$). No effect of age was found. These findings were consistent with the temperament and personality literature on Emotionality or Neuroticism where negatively valued labels emphasize the importance of the negative pole of this dimension (e.g., Rothbart, 1989). In analyzing data from four different personality questionnaires, Ostendorf and Angleitner (1992) found that the Neuroticism factor explained the most variance, and of the 30 items defining Neuroticism, only four were positively phrased words.

Emotional Stability Low. Parents in all countries used more descriptors referring to Emotional *In*stability, when samples from all countries were combined (overall $M = 6.3\%$). Again, no effects of age were found. Emotional Instability was regarded as salient for 3-year-olds as it was for 12-year-olds (see Fig. 7.10).

In three countries, a significant age trend appeared. In Belgium and the Netherlands, parents used more descriptors referring to the low end of Emotional Stability when describing older children (see Fig. 7.11a). In the United States, the trend was reversed: Parents used fewer descriptors when describing older children (see Fig. 7.11b). Although statistically significant age trends occurred in these three countries, there was only small age differences, explaining only between 2% and 5% of the variance.

Emotional Stability was divided in three facets: Emotional Reactivity, Self-Confidence, and Anxiety. Both Self-Confidence (overall $M = 1.1\%$) and Anxiety (overall $M = 0.9\%$) were of minor importance compared to Emotional Reactivity (overall $M = 4.6\%$). The age trend at the main category level for Belgium, the Netherlands, and the United States was

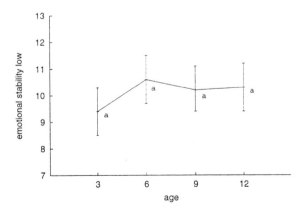

FIG. 7.10. Arcsine transformed means and 95% confidence intervals over countries for Category II, Emotional Stability low. (Note: Means of samples sharing a common letter are *not* significantly different from one another according to post hoc Scheffé tests.)

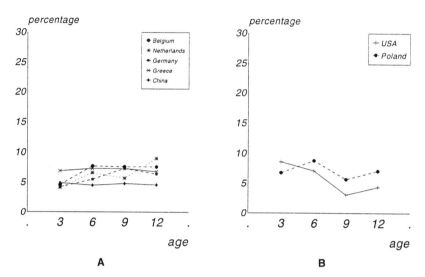

Emotional Stability (low)
home interviews

Emotional Stability (low)
outside of home interviews

A   B

FIG. 7.11. Mean proportions of low Emotional Stability descriptors.

also found for the subcategory of Emotional Reactivity. Again, Belgium and the Netherlands had a small increase in use over age while the U.S. sample had a decrease.

Openness to Experience

Openness to Experience High. Openness to Experience showed the largest discrepancy between proportions of high and low descriptors. On average only 1% of the descriptors was classified at the low end of Openness to Experience. Parents mainly talked about characteristics coded at the high end of Openness, such as intelligent, eager to learn, imaginative, has a good memory. A very small univariate effect of age was found for descriptors coded at the high end of Openness to Experience $F(3, 2237) = 5.5, p < .05$ ($\eta^2 = .07$). The use of descriptors referring to Openness to Experience decreased slightly over age and ranged from 13.4% for 3-year-olds to 10.9% for 12-year-olds. Figure 7.12 depicts this decline, with highly overlapping confidence intervals. Within-country ANOVAs revealed that this decline occurred only in the Chinese and Polish samples (see Table 7.6).

Openness to Experience Low. Descriptors referring to characteristics such as "Not eager to learn," "Slow learner," "Not intelligent" were rarely used, ranging from 0.3% in the U.S. sample to 1.8% in the German sample.

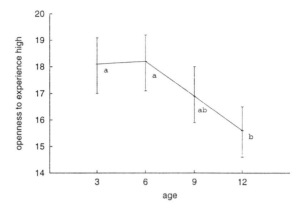

FIG. 7.12. Arcsine transformed means and 95% confidence intervals over countries for Category II, Openness to Experience high. (Note: Means of samples sharing a common letter are *not* significantly different from one another according to post hoc Scheffé tests.)

As discussed in chapter 6, concepts describing Openness to Experience as well as any other concept dealing with intellect have been explicitly excluded from the temperament literature. When parents were given the opportunity to talk freely about the characteristics of their children, however, a substantial part of the description consisted of descriptors referring to intellect and Openness to Experience. Parents found these aspects to be very salient even for very young children.

Age-Related Trends in Eight Additional Categories

To capture a wide range of individual differences, eight additional categories were coded in addition to five main categories. Small proportion of descriptors, however, were coded in each of these additional categories. In most categories, descriptors were not mentioned frequently enough to

TABLE 7.6
Average Proportions of Descriptors in High Openness to Experience

	Age 3	Age 6	Age 9	Age 12	Total	η^2
Belgium	11.0	12.3	11.9	11.5	11.7	.0
Netherlands	10.8	13.7	12.4	10.1	11.6	.02
Germany	15.6	16.1	17.1	14.8	15.9	.01
Greece	12.6	11.3	9.1	8.1	10.3	.02
China	15.2	13.0	12.2	11.0	12.3	.02
U.S.A.	21.2	18.2	22.7	20.2	20.4	.01
Poland	12.0	14.5	8.1	8.1	10.7	.02
Total	13.4	13.7	12.1	10.9	12.5	.02

justify a meaningful analysis (less than 3% of the descriptors in all age groups). No distinctions between the high and low ends of these categories were made. Further, only Independence (VI), School Performance (XI), and Relations With Siblings and Parents (XIII) accounted for as much as 3% of the descriptors. An age effect was found only for School Performance, $F(3, 2213) = 71.7$, $p < .001$ ($\eta^2 = .089$). Parents of 3-year-olds mentioned less school-related characteristics such as "Likes to go to school" and "Does well at school" than did parents of 12-year-olds (overall mean ranging from 1.0% for 3-year-olds to 4.0% for 12-year-olds). This age trend was not surprising; in most countries formal education begins around 4 to 5 years of age. This age trend was found in all seven countries.

CONCLUSION

The free-description approach used in this study proved to be useful for describing age differences in personality across countries. The study of links between culture and personality is the oldest subfield of cross-cultural psychology (Triandis, 1997). Although there were some methodological differences in the collection of parent responses by the collaborating research teams, very similar age differences appeared in the frequency of various personality descriptors. In no way do we believe that our findings support an absolutist position that would assume that traits and psychological processes are universal and unaffected by culture, but we do believe that we have begun to identify some personality traits in children with some representation across cultures. Yet, even if the underlying structure of a trait is common across cultures, the meaning of that trait might be different in each culture.

> For example, the trait "self-reliance" has some common meaning across cultures. What is common in these meanings across cultures is etic. But self-reliance has somewhat different goals in collectivist cultures (e.g., traditional) than in individualistic cultures (e.g., the West). In collectivist cultures it often takes the form "I am self-reliant so I will not burden my group." In individualist cultures it takes the form "I am self-reliant so I can have fun and do my own thing." Clearly, the meaning is different across cultures; thus our task is to measure both the etic and the emic aspects of the construct. (Triandis, 1997, p. 443)

Hence, we continue to have two goals: first, to examine cross-cultural differences or similarities in the structure of personality in childhood; second, to interpret our findings with cultural sensitivity. The analyses of parents' natural-language descriptions of children at different ages in different countries have allowed us to begin this process.

Most meaningful age differences were found in examining the high and low ends of the facets of our dimensions. Analyses of descriptors coded at the low ends of some categories revealed that descriptors referring to socially demanding and disobedient behaviors (like Agreeableness) were used less frequently as children's age increased. Other attributes like sloppiness, laziness, and lacking in ambition (Conscientiousness) tended to increase with age. We used proportional frequencies; as the use of one category increased or decreased, there was necessarily a concomitant change in the proportions of another category or categories. Generally, we found that parents of young children tended to focus more on Manageability (a facet of Agreeableness) including such behaviors as obedience, willingness to follow directions, and cooperation. Descriptions in this facet reflected how well children responded to external control, while parents of older children might be expecting more of their children in terms of internalized control. Hence, parents might describe young children as unmanageable and older children as lacking in conscientiousness. We also found that parents used descriptors referring to ambitious, achievement-oriented behavior (Conscientiousness) more frequently when describing school-age and older children. There was a decrease in the use of descriptors referring to high activity level (coded as an Extraversion facet) when describing older children.

These age-related changes occurred in most of the countries and are consonant with much of the current literature on developmental trends in child behavior and parental concerns. For example, Achenbach and Edelbrock (1981) used the Child Behavior Checklist (CBCL) to gather data on behavioral problems and competencies to assess the prevalence of behavior problems at different ages. Parents of children ranging from 4 to 16 years completed the CBCL. Achenbach and Edelbrock found that certain behaviors such as "Whining," "Asks for a lot of attention," "Disobedient at home," and "Hyperactive" decreased with age. These results were replicated in a Dutch sample of 2,076 children selected from the general population (Verhulst, 1985). Achenbach and Edelbrock's findings are consistent with our data in which parents of young children described them more frequently with terms referring to manageability and activity level than did parents of older children. Younger children are more active and less agreeable than are older children.

The largest age effect, however, was found for Conscientiousness. Our study showed that parents talked about characteristics referring to Conscientiousness or Task Persistence in children from age 3, but nothing like the parents of school-age children for whom the trait was of major importance. Conscientiousness was also the category with the largest age-by-country interaction. For children of age 3, Conscientiousness was of minor importance in all countries; Chinese parents, however, described their children from age 6 in terms such as "Sloppiness," "Easily distracted," and "Lacking in motivation" much more frequently than did parents in the other countries.

To summarize the age trends in the five main categories, characteristics reflecting the interpersonal domain, such as Extraversion and Agreeableness, apparently grew less salient with increasing age, while characteristics under more active cognitive control like those coded in Conscientiousness became more salient with increasing age. The Conscientiousness category also showed the largest cultural difference, which we interpreted to be associated with the influence of cultural values on parental perceptions. The fact that Chinese parents used Conscientiousness descriptors more frequently than did other parents was likely due to the importance of those traits and behaviors in the Chinese culture. Indeed, from a list of 35 value statements, triads consisting of Chinese participants endorsed "Persistence and perseverance" as the most important cultural value; in contrast, U.S. triads endorsed "To be well-adjusted, in harmony with my environment, in good relationship with others" as the most important (Triandis, Bontempo, Leung, & Hui, 1990).

Both ecological theory and lifespan developmental theory have emphasized the importance of contextual conceptualization in human development (Kagitcibasi, 1996). Our free-description method of data collection was sensitive to both age-related changes in personality and cultural differences. It is important to know about parents' beliefs regarding children and childhood because they have an impact on childrearing. Children's socialization is goal directed, and these goals are organized as culturally valued adult characteristics and competence in a society. We found that parents in our sample construed the basic structure of children's personalities in much the same way in every country. The salience of certain characteristics varied with the child's age as well as with cultural demands.

Much research in the field of temperament has focused on the biological underpinnings of behavior (Bates & Wachs, 1994). Instead of exploring the etiology of different temperamental dimensions, as personologists we are attempting to find links between childhood behaviors and adult personality. With the development of our new individual difference measures, we can begin to explore the structure of personality in childhood as well as across cultures. We can then begin the process of systematically examining the construct and the predictive validity of the dimensions we have discovered in the lexicon about children.

REFERENCES

Achenbach, T. M., & Edelbrock, C. S. (1981). Behavioral problems and competencies reported by parents of normal and disturbed children aged four through sixteen. *Monographs of the Society for Research in Child Development*, 46(1).

Ahadi, S. A., Rothbart, M. K., & Renmin, Y. (1993). Children's temperament in the US and China: Similarities and differences. *European Journal of Personality, 7,* 359–377.

Asendorpf, J. B. (1992). A Brunswikean approach to trait continuity: Application to shyness. *Journal of Personality, 60,* 53–77.

Bates, J. E. (1986). The measurement of temperament. In R. Plomin & J. Dunn (Eds.), *The study of temperament: Changes, continuities and challenges* (pp. 1–11). Hillsdale, NJ: Lawrence Erlbaum Associates.

Bates, J. E., & Wachs, T. D. (Eds.). (1994). *Temperament: Individual differences at the interface of biology and behavior.* Washington, DC: American Psychological Association Press.

Bloom, B. (1964). *Stability and change in human characteristics.* New York: Wiley.

Block, J. H., & Block, J. (1980). The role of ego-control and ego-resiliency in the organization of behavior. In W. A. Collins (Ed.), *Development of cognition, affect, and social relations* (pp. 39–101). Hillsdale, NJ: Lawrence Erlbaum Associates.

Bronson, W. C. (1966). Central orientations: A study of behavior organization from childhood to adolescence. *Child Development, 37,* 125–155.

Buss, A. H. & Plomin, R. (1975). *A temperament theory of personality development.* New York: Wiley.

Chen, C., & Stevenson, H. W. (1995). Motivation and mathematics achievement: A comparative study of Asian-American, Caucasian-American, and East Asian high school students. *Child Development, 66,* 1215–1234.

Chen, C., & Uttal, D. H. (1988). Cultural values, parents' beliefs, and children's achievement in the United States and China. *Human Development, 31,* 351–358.

Costa, P. T., & McCrae, R. R. (1985). *The NEO Personality Inventory manual.* Odessa, FL: Psychological Assessment Resources.

Costa, P. T., & McCrae, R. R. (1994). Stability and change in personality from adolescence through adulthood. In C. F. Halverson Jr., G. A. Kohnstamm, & R. P. Martin (Eds.), *The developing structure of temperament and personality from infancy to adulthood* (pp. 139–150). Hillsdale, NJ: Lawrence Erlbaum Associates.

Digman, J. M. (1990). Personality structure: Emergence of the five-factor model. *Annual Review of Psychology, 41,* 417–440.

Digman, J. M. & Inouye, J. (1986). Further specification of the five robust factors of personality. *Journal of Personality and Social Psychology, 50,* 116–123.

Eaton, W. O. (1994). Temperament, development, and the five-factor model: Lessons from activity-level. In C. F. Halverson Jr., G. A. Kohnstamm, & R. P. Martin (Eds.), *The developing structure of temperament and personality from infancy to adulthood* (pp. 173–187). Hillsdale, NJ: Lawrence Erlbaum Associates.

Goldberg, L. R. (1990). An alternative "Description of personality": The Big-Five factor structure. *Journal of Personality and Social Psychology, 59,* 1216–1229.

Goodnow, J. J., Cashmore, J., Cotton, S., & Knight, R. (1984). Mothers' developmental time-tables in two cultural groups. *International Journal of Psychology, 19,* 193–205.

Gretarsson, S. J., & Gelfand, D. M. (1988). Mothers' attributions regarding their children's social behavior and personality characteristics. *Developmental Psychology, 24,* 264–269.

Guerin, D. W., & Gottfried, A. W. (1994). Developmental stability and change in parent reports of temperament: A ten-year longitudinal investigation from infancy through preadolescence. *Merrill–Palmer Quarterly, 40,* 334–355.

Hagekull, B. (1994). Infant temperament and early childhood functioning: Possible relations to the five-factor model. In C. F. Halverson Jr., G. A. Kohnstamm, & R. P. Martin (Eds.), *The developing structure of temperament and personality from infancy to adulthood* (pp. 227–240). Hillsdale, NJ: Lawrence Erlbaum Associates.

Hagekull, B., & Bohlin, G. (1996, October). *Preschool temperament and environmental influences on the Five Factor Model personality dimensions in middle childhood.* Paper presented at the Occasional Temperament Conference, Eugene, OR.

Hess, R. D., Kashiwagi, K., Azuma, H., Price, G. G., & Dickson, W. P. (1980). Maternal expectations for mastery of developmental tasks in Japan and the United States. *International Journal of Psychology, 15*, 259–271.

John, O. P. (1989). Towards a taxonomy of personality descriptors. In D. M. Buss & N. Cantor (Eds.), *Personality psychology: Recent trends and emerging directions* (pp. 261–271). New York: Springer Verlag.

John, O. P., Caspi, A., Robins, R. W., Moffitt, T. E., & Stouthamer-Loeber, M. (1994). The "little five": Exploring the nomological network of the five-factor model of personality in adolescent boys. *Child Development, 65*, 160–178.

Kagan, J. (1980). Perspectives on continuity. In O. G. Brim Jr., & J. Kagan (Eds.), *Constancy and change in human development* (pp. 26–74). Cambridge, MA: Harvard University Press.

Kagan, J., & Moss, H. A. (1962). *Birth to maturity.* New York: Wiley.

Kagitcibasi, C. (1982). *The changing value of children in Turkey* (Publ. No. 60-E). Honolulu, HI: East–West Center.

Kagitcibasi, J. C. (1996). *Family and human development across cultures.* Mahwah, NJ: Lawrence Erlbaum Associates.

Lanthier, R. P., & Bates, J. E. (1995, November). *Infancy era predictors of the Big Five personality dimensions in adolescence.* Paper presented at the Meeting of the Midwestern Psychological Association, Chicago, IL.

Martin, R. P., Wisenbaker, J., & Huttunen, M. (1994). Review of factor analytic studies of temperament measures based on the Thomas–Chess structural model: Implications for the Big Five. In C. F. Halverson Jr., G. A. Kohnstamm, & R. P. Martin (Eds.), *The developing structure of temperament and personality from infancy to adulthood* (pp. 157–172). Hillsdale, NJ: Lawrence Erlbaum Associates.

McCall, R. B. (1986). Issues of stability and continuity in temperament research. In R. Plomin & J. Dunn (Eds.), *The study of temperament: Changes, continuities and challenges* (pp. 13–25). Hillsdale, NJ: Lawrence Erlbaum Associates.

McCrae, R., & Costa, P. T., Jr. (1985). Updating Norman's "adequate taxonomy": Intelligence and personality dimensions in natural language and in questionnaires. *Journal of Personality and Social Psychology, 49*, 710–721.

Moss, H. A., & Susman, E. J. (1980). Longitudinal study of personality development. In O. G. Brim Jr. & J. Kagan (Eds.), *Constancy and change in human development* (pp. 530–595). Cambridge, MA: Harvard University Press.

Ostendorf, F., & Angleitner, A. (1992). On the generality and comprehensiveness of the five-factor model of personality: Evidence for five robust factors in questionnaire data. In G. V. Caprara & G. Van Heck (Eds.), *Modern personality psychology: Critical reviews and new directions.* New York: Harvester Wheatsheaf.

Pedlow, R., Sanson, A., Prior, M., & Oberklaid, F. (1993). Stability of maternally reported temperament from infancy to 8 years. *Developmental Psychology, 29*, 998–1007.

Rosenthal, D., & Bornholt, L. (1988). Expectations about development in Greek- and Anglo-Australian families. *Journal of Cross-Cultural Psychology, 19*, 19–34.

Rothbart, M. K. (1989). Temperament and development. In G. A. Kohnstamm Jr., J. E. Bates, & M. K. Rothbart (Eds.), *Temperament in childhood* (pp. 187–247). Chichester, England: Wiley.

Shweder, R. A. (1990). Toward a theory of the universal content and structure of values: Extensions and cross-cultural replications. *Journal of Personality and Social Psychology, 58*, 878–891.

Strelau, J. (1991). Renaissance in research on temperament: Where to? In J. Strelau & A. Angleitner (Eds.), *Explorations in temperament: International perspectives on theory and measurement* (pp. 337–358). New York: Plenum.

Thomas, A., & Chess, S. (1977). *Temperament and development.* New York: Brunner/Mazel.

Triandis, H. C. (1997). Cross-cultural perspectives on personality. In R. Hogan, J. Johnson, & S. Briggs (Eds.), *Handbook of personality* (pp. 439–464). San Diego, CA: Academic.

Triandis, H. C., Bontempo, R., Leung, K., & Hui, C. H. (1990). A method for determining cultural, demographic, and personal constructs. *Journal of Cross-Cultural Psychology, 21,* 302–318.

Van Lieshout, C. F. M., & Haselager, G. J. T. (1994). The big-five personality factors in Q-sort descriptions of children and adolescents. In C. F. Halverson Jr., G. A. Kohnstamm, & R. P. Martin (Eds.), *The developing structure of temperament and personality from infancy to adulthood* (pp. 293–318). Hillsdale, NJ: Lawrence Erlbaum Associates.

Verhulst, F. C. (1985). *Mental health in Dutch children.* Meppel, Netherlands: Krips Repro.

Parental Personality
Descriptions of Boys and Girls

Filip De Fruyt
University of Ghent

Alain Van Hiel
University of Ghent

Veerle Buyst
University of Ghent

Gender differences in personality test scores have been the subject of considerable debate among personality, developmental, and cross-cultural psychologists. Two questions have been central in the literature on gender and personality (Feingold, 1994): Do men and women differ in their personality trait scores? and How do we explain gender differences in personality ratings? The answer to the first question provides a framework to interpret gender differences in the distribution of descriptors across the (sub)categories of the personality-descriptive lexicon used by our collaborative research group. Knowledge of the nature of gender differences might help to clarify the meaning of observed sex differences across cultures. The current study extends former research on sex differences in children and adults (for a review, see Feingold, 1994; Maccoby & Jacklin, 1974) in two ways: The targets in this study were children between the ages of 3 and 12, freely described by one of their parents, and the focus was on the kind and number of free descriptors assigned to a personality-descriptive category, instead of on a score on a trait or a composite personality scale.

The final aim of the project described in this book is the construction of broadband personality questionnaires to assess the behavior of children aged 3 to 12 (chapter 1). The personality-descriptive lexicons, accommodating the free personality descriptors for four age groups, serve as a database to provide age-specific items to create personality questionnaires for these four age groups. Although a considerable proportion of the items is applicable to all age groups, the results described in chapter 7 underscore the necessity to include age-specific items to tap developmental changes in the behavior of children. In this chapter we investigate the need for gender specificity in the questionnaires.

GENDER DIFFERENCES IN PERSONALITY RATINGS

To our knowledge, there are no separate broadband personality questionnaires or item sets for males and females. In contrast, almost all manuals of personality tests provide gender-specific normative and psychometric data that assume the possibility of gender differences for the measured traits. In general, there are only marginal gender differences in the structure of personality and the psychometric features of the scales, such as internal consistency, test–retest reliability, and validity, but in some cases the scale means and standard deviations differ considerably and require gender-specific normative data.

Maccoby and Jacklin (1974), using qualitative methods, conducted a now classic review of gender differences in personality and concluded that the evidence favored the interpretation that males were more assertive and aggressive, whereas females were more anxious. They found no consistent differences in the self-esteem literature. In a meta-analysis of personality studies published between 1975 and 1983 in major personality journals, Hall (1984) compared studies of personality trait scores of men and women and found women to be more anxious and less internally controlled than were men. No gender differences in levels of assertiveness or self-esteem were found. Comparison of the results of Maccoby and Jacklin's review and Hall's study shows consistent findings for anxiety and self-esteem, but divergent results for assertiveness.

In an extensive meta-analysis, Feingold (1994) further investigated gender differences in personality trait scores published in the personality literature between 1958 and 1992 and in normative data for personality inventories published between 1940 and 1992. Feingold extended Hall's review to include the literature published after 1983 and validated some of Maccoby and Jacklin's (1974) conclusions using a quantitative method of analysis. The meta-analysis of the published studies showed males to be less anxious in general and to be more assertive than females, but the latter findings were valid only for adolescents and adults. There were no differences for social anxiety. Self-esteem was higher for males, but the magnitude of the difference was small. For his meta-analysis of the normative data of widely used personality inventories, Feingold used the Big Five hierarchical framework as described by Costa and McCrae (1992) to accommodate different scales and traits. The meta-analysis was conducted on normative data sets for editions of the Minnesota Multiphasic Personality Inventory (MMPI/MMPI-2), the California Psychological Inventory (CPI, CPI-R), the MMPI-adolescent form (MMPI-A), the Guilford–Zimmerman Temperament Survey (GZTS), Cattell's High School Personality Questionnaire and his 16PF, the Institute for Personality and Ability Testing (IPAT) Anxiety Scale, the NEO-Personality Inventory (NEO-PI & NEO-PI-R), the Gordon Personal Profile and Gordon Personal Inventory, the Comrey Personality Scales (CPS), Eysenck's Maudsley Personality Inventory and the Revised Eysenck Personality Questionnaire (EPQ-R), the Edwards Personal Preference Schedule (EPPS), and finally the Personality Research Form (PRF). The scales of these questionnaires were assigned to nine facets as described in Costa and McCrae's 30-facet NEO model: Anxiety and Impulsiveness (Neuroticism); Gregariousness, Assertiveness, and Activity (Extraversion); Ideas (Openness); Trust and Tender-Mindedness (Agreeableness); and finally Order (Conscientiousness). The results showed that women had higher scores on Anxiety (N), Gregariousness (E), Trust (A), and Tender-Mindedness (A), whereas men scored higher on Assertiveness (E). These results were similar across year of standardization of the test and normative group (subjects enrolled in high school or college or adults). The results of Feingold's meta-analyses are especially relevant for this chapter, because he also made cross-cultural comparisons among data available for the PRF. Effect sizes were compared for student samples from Canada (3 samples), China (1 sample), Finland (2 samples), Germany (2 samples), and Poland (2 samples) and for one Russian sample. Gender differences proved to be generally invariant across different countries.

In one of the most extensive cross-cultural studies of gender and personality, Williams and Best (1990) studied whether there were similarities and differences among 30 countries in the degree to which personality traits were associated with one gender or the other. They had university students in 30 countries rate the 300-adjective Adjective Check List (ACL; Gough & Heilbrun, 1980) for how much each adjective was characteristic of men rather than women (and vice versa). They found remarkable consensus across many countries and languages on the adjectives attributed to men and women. Items associated with men in at least 24 of the 30 countries included Adventurous, Aggressive, Autocratic, Daring, Dominant, Enterprising, Forceful, Independent, Masculine, Robust, Stern, and Strong. Associated with women were adjectives like Affectionate, Dreamy, Feminine, Sensitive, Sentimental, Softhearted, Submissive, and Superstitious. They noted that they were impressed that they could identify clear stereotypes across all the countries studied.

The majority of the empirical studies on gender differences in personality have been based on self- and peer ratings using personality questionnaires. A systematic study of childhood gender differences in personality and temperament has been hampered by the fact that there is no consensus among researchers about a framework to accommodate the different constructs of individual differences (Halverson, Kohnstamm, & Martin, 1994). Furthermore, the available research has shown an inconsistent picture because of the different assessment methods (e.g., questionnaires versus observations) and temperament inventories used.

In a review of the literature on gender-related socialization, Block (1983) described gender differences in personality characteristics in children and adults on seven temperament traits: aggression, activity, impulsivity, susceptibility to anxiety, achievement, self-concept, and social relationships. In general, she concluded that, compared to girls, boys were more aggressive and active, exhibited more curiosity and exploratory behavior, and were less susceptible to anxiety. Further, she cited the literature that showed adult men to be more motivated in ego-involving and challenging situations, to feel more confident in problem-solving situations, and to experience greater personal efficacy than were adult women. She concluded that there were social orientation differences between both groups.

More recent studies have not resolved the inconsistencies in findings on gender differences. Margalit and Eysenck (1990) reported higher levels of psychoticism in young males aged 12 to 16 years, whereas their female peers showed higher scores on Neuroticism, Extraversion, and the lie scale of the Junior Eysenck Personality Questionnaire (EPQ). McClowry, using the School-Age Temperament Inventory (SATI; McClowry, 1995) to assess the personality of children aged 8 to 11 years, concluded that age and gender differences on task persistence, negative reactivity, approach-withdrawal, and activity level were minimal. Persson-Blennow and McNeil (1982) found no gender differences on the nine Thomas and Chess temperament variables at the ages of 6 months, 1 year, and 2 years. In a 10-year longitudinal study on the developmental change and stability of the nine Thomas and Chess temperament dimensions, Guerin and Gottfried (1994) demonstrated only marginal differences between boys and girls in their mean temperament scale scores and their stability coefficients throughout childhood.

Ahadi, Rothbart, and Ye (1993) investigated children's temperament in the United States and China using the Children's Behavior Questionnaire (CBQ). The factor structure of the CBQ was invariant in the two cultures, and in each culture clear gender differences were demonstrated, although such differences were a function of culture. Girls in the United States showed significantly higher levels of Inhibitory Control, Low-Intensity Pleasure, and Perceptual Sensitivity than did their male counterparts, whereas Chinese girls compared to Chinese boys showed the reverse pattern.

The most consistent research findings about gender differences in personality measures have been reported for Holland's vocational personality types (Holland, 1985). Male adults and boys usually obtained higher scores on the Realistic, Investigative, and Enterprising scales, whereas females resembled more the Artistic, Social, and Conventional types (De Fruyt, 1996; Holland, 1985). Using the 15 trait adjectives provided by Holland (1985, pp. 19–23) as descriptors of Holland's types, Hofstee, De Raad, and Goldberg (1992) determined the position of each type in the Abridged Big Five Circumplex Model (AB5C) factor space. If only the primary loadings of traits are taken into consideration, boys scored higher on Extraversion and girls higher on Agreeableness and Conscientiousness.

ETIOLOGY OF GENDER DIFFERENCES

Several hypotheses about the nature of personality differences have been formulated in the past. The discussion of personality differences in general is reflected in the hypotheses about the etiology of gender differences (Feingold, 1994). Adherents of the genetic-biological model explained gender differences by referring to innate temperamental factors, whereas sociocultural theorists explained the differences in terms of differential learning and socialization processes. More recent evidence has shown that both social environment and genes have effects on personality differences (Plomin, 1990). Furthermore, it is now believed that the interaction of genes with the environment results in effects that cannot be accounted for by genes or environment alone. Rowe (1995) has concluded that simultaneous calculation of the effect sizes for all these factors has to be considered as central to the study of the etiology of personality and sex differences.

Genetic–Biological Model

Research bearing on the behavioral genetic model has used twin and adoption studies to disentangle the influence of genes and social environment (Bergeman et al., 1993; Loehlin, 1992; Plomin, 1990). Biologically oriented psychologists have typically correlated personality traits with physiological measures (Cloninger, 1986, 1987; Cloninger, Syrakic, & Przybeck, 1993; Zuckerman, 1991; Zuckerman & Cloninger, 1996) and have explained gender differences in personality by biological sex differences in hormonal-chemical activity or by physiological characteristics. Although behavioral genetic research paradigms have focused on the study of individual differences instead of differences among groups (Plomin, 1990), the comparison of concordance rates between monozygotic and same-sex dizygotic twins allows the evaluation of the contributions of genetic and environmental factors in both genders. Loehlin (1992) combined the results of five large twin studies conducted in Australia (Martin & Jardine, 1986; N = 3,810), Britain (Eaves, Eysenck, & Martin, 1989; N = 475), Finland (Rose, Koskenvuo, Kaprio, Sarna, & Langinvainio, 1988; N = 7,144), Sweden (Floderus-Myrhed, Pedersen, & Rasmusson, 1980; N = 12,898), and the United States (Loehlin & Nichols, 1986; N = 793) and rejected the hypothesis that males and females showed identical heritability and environmental influence in the case of Extraversion. Similar findings were obtained for Neuroticism. As these studies were conducted on three different continents, a legitimate question is whether cultural differences were involved. Analyzing the sample-to-sample differences for Extraversion, Loehlin (1992, p. 19) concluded that "the consistency across studies is more impressive for both males and females than are the inconsistencies." That is, no important cultural differences in environmental and genetic influences were found in either the male or the female samples. Such findings do not imply that the phenotype is the same in these five countries, but that genetic and environmental sources of differences can be thought of as being the same in each country.

Plomin and Rende (1991) concluded that the most important finding in behavioral genetics involved nurture rather than nature; that is, the significant environmental variation leading to individual differences lay in experiences not shared by siblings. Some authors (Loehlin, 1992; Plomin & Daniels, 1987) have even argued that a nonshared environmental factor might be the most influential component of behavioral variation.

The Social–Cultural Model

Sociocultural researchers have assumed that the "appropriate learning conditions" for gender role development were those situations in which children have many opportunities to observe gender role-consistent behavior and those situations in which children's gender-consistent behavior was reinforced (Eagly, 1987; Eagly & Wood, 1991). Several studies have demonstrated that socialization typically encourages interests and activities traditionally associated with a child's own gender. In different independent samples (Block, 1981) and across different cultures (Barry, Bacon, & Child, 1957), parents have been reported to encourage boys to achieve, to compete, and to explore, whereas girls have been encouraged to be nurturant, domestic, and obedient. Observational studies of parental behavior yielded the same evidence. These findings are extended to teachers in classrooms (Serbin, O'Leary, Kent, & Tonick, 1973). Television has also been shown to reinforce these traditional gender roles (e.g., Lovdal, 1989; O'Donnell & O'Donnell, 1978). McGhee and Fruch (1980) have demonstrated a relation between increased television viewing and stronger gender typing.

A. H. Buss (1989) has argued that when gender differences begin to appear later in infancy, their appearance would be consistent with the socialization explanation. Block (1976) suggested that some gender differences do not emerge until adolescence because socialization takes time. If innate gender differences are assumed, however, it should be plausible to note them before long-term socialization processes take place. Such differences should be detectable before age 3 as reflections of basic biological processes. Buss (1989) proposed a genetic basis for temperament, but assumed gender differences to be mostly environmental, as many differences between boys and girls occur at about age 4 years. Kohnstamm (1989) raised two arguments against this hypothesis. First, many gender differences are apparent before age 4 (Eaton & Enns, 1986). Second, changes in temperament traits reflect both genetic and environmental effects. Current interpretations of the data have suggested that gender differences reflect the effects of both biology and culture.

GENDER DIFFERENCES IN FREE DESCRIPTIONS

We investigated gender differences in parents' free descriptions of children as summarized in this book. In general, personality psychologists have favored ratings by others above self-ratings, both to define the structure of personality and to assess someone's personality in particular (Borkenau & Liebler, 1993; Funder & Sneed, 1993; Hofstee, 1994). Developmental psychologists have also often relied on parents as the main source of information about children's personalities. In the free descriptors reported in this book, we go beyond these approaches by assuming that parents are both accurate and reliable observers and judges of the behavior of children and also are good informants as to what are the most characteristic and salient characteristics of their children.

The design of the present project allowed cross-cultural comparisons of the kind and number of descriptors provided for boys and girls. Such information is important for both genetic-biological and sociocultural psychologists. The current investigation can be interpreted as a repeated measures design, in which the occurrence of gender differences in the distribution of descriptors can be examined for cross-cultural replicability. Substantial culture-by-gender interactions would underscore a nurture explanation for gender differences. If, however, gender differences were found to be cross-culturally stable, then the nature hypothesis would be the more parsimonious explanation. Both explanations, however, would have to be interpreted with caution, as both scenarios can be explained by a gene–environment interaction.

When discussing the parental perspective on children's behavior, it is important to remember that the parents interviewed were instructed to describe only what was characteristic for their children. Clearly this was not a comparative perspective in which a child is described in relation to other- or same-gender children. The personality-descriptive lexicon used in this study included a category to assign descriptors where an explicit reference was made to the gender (in)appropriateness of a particular behavior. Less than 2% of the descriptors were assigned to this category, a fact underscoring the hypothesis that parents had no stereotypical gender perspective when describing their children.

In this analysis, we focused on age only when it interacted with gender (see Kohnstamm, 1989). Our objectives were twofold: to investigate the distribution of free descriptions across the categories of the personality-descriptive lexicon for boys and girls, and to examine the cross-cultural replicability of any gender differences found.

Subjects and Analysis

The distribution of free descriptors was examined for 1,222 boys and 1,194 girls. Data of seven research teams were available: Georgia (United States), Bielefeld (Germany), Ghent (Belgium), Leiden (Netherlands), Athens (Greece), Wroclaw and Warsaw (Poland), and Beijing (China). Approximately equal numbers of boys and girls were involved in the different samples: 93 boys versus 109 girls (United States); 124 boys versus 122 girls (Germany); 204 boys versus 223 girls (Belgium); 163 boys versus 159 girls (Netherlands); 234 boys versus 225 girls (Greece); 181 boys versus 178 girls (Poland); and 223 boys versus 178 girls (China). The children were in four age groups, 1 year below and 1 year above the target ages of 3, 6, 9, and 12. The distribution across the different age categories was roughly similar in each data set. All ANOVA analyses were conducted on arcsine transformed proportion scores per subject to account for the dependency of means and standard deviations of proportion scores and to stabilize sample variances.

Gender Differences for Big Five Categories

The results for ANOVA for proportions, with sex, age group, and country as the independent variables, are described here. There were only two gender effects: for high- and low-end Conscientiousness. Boys received significantly more low-end descriptors than did girls (5.2 vs. 4.0, $F = 6.5$, $p < .05$) and fewer high-end descriptors than did girls (5.2 vs. 6.0, $F = 5.7$,

$p < .05$). Clearly, at the broad category level, there were no overwhelming gender differences.

Facet Analyses. Although there were no gender differences in overall Extraversion, analyses at the facet level showed that girls were more Sociable (Ia; 10.8 vs. 9.3, $F = 9.6$, $p < .01$) and Dominant (Ib; 4.0 vs. 3.0, $F = 11.8$, $p < .01$), whereas boys were significantly more Active (Ic; 7.8 vs. 5.6, $F = 29.8$, $p < .01$). There were no main or interaction effects for the Agreeableness facets. The overall gender effect observed for Conscientiousness was due mainly to girls' being higher in high-end Carefulness descriptors (IIIa; 2.1 vs. 1.7, $F = 4.4$, $p < .05$), whereas boys were described with more low-end Diligence descriptors (IIIc; 2.7 vs. 2.0, $F = 4.7$, $p < .05$). Finally, boys were assigned somewhat more high-end Openness descriptors than were girls (Va; 3.8 vs. 3.1, $F = 4.4$, $p < .05$).

The analyses in other chapters show that age group and country differences were clearly more important than was gender in describing the distribution of descriptors across the five major categories of the lexicon. Interactions in which gender was involved were small with small effect sizes, a fact underscoring the notion that gender differences were mostly culturally similar.

Gender Differences Beyond the Big Five

The results for the eight smaller categories showed that there were significant gender differences for the high ends of Independence (VI) and Gender-Appropriate Behavior (X) and the low ends of Mature for Age (VII) and School Performance (XI). Briefly, girls were ascribed more Independence descriptors (VI; 2.3 vs. 1.9, $F = 7.4$, $p < .01$), whereas boys were characterized with more phrases referring to Immaturity for Age (VII; 0.8 vs. 0.4, $F = 13.5$, $p < .01$), Gender-Appropriate Behavior (X; 0.6 vs. 0.1, $F = 26.4$, $p < .01$), and references to performance problems at school (XI; 0.9 vs. 0.5, $F = 13.5$, $p < .01$). These differences were all based on very small proportions and very small differences between boys and girls. Although each was reasonable and expectable, we did not place much importance on the differences in these very small categories.

DISCUSSION

When comparing the differences we found with the results reported in the literature on gender differences, we assumed that the parental free-description procedure was a reasonable approach to assess gender differences of the target children. The validity of this assumption can be indirectly inferred from the extent to which we replicated gender differences obtained with personality questionnaires.

Although the research on gender differences in personality is not un-equivocal, some findings have been consistently reported for different age groups. In general, women have been found to be more anxious (Block, 1983; Feingold, 1994; Hall, 1984; Maccoby & Jacklin, 1974), whereas men have usually obtained higher scores on scales assessing assertiveness and aggressiveness (Block, 1983; Feingold, 1984; Maccoby & Jacklin, 1974), activity (Block, 1983; Eaton & Enns, 1986), and curiosity and exploratory behavior (Block, 1983). Some of these differences mesh with what we found and suggest that at least some findings on gender differences for adults and adolescents can be replicated in free descriptors of children. Generalizability across age cohorts and methods was limited, however. Indeed, boys were described as more active, but the free-description data failed to support the well-documented findings of females being higher on anxiety (Block, 1983; Feingold, 1994; Hall, 1984; Maccoby & Jacklin, 1974; Margalit & Eysenck, 1990) and boys being more assertive (Block, 1983; Feingold, 1994; Maccoby & Jacklin, 1974). Surprisingly, there were no gender effects for the three Emotional Stability facets, and the results for Dominance were reversed; that is, girls received *more* descriptors referring to Dominance. Besides these well-documented gender differ-ences, the free-description approach did provide additional support for the generalization that girls are more sociable and for Block's (1983) suggestion that boys are more curious and eager to learn and explore.

Feingold (1994) concluded that gender differences seem to be mostly invariant across different countries, whereas Ahadi et al. (1993) demon-strated clear cultural differences in infant temperament. The results of our ANOVAs showed a number of small gender-by-country interactions (for 4 of the 15 subcategories), a finding consistent with Feingold's contention (1994) that gender differences on many dimensions are universal.

The analysis of gender differences at the main category level did not show differences for Extraversion. An analysis at the facet level, however, provided significant main effects for all facets. The effects were counter-balanced, with girls characterized by more dominance and sociability descriptors and boys by more activity descriptors. Such findings point to the necessity to go beyond the level of broad categories in the search for useful individual differences. These observations are in line with devel-opments in the assessment of adult personality, including the assessment of both domains and facets (Costa & McCrae, 1992; Hogan, 1986). Probably part of the controversy in research findings on personality gender differ-ences in adults and children can be attributed to these different levels of analysis and comparison.

The gender differences observed beyond the Big Five categories were in line with the findings obtained for the Big Five categories. Parents provided significantly more negative Conscientiousness descriptors to characterize their sons and also made more references to problems at school, a conceptually related category. Girls were described as more dominant, but also received more Independence descriptors. The differences obtained for Maturity for Age and Behaving in Gender-Appropriate Ways were difficult to interpret as personality or temperament gender differences.

As for our main objective, the construction of personality questionnaires for children aged 3 to 12, these analyses of gender differences in parental free descriptions illustrate that the behavior of boys and girls is described using an almost identical vocabulary in terms of the frequency of use of the Big Five personality categories. Furthermore, the analysis at the main and the facet levels underscored the necessity to develop questionnaires assessing domains and facets that are defined *across* boys and girls. We can then examine differences in identically defined scales and assess differences between boys and girls on means for domains and facets.

REFERENCES

Ahadi, S. A., Rothbart, M. K., & Ye, R. (1993). Children's temperament in the United States and China: Similarities and differences. *European Journal of Personality, 7*, 359–377.

Barry, H., Bacon, M. K., & Child, I. L. (1957). A cross-cultural survey of some sex differences in socialization. *Journal of Abnormal and Social Psychology, 55*, 327–332.

Bergeman, C. S., Chipuer, H. M., Plomin, R., Pedersen, N. L., McClearn, G. E., Nesselroade, J. R., Costa, P., Jr., & McCrae, R. R. (1993). Genetic and environmental effects on Openness to Experience, Agreeableness, and Conscientiousness: An adoption/twin study. *Journal of Personality, 61*, 159–179.

Block, J. H. (1976). Debatable conclusions about sex differences. *Contemporary Psychology, 21*, 517–522.

Block, J. H. (1981). Gender differences in the nature of premises developed about the world. In E. Shapiro & E. Weber (Eds.), *Cognitive and affective growth: Developmental interaction.* Hillsdale, NJ: Lawrence Erlbaum Associates.

Block, J. H. (1983). Differential premises arising from differential socialization of the sexes: Some conjectures. *Child Development, 54*, 1335–1354.

Borkenau, P., & Liebler, A. (1993). Consensus and self–other agreement for trait inferences from minimal information. *Journal of Personality, 61*, 477–496.

Buss, A. H. (1989). Temperaments as personality traits. In G. A. Kohnstamm, J. E. Bates, & M. K. Rothbart (Eds.), *Temperament in childhood* (pp. 49–58). New York: John Wiley & Sons.

Cloninger, C. R. (1986). A unified biosocial theory of personality and its role in the development of anxiety states. *Psychiatric Developments, 3*, 167–226.

Cloninger, C. R. (1987). A systematic method for clinical description and classification of personality variants. *Archives of General Psychiatry, 44*, 573–588.

Cloninger, C. R., Syrakic, D. M., & Przybeck, T. R. (1993). A psychobiological model of temperament and character. *Archives of General Psychiatry, 50*, 975–990.

Costa, P. T., & McCrae, R. R. (1992). *NEO PI-R professional manual: Revised NEO Personality Inventory (NEO PI-R) and NEO Five-Factor Inventory (NEO-FFI).* Odessa, FL: Psychological Assessment Resources.

De Fruyt, F. (1996). *Personality and vocational interests: Relationship between the Five-Factor Model of personality and Holland's RIASEC typology.* Unpublished doctoral dissertation, University of Ghent, Belgium.

Eagly, A. H. (1987). *Sex differences in social behavior: A social-role interpretation.* Hillsdale, NJ: Lawrence Erlbaum Associates.

Eagly, A. H., & Wood, W. (1991). Explaining sex differences in social behavior: A meta-analytic perspective. *Personality and Social Psychology Bulletin, 17,* 306–315.

Eaton, W. O., & Enns, L. R. (1986). Sex differences in human motor activity level. *Psychological Bulletin, 100,* 19–28.

Eaves, L. J., Eysenck, H. J., & Martin, N. G. (1989). *Genes, culture and personality—An empirical approach.* London: Academic Press.

Feingold, A. (1994). Gender differences in personality: A meta-analysis. *Psychological Bulletin, 116,* 429–456.

Floderus-Myrhead, B., Pedersen, N., & Rasmusson, I. (1980). Assessment of heritability for personality, based on a short form of the Eysenck Personality Inventory. *Behavior Genetics, 10,* 153–162.

Funder, D. C., & Sneed, C. D. (1993). Behavioral manifestations of personality: An ecological approach to judgmental accuracy. *Journal of Personality and Social Psychology, 64,* 479–490.

Gough, H. G., & Heilbrun, A. B. (1980). *The adjective check list manual.* Palo Alto, CA: Consulting Psychologists Press.

Guerin, D. W., & Gottfried, A. W. (1994). Developmental stability and change in parent reports of temperament: A ten-year longitudinal investigation from infancy through preadolescence. *Merrill–Palmer Quarterly, 40,* 334–355.

Hall, J. A. (1984). *Nonverbal sex differences: Communication accuracy and expressive style.* Baltimore: Johns Hopkins University Press.

Halverson, C. F., Jr., Kohnstamm, G. A., & Martin, R. P. (Eds.). (1994). *The developing structure of temperament and personality from infancy to adulthood.* Hillsdale, NJ: Lawrence Erlbaum Associates.

Hofstee, W. K. B. (1994). Who should own the definition of personality? *European Journal of Personality, 8,* 149–162.

Hofstee, W. K. B., De Raad, B., & Goldberg, L. R. (1992). Integration of the Big Five and circumplex approaches to trait structure. *Journal of Personality and Social Psychology, 63,* 146–163.

Hogan, R. (1986). *Hogan Personality Inventory manual.* Minneapolis, MN: National Computer Systems.

Holland, J. L. (1985). *Making vocational choices: A theory of vocational personalities and work environments.* Englewood Cliffs, NJ: Prentice-Hall.

Kohnstamm, G. A. (1989). Temperament in childhood: Cross-cultural and sex differences. In G. A. Kohnstamm, J. E. Bates, & M. K. Rothbart (Eds.), *Temperament in childhood* (pp. 483–508). New York: John Wiley & Sons.

Loehlin, J. C. (1992). *Genes and environment in personality development.* London: Sage.

Loehlin, J. C., & Nichols, R. C. (1976). *Heredity, environment, and personality.* Austin: University of Texas Press.

Lovdal, L. (1989). Sex role messages in television commercials: An update. *Sex Roles, 21,* 715–724.

Maccoby, E. E., & Jacklin, C. N. (1974). *The psychology of sex differences.* Stanford, CA: Stanford University Press.

Margalit, M., & Eysenck, S. (1990). Prediction of coherence in adolescence: Gender differences in social skills, personality, and family climate. *Journal of Research in Personality, 24,* 510–521.

Martin, N., & Jardine, R. (1986). Eysenck's contributions to behavior genetics. In S. Mogdil & C. Mogdil (Eds.)., *Hans Eysenck: Consensus and controversy* (pp. 13–47). Philadelphia: Falmer Press.

McClowry, S. G. (1995). The development of the School-Age Temperament Inventory. *Merrill–Palmer Quarterly, 41*, 271–285.

McGhee, P. E., & Fruch, T. (1980). Television viewing and the learning of sex role stereotypes. *Sex Roles, 6*, 179–188.

O'Donnell, W. J. & O'Donnell, K. J. (1978). Update: Sex-role messages in TV commercials. *Journal of Communications, 28*, 156–158.

Persson-Blennow, I., & McNeil, T. F. (1982). Temperament characteristics of children in relation to gender, birth order, and social class. *Annual Progress in Child Psychiatry and Child Development*, 317–322.

Plomin, R. (1990). *Nature and nurture: An introduction to human behavioral genetics.* Belmont, CA: Brooks/Cole.

Plomin, R., & Daniels, D. (1987). Why are children in the same family so different from each other? *Behavioral and Brain Sciences, 10*, 1–16.

Plomin, R., & Rende, R. (1991). Human behavioral genetics. *Annual Review of Psychology, 42*, 161–190.

Rose, R. J., Koskenvuo, M., Kaprio, J., Sarna, S., & Langinvainio, H. (1988). Shared genes, shared experiences and similarity of personality. *Journal of Personality and Social Psychology, 54*, 161–171.

Rowe, D. C. (1995). The limits of family influence: A response. *Psychological Inquiry, 6*, 174–182.

Serbin, L. A., O'Leary, K. D., Kent, R. N., & Tonick, I. J. (1973). A comparison of teacher response to the preacademic and problem behavior of boys and girls. *Child Development, 44*, 796–804.

Williams, J. E., & Best, D. L. (1990). *Measuring sex stereotypes: A multination study.* Newbury Park, CA: Sage.

Zuckerman, M. (1991). *Psychobiology of personality.* Cambridge, England: Cambridge University Press.

Zuckerman, M., & Cloninger, R. C. (1996). Relationships between Cloninger's, Zuckerman's, and Eysenck's dimensions of personality. *Personality and Individual Differences, 21*, 283–285.

9

How African American Parents Describe Their Children

James B. Victor
Hampton University

Harold E. Dent
Hampton University

Barbara Carter
Hampton University

Charles F. Halverson, Jr.
University of Georgia

Valerie L. Havill
University of Georgia

WHY AN AFRICAN AMERICAN HOMOGENEOUS STUDY?

Issues have been raised about how to study American minorities (Garcia-Coll, Lamberty, Jenkins, McAdoo, Crnic, Wasik, & Vasquez-Garcia, 1996; Gordon, 1976; Guthrie, 1976). African American children historically and currently are the most studied of U.S. minority children (Caplan & Nelson, 1973; McLoyd, 1990; Wiese, 1992). Among U.S. minorities, African American children have remained at the center of the debate over methodological issues, although there is also interest in studying Hispanic American and Native American children (Powell, Yamamoto, Romero, & Morales, 1983).

Of greatest concern are the appropriateness of comparing the behavior of African American children to that of majority (Anglo) children; of interpreting differences found between these two groups as deficits; and of using tests normed on majority children to assess the cognitive abilities (Dent, 1976, 1996) and development of African American children (Myers, Rana, & Harris, 1979; Washington & McLoyd, 1982). The marker of research with African American children receiving the most criticism is the race-comparative paradigm (McLoyd, 1990). Critics have argued that a preoccupation with differences between African American children and majority children has focused on negative behaviors and has fostered the view that African American children are abnormal or incompetent. This preoccupation with race comparison has consequently drawn attention from the structural forces that are important to the children's development (McLoyd & Randolph, 1985). McLoyd (1990) has cogently argued that focusing on the race-comparative paradigm has fostered a tendency to ignore intragroup variability and that consequently very little is known about individual differences among African American children or about the sources of variability in development in the African American population. The importance of intragroup variation has been pointed out by research demonstrating that the variables that best explain differences in certain minority groups (e.g., in achievement) are sometimes different from the variables that best explain differences between racial–ethnic groups (Howard & Scott, 1981).

Thoughtful reviews have highlighted the complexities in conducting developmental research with culturally different groups (Garcia-Coll et al., 1996; Ogbu, 1981; Washington & McLoyd, 1982). Washington and McLoyd (1982) have argued that validity in developmental research involving African Americans has focused on a mechanistic or causal approach of internal and external validity (i.e., after Bracht & Glass, 1968; Campbell & Stanley, 1963; Hultsch & Hickey, 1978), which emphasizes theory, measurement, and intersubjective agreement in searching for similarities and differences across and between cultures. These authors have contended that a more complete understanding of cultural differences could be attained by combining the mechanistic or causal approach with a teleological or intentional approach that emphasizes the goal directness of human actions and the unique meanings that different cultural groups give to their experiences. This distinction of behavior accounting for a perspective from within the system as opposed to behavioral accounts of perspectives from outside the system parallels the distinction between an emic and an etic approach (Davidson, Jaccard, Triandis, Morales, & Diaz-Guerrero, 1976; Pike, 1966). Washington and McLoyd (1982) concluded that the failure to develop procedures that include these additional dimensions of external validity (from a teleological or intentional perspective) has left the impression that developmental researchers ignore the cultural context of experience and are insensitive to the view of U.S. minorities.

We concur with Washington and McLoyd that the question of whether to utilize the words, motives, and purposes of informants or instead to give priority to the interpretations of social scientists is a critical methodological question in comparative research. Washington and McLoyd (1982) have argued that "it is especially important that comparative research involving African Americans provide an opportunity for the participants to provide their interpretations of the issues at hand." These authors believed that racism's myths and stereotypes have affected and touched every aspect of the African American experience (family life, parenting, sexuality, education, housing, medical care, etc.). We believe that personality-temperament, behavior problems, and other person-centered variables also need to include the intentional approach that takes into account African American interpretations of their own experiences. We are aware that social scientists tend to link person-centered characteristics and problematic situations while ignoring situationally relevant factors (i.e., racism) and that they tend to attribute causal significance to person-centered variables found in statistical association with social problems (Caplan & Nelson, 1973). We believe that allowing the opportunity for African Americans to provide their own interpretations of their own experiences can provide necessary new information for the scientific interpretation of the meaning of experience.

Early writings have provided a historical understanding of a distinctive African American culture (Blassingame, 1971; Genovese, 1974; Gutman, 1976; Herskowitz, 1941). Washington and McLoyd (1982) speculated that the vast majority of African Americans learn two different cultural experiences, mainstream European American and African American, and that their experience is more considerable in the African American community, while their understanding of the mainstream community remains underdeveloped because there are few opportunities to practice such cultural experiences. Empirical evidence for a bicultural interpretation has come from the study of perceptions of the social environment within and between both White and African American subjects (Triandis, 1976). Although there were many similarities in response and both groups were extremely variable, there were systematic differences that he attributed to differences in the two groups' subjective cultures.

In presenting his cultural ecological perspective, Ogbu (1981) argued that African Americans represent two distinct groups and that urban "ghetto" African Americans have unique vocabulary categories and perceptions and might represent a uniquely different culture from other groups of African Americans. Important to this discussion is Ogbu's conceptual framework for the causal relation between competencies and childrearing practices. In contrast to conventional thinking that differences in competencies between members of two populations (e.g., middle-class Whites and urban ghetto Blacks) result from differences in childrearing practices, Ogbu, using cross-cultural studies (see Ogbu, 1981) argued that the nature of the instrumental competencies in a population might determine the techniques that parents and parent surrogates employ to raise children. Using examples from an older study in this country (Kohn, 1977), Ogbu showed that middle-class bureaucratic and professional jobs versus working-class jobs differ greatly with respect to the personal attributes (*personality descriptors*) associated with them. Examples of personal attributes of the former (middle-class jobs) are self-direction and ability to manipulate interpersonal relations, ideas, and symbols; examples of personal attributes related to the latter (working-class jobs) are respect for authority and conformity to externally imposed rules.

These ideas are similar to Triandis's (1989) distinction of childrearing patterns in collectivist cultures versus individualist cultures. In collectivist cultures, the primary concerns of parents are obedience, reliability, and proper behavior. The primary concerns of parents in individualistic cultures are self-reliance, independence, and creativity. Ogbu (1981) asserted that "members of a population learn which strategies are effective and appropriate in exploiting their subsistence resources and which competencies facilitate the use of the strategies, they also learn how best to inculcate these instrumental competencies in their children" (p. 419). Applying these concepts to personality descriptors, we reason that differences between middle-class and lower-class African Americans' personality descriptors might be at descriptor level (the actual descriptors might be different in a population) or at the meaning or value level (the same descriptors might have different meaning or value in a population). We believe an emic approach allows us to learn where such differences occur.

Understanding the African American experience is a complex task, and researchers have often ignored the sheer diversity in the African American community (Valentine, 1971; Washington & McLoyd, 1982). Several authors have however stressed the need to consider social stratification in the African American community in comparative inquiry and have emphasized that social stratification in the United States should include the influence of class and caste (Berreman, 1972; Ogbu, 1978). Studies in social perceptions (Triandis, 1976) and family and school achievement (Tulkin, 1968) compared African Americans and White Americans and showed that middle-class African Americans and White Americans were comparable but that the lower classes were distinctly different from each other. Tulkin noted that when both groups were equated with regard to class, they still differed with respect to family structure and maternal employment. Ogbu (1994) proposed a provocative conceptualization of African Americans as "involuntary immigrants" whose perspective has been developed over several hundred years in opposition to oppression. He compared this situation to that of "voluntary immigrants" whose perspective has arisen in comparison to a past experience most often viewed as offering fewer opportunities. Ogbu believed that these different comparative perspectives have implications for the way groups evaluate their experiences. For example, Asian American immigrants (voluntary immigrants) might view a U.S. inner city school as much superior to previous school experiences in offering new educational opportunities. In contrast, African Americans (involuntary immigrants) might view the same school as representing little or no opportunity.

Washington and McLoyd (1982) suggested that researchers address the problem of equating the socioeconomic standing of African Americans and White Americans. Pointing out that developmental psychologists have tended to rely on outdated measures of socioeconomic status, several researchers have provided developmental psychologists with guidelines that offer more stable measures of socioeconomic status (Entwisle & Astone, 1994; Hauser, 1994; Mueller & Parcell, 1981). Our model treats each of two social-class groups of African Americans as though it was culturally different. We are careful to assure that the social-class groups are distinctly different (no overlap) and sampled to represent each African American group (lower- and middle-class census tract projections).

WHY THE FIVE-FACTOR APPROACH
FOR AN AFRICAN AMERICAN STUDY?

Kohnstamm, Halverson, Mervielde, and Havill (see Introduction and chapter 1 of this book) have discussed the issues that have driven this multinational collaboration to use the Five-Factor Model (FFM) as a target for studying children's unfolding development from infancy to adulthood. There is strong convergence with the issues we view as important in studying African American children and the issues important to other authors of this book, namely that "traits parents come to see in their children depend partly on the saliency of those traits in the behavior of their children, partly on their family history, and partly on the prevailing belief systems or collective ideas about what traits are important for children in their particular culture."

Another issue that has given rise to our work is the lack of agreement on the personality and temperament dimensions or structure to apply to the developmental study of children. Parke and Asher's (1983) review of "personality development" entirely neglected the issues of personality structure, and current textbooks in child development have shown almost no interest in personality structure beyond the summary of temperament based on the nine-dimensional structure proposed by Thomas and Chess (1977). Undoubtedly, one of the effects of the etic, top-down, theory-driven approach to construct and test development in child temperament and personality research has been the plethora of dimensions that have emerged. Although parents and others (teachers, child caregivers) have often given personality descriptions of children, the descriptions are mostly obtained using theory-driven standardized procedures such as questionnaires, Q sorts, or checklists. These questionnaires can be directed at behavior problems (e.g., the Child Behavior Checklist [CBCL]; Achenbach & Edelbrock, 1981), at "normal" social and emotional characteristics (e.g., Carey & McDevitt, 1989; Chess & Thomas, 1984; Windle, 1989; Windle & Lerner, 1986), or at personality differences measured from questionnaires like the Eysenck Personality Questionnaire (EPQ: e.g., Eysenck & Eysenck, 1975). Consensus on the broadband dimensional structure underlying these descriptions exists *only* for behavior problems, such as the distinction between "externalizing" and "internalizing" problems (Achenbach, Howell, Quay, & Connors, 1991). Kohnstamm, Bates, and Rothbart (1989) reviewed the measures and constructs of temperament in childhood. Strelau (1991), referring to the "uncontrolled growth" in temperament research, reported that there are over 30 psychometric measures of early temperament, sampling over 40 different individual difference constructs. Thomas and Chess's nine-dimensional scheme has been the operational basis for many different questionnaires.

With Thomas and Chess as an example, most of the studies we have mentioned used either the original Thomas and Chess (1977) items or adaptations and translations of the original items. It is not known whether some important personality dimensions were not obtained because Thomas and Chess were not interested in them or dimensions were obtained because researchers wrote many items to measure what they believed to be important. These questions can be applied to most theory-driven personality dimensions. This discrepancy between top-down, theory-driven tests (like virtually *all* tests describing personality in children) and bottom-up, language-frequency–based tests reflects the etic–emic distinctions previously discussed under validity issues involving African American children. Many have preferred the emic (cultural-specific–informant-based) approach to instrument construction. When researchers use a scheme like Thomas and Chess's, they get out of analyses what they put into them (even if they are not the original nine factors), because parents rate what is given to them—even if they never otherwise use such terms in describing their own children. A key question is: Does the test constructor base the instrument on what the *theorist* thinks important (etic) or on what *informants* such as parents and teachers use as frequent descriptors (emic)?

As described in this book's introduction, Oliver John (1990) began obtaining personality descriptors from the natural language by using a free-description method. This emic approach to obtaining personality descriptors of children from natural language has provided an ideal method to develop a lexical manual that can be used across language and culture. The convergence between the issues related to studying personality descriptors across language and culture and validity issues for studying African American children raised by Washington and McLoyd (1982) was striking to us. We subsequently came to believe that obtaining natural-language free descriptions was the preferred method for our project.

As stated earlier, consensus on the broadband dimensional structure exists *only* for behavior problems (Achenbach et al., 1991). We have been concerned for some time (Victor & Halverson, 1975, 1976) about this negative halo effect in measuring children with instruments like the Achenbach and the Quay scales that allow raters only to mark negative behaviors. Until recently, only Digman and his colleagues (Digman, 1990; Digman & Inouye, 1986; Digman & Takemoto-Chock, 1981) have applied the Five-Factor approach to issues related to developmental processes. They have shown the Big Five factors to be robust and stable and predictive of academic achievement in school-age populations. In an earlier article, Victor (1994) presented data for fifth- and sixth-grade children, using Digman's adjective procedures that replicated his five-factor structure in school-age children. We included in our assessment measures standardized academic achievement and a commonly used, factor analytically derived Behavior Problem checklist (Quay & Peterson, 1987). *Analyses indicate that the commonly endorsed "behavior problems" load on early analogs of the Big Five—in fact, on four of the five, and form no separate factor.* As in the Digman studies, personality was a better predictor of achievement than was aptitude. Openness to Experience as the personality marker (not Conscientiousness) formed the fifth factor across personality, behavior problems, and achievement. Digman had used teacher grades in his analysis, and we speculated that if both standardized achievement and grades had been used in the same analysis, then Conscientiousness would show a stronger relation to grade point average (GPA), and Openness to Experience would better predict standardized achievement.

We have recently obtained 6-year follow-up measures for this sample of students, who are now high school juniors and seniors. In a multiple regression analysis, we found that Conscientiousness and Openness to Experience accounted for 17% of the variance in GPA 6 years later ($R = .41$, df 2, 99, $F = 10.08$, $p < .0001$). Over the 6-year period, Conscientiousness, not Openness, showed the stronger correlations ($r = .33$, $p < .001$, $r = 22$, $p < .02$, respectively). Concurrently, teacher-rated dimensions of Conscientiousness and Openness to Experience (rated when the students were juniors and seniors in high school) continued to show statistically significant correlations to GPA ($r = .51$, $p < .001$, $df = 107$). We now believe that it is important to characterize both personality and behavior problems to understand the overlap (contamination) between the way the two constructs are measured. Only then can we know when behavior problems are contributing new information. Unlike cognitive measures, Five-Factor personality scales might be less prone to racial discrimination concerns (Goldberg, 1993; Hogan, 1991). The importance of the Five-Factor approach for developmentalists is that it provides a total picture of children, and when tracking the same children over time, we can understand not only the risk factors of young children, but the supportive factors as well (Garmezy & Masten, 1991; Masten, 1994; Werner & Smith, 1982). We hope that such an approach not only answers important basic developmental research questions but also provides school and mental health workers with the individual difference information they need to provide optimal program support for children at risk.

DIMENSIONS OF PERSONALITY IN AFRICAN AMERICAN CHILDREN: CONCEPTUAL FRAMEWORK

These issues have driven our own research directions. In summary, the conceptual framework for the Dimensions of Personality in African American Children project is based on five interrelated ideas: a gap in the literature about *the lack of consensus in the structure of personality* for children; applying to children the lexical hypothesis, which has led to the FFM in adult personality research; an emic approach to obtain personality descriptors from natural language to allow comparison within language, culture, and age and an emic approach that allows for the identification of cultural universals; a race-homogeneous design to study African American intragroup differences for children; and using social class as a quasi-independent variable to untangle social class and race–ethnicity differences. We echo Washington and McLoyd's view: "What we are searching for is not a perfect translation system but one which more closely approaches the goal of equating the meaning of concepts across cultures." For Ogbu (1981), race-comparative research can be justified *only* after the within-race issues have been addressed.

By studying African American children through a homogeneous sample, we can better understand within-group variations and begin to disentangle social class and ethnicity and the use of an emic versus etic approach. Thus our project studies within-group differences; the broad, international cultural samples allow for distinctly different comparisons from those typical for African American studies.

The Larger Project

The long-term goal of the personality project is the development of a series of instruments that measure the dimensional structure of personality in young African American children and that function as the African

American component of the multinational project. The project has three phases or components: collecting and coding parents' and teachers' free descriptions of African American children; assembling and testing questionnaires; conducting comparison and validity studies across social class, language, and culture.

The significance of this research is based on our addressing African American cultural issues in a cross-cultural context while simultaneously addressing the lack of consensus about the main dimensions of child personality (and/or temperament). Using a race–ethnic-homogenous design, we are examining how two groups of African American parent informants, differing in social class, describe their children. Simultaneously using the same methodology, we study teacher descriptors of personality structure in African American children. We are using a variety of techniques common to cross-cultural research and research with indigenous populations to ensure conceptual equivalence and cultural sensitivity (social-class–relevant focus groups to back-translate, sort descriptions, and label categories and to perform prototype analysis). When we have completed the "African American dictionaries" for the two social-class groups, we will study the commonalties and differences in the "natural-language dictionaries" that have been obtained through the two U.S. research teams (Hampton University and the University of Georgia). This will allow us to determine the number of common and different items we need to use when we construct and test our instruments.

After we have constructed our instruments, we will assess the robustness of our lexically based structural models across the two African American social-class groups and with other lexically derived models in the United States and other countries. In the third phase of our project, we will begin to initiate cross-cultural and developmental studies of the validity of these new instruments. Using a race-homogenous design will allow us to explore intragroup variability, individual differences, and sources of deviation in the African American child population. Through adopting the lexical natural-language approach and collaborating with multinational research teams, we hope to contribute to the unification of the study of personality development from childhood to adulthood.

Common Elements Across Research Teams

Across research teams the common elements of the study design include using the same age groups of children, interviewing mothers and fathers, including similar numbers of boys and girls, and using the same free-description interview technique. In the Hampton project, parents in two social-class groups were asked to describe their children (fathers and mothers, similar numbers of boys and girls, ages 3, 6, 9, and 12). African American interviewers simply asked parents to describe their children using their natural language. Parents were given prompts such as: "What is your child like?" "What is typical for her or him?" "How is he or she similar to or different from other children?" All interviews were audiotaped, and the descriptions were transcribed verbatim. African American research team members coded the descriptions using the Natural-Language Child Personality Lexicon developed collaboratively by the U.S. and Dutch teams. (See Havill, Allen, Halverson, & Kohnstamm, 1994, for coding procedures.) The lexicon is made up of categories based on the Five-Factor Adult Personality categories of Extraversion, Agreeableness, Conscientiousness, Emotional Stability, and Openness to Experience. All interviews were by appointment; a few were conducted in the home, but the vast majority were conducted at the university in an interview setting. All interviews were conducted by interviewers of same race, who recorded the entire interview. The interviews were transcribed verbatim and coded by the research team. One of the authors trained the coders and checked the coding for reliability.

Population of African Americans Studied

The Hampton Roads area of Virginia is a Standard Metropolitan Statistical Area of 1,396,107 people made up of the cities of Hampton, Newport News, and Poquoson, Williamsburg on the Peninsula, and Norfolk, Virginia Beach, Chesapeake, Portsmouth, and Suffolk on the Southside. There are also four rural counties in the Hampton Roads Standard Metropolitan Statistical Area: Gloucester, Mathews, James City County on the North or Peninsula side, and Isle of Wight on the south side. All these communities are within 30 minutes of Hampton University. The area is one of the fastest growing in Virginia, with a 19.2% growth rate from 1980 to 1990 as compared to 15.7% for the state of Virginia. The 1990 minority population in Hampton Roads was 34.1% as compared to 22.6% for the state of Virginia. The area is the home for a number of large military installations and several universities including two historically Black universities, which contribute to a broad distribution of socioeconomic status among the African Americans living in the Hampton Roads area. Consequently this is an excellent region to study diversity in African Americans.

HOW SOCIAL CLASS MODERATES AFRICAN AMERICAN PARENTAL DESCRIPTIONS

The Hampton Sample

This sample represented our first data from parental interviews for 205 African American children. We discuss two social-class subsamples. The first group, labeled the *middle-class sample*, consisted of a diverse group of parents describing their children. Parents of 149 African American children were recruited from working-class neighborhoods, public schools, and preschool programs and from Hampton University and other nearby university communities. This group of parents was very diverse in education and occupation level. For example, of 139 parents, 2 had less than a high school education, 20 had graduated from high school, 46 had some college (2 years or less), 46 had completed a bachelor's degree, 19 had completed master's degrees, and 6 held doctorate degrees.

The group labeled the *low socioeconomic (SES) sample* consisted of parents who lived in public housing projects and worked at unskilled jobs. Many of these parents had not moved into the active workforce. The social-class comparisons made here are between a diverse group of African Americans labeled "middle class" and the low SES group (public housing). Comparisons were then made to the international samples presented in this book. Thus, we made what Ogbu (1981) discussed as a class and caste distinction (between mobile and immobile poor).

International Consortium Samples

Since the international data set has been described in detail in the other chapters, we do not discuss those differences here. Rather, we show the comparison data from the two Hampton subsamples with the samples from seven research teams in seven countries (United States, Netherlands, Belgium, Germany, Poland, Greece, and China). Table 9.1 shows these comparisons. The Georgia sample size ($N = 400$) was different from the data set for Georgia presented in the other chapters of this book. As our interviewing procedures were similar, we used the entire Georgia sample when making comparisons. Values shown are mean percentages for total descriptors across clusters for each factor. Before performing ANOVAs, data were normalized using an arcsine transformation, although for clarity, all means are presented as raw proportions.

Some Preliminary Findings

There were no differences between the two Hampton samples for parent gender, child gender, or age of child. There were, however, large differences in the number of descriptors that parents used across the two African American social-class groups, with middle-class parents using significantly more descriptors across all personality categories than did the public housing parents (middle-class group, $N = 149$, $M = 13.2\%$; Low SES group, $N = 56$, $M = 7.0\%$, $F = 75.10$, $p < .0001$). Social class accounted for a large amount of the variance in the number of descriptors that

TABLE 9.1

Proportions of Descriptors Categorized in Hampton Sample Compared to Main Categories of Coding Scheme for Other Countries

	Belgium	Holland	Germany	Greece	China	Poland	U.S.A. (N = 400)	Hampton Middle Class (N = 149)	Hampton Public Housing (N = 56)
					Percentage				
I. Extraversion	27.7	28.5	29.9	25.0	27.2	29.7	29.0	32.7	33.7
II. Agreeableness	19.6	18.9	21.3	25.5	17.4	23.7	21.2	19.2	24.9
III. Conscientiousness	7.9	6.8	8.3	10.7	19.4	8.1	8.3	5.5	2.4
IV. Emotional Stability	9.2	9.9	8.0	8.7	7.1	8.4	7.9	5.7	2.7
V. Openness-Intellect	12.6	12.2	17.6	11.1	14.1	11.5	19.9	20.1	15.5

African American parents used to describe their children (η^2 was .27). We compared the number of descriptors used by African American parents with the predominantly White Georgia sample and found no difference between the African American middle-class group and the Georgia sample (Hampton middle-class group, M = 13.2%; Georgia, M = 14.2%, F = 2.82, n.s.). The difference between the Georgia dominant-culture sample and the African American Low SES group, however, was statistically significant (Georgia M = 14.2%; Hampton low SES group, M = 7.0%, F = 73.24, p < .0001). The effect size was again quite large between the Hampton low SES sample and the Georgia middle-class sample (η^2 was .14). The effect size between the African American social-class groups (27%) was nearly twice as large as the effect size between the White middle-class group and the African American low SES group (14%), a finding indicating that, in these samples, social class contributed more than did race to the number of descriptors parents used to describe their children.

There were no statistically significant differences for the dimensions of Extraversion and Agreeableness between the two Hampton social-class groups. There were significant differences between the number of personality descriptors that African American parents differing in social class used to describe their children in the categories of Conscientiousness, Emotional Stability, and Openness to Experience. We now focus on these dimensions and present the results of the comparisons between the African American social-class samples and the Georgia dominant-culture middle-class sample.

Conscientiousness. African American middle-class parents used more Conscientiousness descriptors when describing their children than did the low SES parents (middle-class sample M = 5.5%; low SES sample, M = 2.4%, F = 9.04, p < .003), although the effect size was rather modest (η^2 = .043). Dominant-culture parents used more Conscientiousness descriptors than did African American middle-class parents (Georgia M = 8.3%; Hampton middle-class sample M = 5.5%, F = 14.09, p < .0002), although the effect size was again small (η^2 = .025). The difference between the number of Conscientious descriptors used by White middle-class parents was greater than for low SES African American parents (Georgia M = 8.3%; Hampton low SES sample M = 2.4%, F = 31.58, p < .0001). The effect size was more meaningful (η^2 = .065).

What was the effect of our social-class grouping when making cross-cultural comparisons with the international consortium samples? For the Conscientious dimension, an analysis of Hampton parents (when making comparisons with the total sample, N = 205) was statistically different from all the countries and, for many of these differences, the effect sizes were substantial (Poland, .031; Netherlands, .046; Georgia, .050; Belgium,

.058; Germany, .092; Greece, .096; and China .298). When the low SES group was removed, the differences between Poland and Netherlands disappeared, and the effect size was decreased below 4% for Georgia, Belgium, Germany, and Greece. The difference between China and Hampton remained strong (η^2 = .233, a decrease of 6.5%). There is no way to disentangle the effects of social class and cultural differences in these data. It is difficult, therefore, to create *comparable* social-class distinctions in all the international consortium samples.

Emotional Stability. The pattern of results was quite similar for the way African American parents used Emotional Stability descriptors to describe their children (middle-class M = 5.7%; low SES sample M = 2.7%, F = 8.03, p < .005), and the effect size was modest (η^2 = .038). Again, White parents used more Emotional Stability descriptors than did African American middle-class parents (Georgia M = 7.9%; Hampton middle-class sample M = 5.7%, F = 10.96, p < .001), and the effect size was again small (η^2 = .020). Similarly, the difference between the number of Emotional Stability descriptors used by White middle-class parents was greater than that for low SES African American parents (Georgia M = 7.9%; Hampton low SES M = 2.7%, F = 28.07, p < .0001), and the effect size was larger (η^2 = .058).

Analyses of Emotional Stability showed that Hampton parents (when making comparisons with the total sample, N = 205) used fewer descriptors than did parents in *all* the countries, and for many of these differences the effect sizes were substantial (China, .024; Poland, .036; Georgia, .041; Greece, .079; Belgium, .099; Germany, .102; and Netherlands, .132). When the low SES group was removed, the differences between China, Poland, and Georgia disappeared, and the effect sizes decreased by 3.4 to 4.3% for Greece, Belgium, Germany, and Netherlands. The difference between Netherlands and Hampton, however, remained strong (η^2 = .089).

Openness to Experience. African Americans differing in social class showed a small but statistically significant difference in the use of Openness to Experience descriptors when describing their children. The effect size was, however, less than 2% (middle-class M = 20.1%; low SES M = 15.5%, F = 3.81, p < .05, η^2 = .018). The difference between the means for the African American middle-class and White middle-class parents was not statistically significant. Finally, White parents used more Openness to Experience descriptors than did low SES African American parents when describing their children (Georgia M = 18.9%; Hampton low SES M = 15.5%, F = 4.92, p < .03, η^2 = .011). Social class had a statistically significant but very weak effect both in African American samples and between race samples.

The proportion of Openness to Experience descriptors for the total Hampton sample when compared with the total consortium sample showed that there were no differences between Georgia, Germany, China, Belgium, and Netherlands. There were statistically significant differences, however, for Greece and Poland. The effect sizes were small ($\eta^2 = .039$ and .040, respectively). When the low SES group was removed, differences were greater, and China, Belgium, and Netherlands showed statistically significant differences from Hampton. The effect sizes were small (from 1 to 1.5%).

CONCLUSIONS

These data illustrate that social class, particularly extreme poverty that might be defined by immobility, moderated the way parents described their children. We believe that our social-class comparisons were very conservative in that our middle-class sample was fairly heterogeneous in education. As we complete our free-description sample, we will be able to make some finer social-class comparisons. Some of the reported differences were moderated by social class but less so by ethnicity. The largest effect was found for Conscientiousness. African American middle-class parents used more Conscientiousness descriptors when describing their children than did low SES parents (a modest social class within-race effect, 4.3%), and White middle-class parents used more Conscientious descriptors than did African American middle-class parents when describing their children (a weak race effect, 2.5%). Of course, White middle-class parents used more Conscientiousness descriptors than did low SES African American parents. Inclusion of the poor sample increased the differences between the Hampton sample and those of other countries, from 2.5% (Georgia) to 6.5% (China). The greatest differences were between the Chinese sample and the Hampton sample. Chinese parents used many more Conscientiousness descriptors than did anyone else when describing their children. The Hampton sample provided fewest Conscientious descriptors of any sample, and, in the African American sample, poor parents mentioned Conscientiousness less frequently than did the higher SES sample. These results dramatically illustrate how our free-description methodology was sensitive to an important class-related dimension in a subsample of Americans. The salience of Conscientiousness, although low for U.S. parents generally when compared with other countries, was even lower for poor, inner-city African Americans. The importance of this low level of salience might be obvious in that there is much research linking social mobility to school success and achievement-related themes of which Conscientiousness is a part. It appears that as social mobility becomes important in middle-class samples and in emerging industrialized countries, Conscientiousness can become increasingly salient as a dimension for describing children.

The interpretation for Emotional Stability descriptors is similar to that of Conscientiousness: Middle-class African American parents used more Emotional Stability descriptors when describing their children than did low-SES African American parents. White middle-class parents used even more Emotional Stability descriptors than did African American middle-class parents when describing their children. In contrast, when controlling for social class, African American parents used Openness to Experience descriptors in a way more similar to their White American counterparts.

Although we recognize that many effect sizes were rather small, we believe that our research question is worth pursuing and that these data lend some support to the usefulness of a homogenous design to study within-group differences in African American children. The differences might be rather conservatively estimated as our comparison group was somewhat diverse in social class. Contrasts between immobile poor and highly educated African Americans might show even greater differences than we found, and these differences might be stronger when making comparisons with middle-class White parents. A number of authors have noted the complexity of understanding the socioeconomic status differences between African American and U.S. White samples (Entwisle & Astone, 1994; Hauser, 1994; Mueller & Parcell, 1981). In the current data set, it appears that the differences in social class were greater between the White and Black samples than they were in the African American sample.

An immobile poor African American family is likely to live in a high-risk environment. Baldwin, Baldwin, and Cole (1990) used four variables to measure distal risk in families: family occupation level, family education level, minority status, and absence of the father. They found that high-risk families were more restrictive, more severe in punishment, less democratic, and reasoned less with their children than did low-risk families. Parents in high-risk families ranked Kohn's (1977) 13 values differently from parents in low-risk families. The primary value in the high-risk group was Obedience, followed by Honest and Good manners. With our coding system, all three values would be scored in the dimension of Agreeableness. The three lowest ranked values were Interested in how things work, Peer sociability, and Neat and clean. These values would be coded as Openness to experience, Extraversion, and Conscientiousness, respectively. In contrast, low-risk parents ranked Honest, Considerate, and Responsible as their highest values. The first two would be coded as Agreeableness, while Responsible falls in the category of Conscientiousness. Their lowest ranked values were Behaves the way a boy (or girl) should, Neat and clean, and Good manners. As these two groups differed in what they valued in a child, we might also expect to find social-class differences in the way children are described by their parents. Findings like these show the link between values and personality characteristics that families use to describe their children. Lower-class or at-risk families might find themselves in very different environments and circumstances in which different behaviors and personal characteristics promote resilience and success. When a larger sample is complete, we hope to begin to disentangle social class from racial differences.

ACKNOWLEDGMENTS

This project was supported by Grant RO1 MH53272-01 from the National Institute of Mental Health. The authors are indebted to Janice Bell, Derrick Franklin, Kelly Y. Lane, and Cathy Turner for their dedicated work in conducting the interviews and scoring the data.

REFERENCES

Achenbach, T. M., & Edelbrock, C. (1981). Behavioral problems and competencies reported by parents of normal and disturbed children aged four to sixteen. *Monographs of the Society for Research in Child Development, 46* (Serial No. 188).

Achenbach, T. M., Howell, C. T., Quay, H. C., & Connors, C. K. (1991). National Survey of problems and competencies among four to sixteen-year-olds. *Monographs of the Society for Research in Child Development, 56* (Serial No. 225).

Baldwin, A. L., Baldwin, C., & Cole, R. E. (1990). Stress-resistant families and stress-resistant children. In J. Rolf, A. S. Masten, D. Cicchetti, K. H. Nuechterlein, & S. Weintraub (Eds.), *Risk and protective factors in the development of psychopathy* (pp. 257–280). Cambridge, England: Cambridge University Press.

Berreman, G. D. (1972). Social categories and interaction in urban India. *American Anthropologist, 74,* 567–586.

Blassingame, J. W. (1971). *The slave community.* New York: Oxford Press.

Bracht, G. H., & Glass, G. V. (1968). The external validity of experiments. *American Educator Research Journal, 5,* 437–474.

Campbell, D. T., & Stanley, J. C. (1963). Experimental and quasi-experimental designs for research on teaching. In N. L. Gage (Ed.), *Handbook of research on teaching* (pp. 171–246). Chicago: Rand McNally.

Caplan, N., & Nelson, S. D. (1973). On being useful: The nature and consequences of psychological research on social problems. *American Psychologist, 28,* 199–211.

Carey, W. B., & McDevitt, S. C. (Eds.). (1989). *Clinical and educational applications of temperament research.* Amsterdam/Lisse: Swets & Zeitlinger.

Chess, S., & Thomas, A. (1984). *Origins and evolution of behavior disorders.* New York: Brunner/Mazel.

Davidson, A. R., Jaccard, J. J., Triandis, H. C., Morales, M. L., & Diaz-Guerrero, R. (1976). *International Journal of Psychology, 11,* 1–3.

Dent, H. E. (1976). Assessing Black children for mainstream placement. In R. L. Jones (Ed.), *Mainstreaming the minority child* (pp. 77–91). Minneapolis: University of Minnesota Press.

Dent, H. E. (1996). Nonbiased assessment or realistic assessment. In R. L. Jones (Ed.), *Handbook of tests and measurements for black populations* (pp. 103–122). Hampton, VA: Cobb & Henry.

Digman, J. M. (1990). Personality structure: Emergence of the five factor model [Special issue]. In M. R. Rosenzweig & L. W. Porter (Eds.), *Annual Review of Psychology, 41,* 417–440.

Digman, J. M., & Inouye, J. (1986). Further specification of five robust factors of personality. *Journal of Personality and Social Psychology, 50*, 116–123.

Digman, J. M., & Takemoto-Chock, N. K. (1981). Factors in the natural language of personality: Re-analysis, comparison, and interpretation of six major studies. *Multivariate Behavioral Research, 16*, 149–170.

Entwisle, D. R., & Astone, N. M. (1994). Some practical guidelines for measuring youth's race/ethnicity and socioeconomic status. *Child Development, 65*, 1521–1540.

Eysenck, H. J., & Eysenck, S. B. C. (1975). *Manual of the Eysenck Personality Questionnaire*. London: Hodder & Stoughton; San Diego: EDITS.

Garcia-Coll, C., Lamberty, G., Jenkins, R., McAdoo, H. P., Crnic, K., Wasik, B. H., & Vasquez-Garcia, H. (1996). An integrative model for the study of developmental competencies in minority children. *Child Development, 67*, 1891–1914.

Garmezy, N., & Masten, A. (1991). The protective role of competence indicators in children at risk. In E. M. Cummings, A. L. Green, & K. H. Karraker (Eds.), *Life span developmental psychology: Prospective on stress and coping* (pp. 151–174). Hillsdale, NJ: Lawrence Erlbaum Associates.

Genovese, E. (1974). *Roll, Jordan, roll: The world the slaves made*. New York: Pantheon Books.

Goldberg, L. R. (1993). The structure of phenotype personality traits. *American Psychologist, 48*, 26–34.

Gordon, T. (1976). Notes on white and black psychology. *Journal of Social Issues, 29*, 87–95.

Guthrie, R. V. (1976). *Even the rat was white: A historical view of psychology*. New York: Harper & Row.

Gutman, H. G. (1976). *The black family in slavery and freedom 1750–1925*. New York: Random House.

Hauser, R. M. (1994). Measuring socioeconomic status in studies of child development. *Child Development, 65*, 1541–1545.

Havill, V. L., Allen, K., Halverson, C. F., Jr., & Kohnstamm, G. A. (1994). Parents' use of Big Five Categories in their natural language descriptions of children. In C. F. Halverson Jr., G. A. Kohnstamm, & R. P. Martin (Eds.), *The developing structure of temperament and personality from infancy to adulthood* (pp. 371–386). Hillsdale, NJ: Lawrence Erlbaum Associates.

Herskowitz, M. (1941). *Myth of the Negro past*. Boston: Beacon Press.

Hogan, R. (1991). Personality and personality measurement. In M. D. Dunnette & L. M. Hough (Eds.), *Handbook of industrial and organizational psychology* (2nd ed., Vol. 2; pp. 873–919). Palo Alto, CA: Consulting Psychology Press.

Howard, A., & Scott, R. A. (1981). The study of minority groups in complex societies. In R. H. Monroe, R. L. Monroe, & B. B. Whiting, *Handbook of cross cultural human development* (pp. 113–152). New York: Garland.

Hultsch, D. F., & Hickey, T. (1978). External validity in the study of human development: Theoretical and methodological issues. *Human Development, 21*, 76–91.

John, O. P. (1990). The "Big Five" factor taxonomy: Dimensions of personality in the natural language and in questionnaires. In L. A. Pervin (Ed.), *Handbook of personality: Theory and research* (pp. 66–100). New York: Guilford.

Kohn, M. L. (1977). *Class and conformity: A study in values* (2nd ed.). New York: Plenum.

Kohnstamm, G. A., Bates, J. E., & Rothbart, M. K. (Eds.). (1989). *Temperament in childhood*. Chichester, England: Wiley.

Masten, A. S. (1994). Resilience in individual development: Successful adaptation despite risk and adversity. In M. Wang & E. Gordon (Eds.), *Educational resilience in inner-city America: Challenges and prospects* (pp. 3–25). Hillsdale, NJ: Lawrence Erlbaum Associates.

McLoyd, V. C. (1990). Minority children: Introduction to the special issue. *Child Development, 61*, 263–266.

McLoyd, V. C., & Randolph, S. (1985). Secular trends in the study of Afro-American children: A review of child development. In A. B. Smuts & J. W. Hagen (Eds.), *History and research in child development. Monographs of the Society for Research in Child Development, 50* (4–5, Serial No. 211).

Mueller, C. W. & Parcell, T. L. (1981). Measures of socioeconomic status: Alternatives and recommendations. *Child Development, 52,* 13–30.

Myers, H. F., Rana, P. G., & Harris, M. (1979). *Black child development in America 1927–1977.* Westport, CT: Greenwood Press.

Ogbu, J. U. (1978). Minority education and caste: *The American system in cross-cultural perspective.* New York: Academic Press.

Ogbu, J. U. (1981). Origins of human competence: A cultural ecological perspective. *Child Development, 52,* 413–429.

Ogbu, J. U. (1994). From cultural differences to differences in cultural frame of reference. In R. M. Greenfield & R. R. Cocking (Eds.), *Cross-cultural roots of minority child development* (pp. 365–391). Hillsdale, NJ: Lawrence Erlbaum Associates.

Parke, R. D., & Asher, S. R. (1983). Social and personality development. *Annual Reviews of Psychology, 34,* 465–509.

Pike, R. (1966). *Language in relation to a unified theory of the structure of human behavior.* The Hague: Mouton.

Powell, G., Yamamoto, J., Romero, A., & Morales, A. (Eds.). (1983). *The psychosocial development of minority group children.* New York: Brunner/Mazel.

Quay, H. C., & Peterson, R. R. (1987). *The Revised Behavior Problem Checklist.* Unpublished manual, University of Florida, Coral Gables.

Strelau, J. (1991). Renaissance in research on temperament: Where to? In J. Strelau & A. Angleitner (Eds.), *Explorations in temperament: International perspectives on theory and measurement* (pp. 337–358). New York: Plenum.

Thomas, A., & Chess, S. (1977). *Temperament and development.* New York: Brunner/Mazel.

Triandis, H. C. (1976). *Variations in black and white perceptions of the social environment.* Urbana: University of Illinois Press.

Triandis, H. C. (1989). The self and social behavior in differing cultural contexts. *Psychological Review, 96,* 506–520.

Tulkin, S. R. (1968). Race, class, family and school achievement. *Journal of Personality and Social Psychology, 9,* 31–37.

Valentine, C. A. (1971). Deficit, difference and bicultural models of Afro-American behavior. *Harvard Educator Review, 41,* 137–157.

Victor, J. B. (1994). The Five Factor Model applied to individual differences in school behavior. In C. F. Halverson Jr., G. A. Kohnstamm, & R. P. Martin (Eds.), *The developing structure of temperament and personality from infancy to adulthood* (pp. 355–366). Hillsdale, NJ: Lawrence Erlbaum Associates.

Victor, J. B., & Halverson, C. F., Jr. (1975). Distractibility and hypersensitivity. *Journal of Abnormal Child Psychology, 3,* 83–94.

Victor, J. B., & Halverson, C. F., Jr. (1976). Behavior problems in elementary school children: A follow up study. *Journal of Abnormal Child Psychology, 4,* 17–29.

Washington, E. D., & McLoyd, V. C. (1982). The external validity of research involving American minorities. *Human Development, 25,* 324–339.

Werner, E. E., & Smith, R. S. (1982). *Vulnerable but invincible: A longitudinal study of resilience in children and youth.* New York: Marrow Hill.

Wiese, M. R. (1992). Racial/ethnic minority research in school psychology. *Psychology in the Schools, 29,* 267–272.

Windle, M. (1989). Temperament and personality: An exploratory inventory study of the DOTS-R, EASI-II, and EPI. *Journal of Personality Assessment, 53,* 487–501.

Windle, M., & Lerner, R. M. (1986). Reassessing the dimensions of temperament individuality across the life span: The Revised Dimensions of Temperament Survey (DOTS-R). *Journal of Adolescent Research, 1,* 213–230.

Validity of Results Obtained by Analyzing Free Personality Descriptions

Ivan Mervielde
University of Ghent

THE SCIENTIFIC STATUS OF FREE DESCRIPTIONS

The lexical personality paradigm considers personality-descriptive terms listed in dictionaries to be the main database for research on the Big Five taxonomy. The rationale for using the dictionary as the definitive database is that lexical researchers believe the importance of a trait to be proportional to the number of terms in a language used to encode it (Goldberg, 1981). Most language speakers obviously use only a small subset of the traits listed in the dictionary, however. Therefore, we tend to agree with Pervin's (1994) criticism of the lexical approach in which he claimed that trait adjectives as a category were not sufficient to capture all the meaning of our person-descriptive language.

Claeys, De Boeck, Van Den Bosch, Biesmans, and Bohrer (1985) were among the first investigators to study the concurrent validity of free personality descriptions by comparing free self-descriptions with more traditional methods of personality assessment. John (1990) also studied the structure of free personality descriptions and illustrated that the factors emerging from a factor analysis of ratings based on free descriptions were very similar to the Big Five dimension arising from a factor analysis of trait adjectives. Similarly, Mervielde (1994) classified teachers' personal constructs about individual differences among children and showed that about 60% of these constructs were part of the trait adjectives in the Dutch Abridged Big Five Circumplex Model (AB5C) taxonomy (Hofstee & De

Raad, 1991). Both these studies, however, focused only on trait adjectives and ignored other potentially useful descriptive information contained in free descriptions of personality.

There are several reasons that the study of free descriptions of personality could increase or enhance the validity of personality measurement of children. In comparison with the lexical approach, free descriptions sample the active- instead of the passive-person descriptive vocabulary. The *active* personality vocabulary (the one actually used by an informant) is certainly more limited in size, but the major question to be answered is whether the scope of free descriptions is broader or narrower than that of trait-descriptive adjectives culled from dictionaries. Moreover, the *passive* personality lexicon is for the most part less salient overall, plays a minor role in encoding experiences, and might, therefore, be less suitable as a cue for the retrieval of stored person-related information than is the active vocabulary. An obvious disadvantage of free descriptions is that each informant is bound to provide a selective and personally biased description of the target person. This criticism, however, applies only to analysis of single-person descriptions. The analysis of cumulative samples of free descriptions is less susceptible to perceiver-directed selectivities.

Free descriptions of children consisted of short sentences or utterances referring to one or more personality terms or perhaps to none at all. Although it is not obvious to which trait adjective descriptions such as Likes to watch television, Enjoys video games, and Never finishes his meal refer, it would be premature to reject these as personality-irrelevant items. Free descriptions are, to some extent, comparable to questionnaire items inasmuch as they are less abstract and more contextual and conditional than are trait adjectives. They differ from questionnaire items because they are not intended to reflect some underlying theoretical concept and therefore tend to be more varied in both content and grammatical structure.

Another important difference between the lexical approach, based on trait adjectives culled from dictionaries, and the analysis of free descriptions is that lexical analysis is sensitive only to the range of personality terms for a given trait dimension. Analysis of free descriptions can take into account both range *and* frequency of use. A dimension for which only a few but frequently used terms are available can be given equal weight to one for which there are many different but rarely used terms. Mervielde's (1994) analysis of teachers' personal constructs showed that although there was an overall similarity in the outcomes of both procedures (the dictionary approach and free descriptions), interesting differences remained. In Dutch, the AB5C category A+E+, combining terms loading primarily on Agreeableness and also substantially on Extraversion, was the largest AB5C category, containing 28 terms (De Raad,

Hendriks, & Hofstee, 1994). Only a few of these terms, however, tended to be used by teachers, but with a very high frequency. Extraversion (E+E+) on the other hand was a small AB5C category composed of only three terms, but these terms had the second largest frequency of use for teachers.

Cross-Cultural and Developmental Sensitivity

One of the most obvious advantages of a free-description methodology is of course that it yields a sample of natural-language personality descriptions not framed in the language proposed by the researcher (top-down), but rather in the language preferred by lay perceivers to encode their everyday experiences (bottom-up). This technique can be readily adopted in different cultures and guarantees a more emic approach to personality assessment. The comparability across cultures can be assured by adopting a common classification system while the classification itself remains sensitive to culture-specific behaviors and meanings.

Free descriptions tend to be phrased in behavioral terms, whereas the specification of the contextual and behavioral referents implicit in a trait adjective must be provided by the rater. Because free descriptions often include an explicit behavioral referent, their classification often depends less on the implicit personality theory of the rater or the judge than do trait adjectives. Free descriptions are more embedded in a specific culture or subculture and are more likely to yield culture-specific manifestations of traits. An analysis of the structure of free descriptions in many cultures should provide an additional, culturally sensitive, stringent test of the universality of the Big Five.

Developmental psychologists have stressed age-specific changes in children's behavioral repertoire. It is hard to imagine how these shifts in behavioral repertoire can be adequately captured by trait adjectives. A trait such as Extraversion can be inferred from different age-specific behaviors in the course of development. Whether trait adjectives can capture developmental variance is ultimately an empirical question, but the odds are probably in favor of behavioral descriptions as the best way to delineate and mark developmental trends.

CONTENT VALIDITY OF FREE DESCRIPTIONS

To evaluate to what extent the content of free personality descriptions is representative of the person-descriptive language is a difficult task because there is no consensus about the target domain of personality-descriptive language. Traditional lexical research has restricted the domain to trait adjectives although some researchers have argued that verbs and nouns can be included as well (De Raad & Hoskens, 1990; De Raad, Mulder, Kloosterman, & Hofstee, 1988). Moreover, the free descriptions used in this collaborative research project were a sample of a rather broadly defined domain. Because the free-description method was chosen as an alternative to using trait adjectives, it seemed appropriate to compare free descriptions to the dimensions that have emerged from the lexical analysis of trait adjectives. Questionnaires or rating scales based on the trait-adjective approach have been constructed to cover each of the five broad domains; free descriptions were expected to cover at least the same content.

The collected free descriptions for each of the collaborating research groups were classified by trained judges into 14 major categories. The first 5 of these corresponded to the Big Five dimensions emerging from lexical research based on trait adjectives. The correspondence in terms of content can be assessed in at least two ways: first, a collective strategy, calculating the percentage of free descriptions that was classified as instances of the Big Five, aggregated over all children in a particular sample and disregarding individual differences among children and parental informants; second, an individual strategy, calculating for each parent–child pair how many of the Big Five categories were used at least once and eventually assessing which combinations or patterns of categories were used to describe the child.

Assessing the content validity by the collective strategy revealed that from 77 to 85% of the parental descriptors were classified by the different teams as instances of the first five categories (see chapter 1, this volume). The remaining nine categories accounted for only a small number of descriptors. Evidently the first five categories were broader than the remaining eight content categories. Each of the first five categories has three facets that are further subdivided in three segments—positive (high end), neutral, negative (low end)—thus bringing the total number of subcategories to 45. Eight of the remaining nine categories are subdivided in positive, neutral, and negative subcategories, bringing that total to 25, including Category XIV, Ambiguous Descriptors. Each of the participating research groups obtained a percentage of Big Five classified descriptors higher than the expected 64%, a result that confirmed the importance of these categories for covering the content of free parental personality descriptors. Of course, one cannot rule out that the non-Big Five categories were less well chosen and that another set of categories might change the distribution of descriptors. The relatively small number of unclassified or ambiguous descriptors (see chapter 1, Table 1.2) indicated, however, that the eight additional categories were useful enough to code a sizable proportion of the descriptors. The fact that all seven research groups classified a higher than expected percentage of descriptors as instances of the first five broad categories underscores the cross-cultural saliency of the Big Five as categories for encoding parental perceptions of children's personality.

A major disadvantage of parental free descriptions is that they reflect the perspective of the parents and tend to cover only the salient characteristics of the children at a particular time. To assess the content validity at the individual level of analysis, Big Five category coverage for the 2,416 parental descriptions collected in the seven samples was assessed. For each described child, I counted how many of the first five categories were used at least once to describe the child. Table 10.1 lists the individual category coverage for the combined high- and low-end categories. A Big Five category was counted as covered *when at least one descriptor* was classified as an instance of one of the six (three high-end and three low-end) facets. Table 10.1 illustrates that category usage depends on the sample ($F = 41.5$ [5,2409] $p < .001$). For the U.S. sample, descriptions covering less than three categories were excluded (see note in Table 10.1). The average number of Big Five categories used at least once to describe a child varied from 3.41 for the Polish sample to 4.39 for the German sample. Only 8% of the U.S. parents used all five categories whereas 50% of the German parents and 42% of the Dutch parents used each of the Big Five categories in their free descriptions. A post hoc comparison of means with a Scheffé test showed three distinct, nonoverlapping country groupings: one combining the Polish and U.S. sample, one with China, Greece, Netherlands, and Belgium, and a third with the German sample.

TABLE 10.1
Percentage of Parents Referring With at Least One Descriptor
to Subsets of First Five (Big Five) Categories ($N = 2,416$)

Country	N	Percentage Big Five Category Usage					
		All 5	4 of 5	3 of 5	2 of 5	1 of 5	Average
Belgium	427	36.8	38.6	19.0	5.2	0.5	4.06
Netherlands	322	41.6	31.4	18.0	8.1	0.9	4.05
Germany	246	50.0	40.2	8.9	0.8	0.0	4.39
Greece	459	35.5	37.9	17.0	8.5	1.1	3.98
China	401	24.4	42.4	25.7	6.7	0.7	3.83
Poland	359	15.3	32.6	32.9	16.2	3.1	3.41
U.S.A.	202	7.9	31.2	60.4	0.5	0.0	3.46
Total Sample	2,416	30.9	36.9	24.1	7.2	1.0	3.89

Note. For the U.S. sample only those descriptions were selected that covered at least three out of five Big Five categories. See chapter 1 for an explanation. Evidently, one "2 out of 5" description was not eliminated.

The differences in coverage among the countries, as explained in chapter 1, was to some extent related to variability in interview length. It is not clear to what extent these differences in interview length and comprehensiveness were due to cultural and procedural differences. For example, the Chinese sample had overall short interviews, and yet the number of categories used was higher than in Poland or the United States, both of whom had, on the average, short interviews of similar length.

For the entire sample, and for most of the countries, the mode for the distribution of category usage in parental child descriptions was using four categories. Separate analysis for usage of high-end (positive) versus low-end (negative) categories showed that parents tended to generate a larger variety of high-end descriptors. Most parents described their children more in high-end than in low-end terms, and the high-end terms covered a broader spectrum of traits. Moreover, close to 31% of the parents provided at least one descriptor for all five of the first five categories.

Analysis of category usage for describing girls and boys showed that the number of Big Five categories used at least once did not depend on gender of the target ($F = 3.23$ [1,2414] n.s.). Category usage did change with the age of the child. The average number of categories used for the four age groups was 3.69, 3.83, 4.09, and 3.95 ($F = 18.65$ [3,2412] $p < .001$). Apparently, the increasing diversity of the children's behavioral repertoire was reflected in the expanded coverage of coded parental descriptions using the Big Five terms. A post hoc analysis of differences among age groups by means of a Scheffé test did not show distinct groups of countries.

The results reported in Table 10.1 confirmed the usefulness of the global analysis strategy. At the individual level, the classified free descriptions captured a broad range of Big Five-related content. Almost 68% of the parents referred to at least four out of the first five categories.

It would be premature, in view of the significant variation among parents in category usage, to consider the free-description method as a valid alternative diagnostic tool for questionnaires or rating scales. The vulnerability of such an approach was illustrated by the positively skewed distributions of the descriptors per category. For three of the five combined high- and low-end categories (III, IV, and V) the mode was zero descriptors. Only descriptors categorized as instances of Extraversion or Agreeableness had distributions low on skew. These results nicely confirmed the greater coverage, in terms of adjectives, observed in lexical research based on representative sets of traits (Peabody & Goldberg, 1989). The results also corroborated the importance assigned to Factors I and II in dyadic interactional models of personality such as the Wiggins circumplex structure (Wiggins & Trapnell, 1996).

The bias in category usage at the individual level should caution us about considering the free-description methodology as a content-valid procedure for individual diagnosis. The aggregated sample of descriptors, however, provided a highly differentiated collection of descriptors that covered a broad range of content in terms of the Big Five. Such a collection is a viable alternative to the dictionary approach for specifying the personality-descriptive language for children and a good starting point for delineating the range of perceived individual differences among children. Our results confirmed our original supposition that parental free descriptions can provide the basis for the development of new personality questionnaires tapping individual differences in children.

CONVERGENT VALIDITY OF FREE DESCRIPTIONS

Some indirect evidence for the convergent validity of the free descriptions can be derived from a comparison of age-related trends reported in chapter 7 and those obtained through other assessment methods. The age-related decrease in low Agreeableness descriptors, in particular those referring to Manageability, is compatible to the known decrease in scores on checklists for behavioral problems. The significant increase in both high and low Conscientiousness descriptors between ages 3 and 9, observed in almost all the countries, suggests that the demands introduced by the start of formal education at age 6 were reflected in the free parental descriptions. The high percentage of negative or low-end descriptors for Emotional Stability is compatible with the results of lexical studies showing a similar bias in the distribution of trait adjectives. Finally, the remarkable correspondence in the distribution of free descriptions over categories among the seven countries, as well as the similar age-related trends for many categories, surely confirms the convergent validity of the results of the free-description approach.

The most direct evidence for the convergent validity of the free descriptions requires, however, a comparison of classified free descriptions with other assessment methods on the same sample. Classification might provide some indication for the relevance of the five factors as dimensions for organizing natural-language personality description, but it has some methodological limitations. Judges tend to fit the segmented descriptors to the available categories. In principle, one cannot exclude the possibility that relevant categories were not part of the system. In fact, Category XIV (Ambiguous) was designed to provide for the possibility of new, emergent categories arising from the descriptors, that could not be classified by our coding scheme. The small proportion of descriptors classified as Ambiguous (Category XIV), however, suggested that no important categories were missing, nor did any new categories emerge from an analysis of the descriptors coded in XIV.

The classification of free descriptors is also at a low level of measurement that needs to be corroborated by measurement procedures that go beyond the nominal scale level. One way to accomplish this is by comparing the categorized free-description data with ratings of the same children on independently selected scales aimed at measuring the Big Five factors. Such a comparison was available for the entire Belgian sample.

After providing free descriptions, all Flemish parents rated their children on the B5BBS25, a Flemish set of 25 bipolar nine-point scales used to measure the Big Five personality factors (Mervielde, 1992). The Flemish scales together with their English translations are described in Table 10.2.

To avoid induction of terms, the bipolar rating scales were consistently presented *after* the natural-language descriptions had been given. Principal component analysis of the 25 scales suggested that six components could be extracted and rotated. One scale (unsteady-steady) had its high-

TABLE 10.2
Selected Flemish Bipolar Big Five Rating Scales (B5BBS-25)

Factor I: Extraversion
    EXT-1: *Bedeesd - zelfzeker* (Timid - self-confident)
    EXT-2: *Stil - spraakzaam* (Silent - talkative)
    EXT-3: *Onderdanig - assertief* (Submissive - assertive)
    EXT-4: *Geremd - spontaan* (Inhibited - spontaneous)
    EXT-5: *Introvert - extravert* (Introvert - extravert)
Factor II: Agreeableness
    AGR-1: *Koel - hartelijk* (Cold - warm)
    AGR-2: *Onvriendelijk - vriendelijk* (Unkind - kind)
    AGR-3: *Zelfzuchtig - onzelfzuchtig* (Selfish - unselfish)
    AGR-4: *Tegenwerkend - meewerkend* (Uncooperative - cooperative)
    AGR-5: *Strak - soepel* (Inflexible - flexible)
Factor III: Conscientiousness
    C1: *Onnauwkeurig - nauwkeurig* (Inaccurate - accurate)
    C2: *Achteloos - nauwgezet* (Negligent - conscientious)
    C3: *Nalatig - grondig* (Neglectful - thorough)
    C4: *Onzorgvuldig - zorgvuldig* (Careless - careful)
    C5: *Lui - ijverig* (Lazy - industrious)
Factor IV: Stability
    S1: *Zenuwachtig - rustig* (nervous - quiet)
    S2: *Nerveus - op zijn gemak* (Nervy - at ease)
    S3: *Gespannen - ontspannen* (Tense - relaxed)
    S4: *Onstandvastig - standvastig* (Unsteady - steady)
    S5: *Opvliegend - kalm* (Angry - calm)
Factor V: Intellect-Openness
    I1: *Onintelligent - intelligent* (Unintelligent - intelligent)
    I2: *Onverstandig - verstandig* (Insensible - sensible)
    I3: *Ongeïnteresseerd - leergierig* (Uninterested - eager to learn)
    O1: *Fantasieloos - fantasierijk* (Unimaginative - imaginative)
    O2: *Oncreatief - creatief* (Uncreative - creative)

est loading on the wrong factor, loading .46 on Intellect instead of loading on Stability. The six components were identified as Conscientiousness, Extraversion, Agreeableness, Stability, Intellect, and Openness. The traditional fifth factor bifurcated into scales tapping Intellect and Openness. The factorial structure of the scales was independently confirmed in a study of teacher ratings of more than 2,000 children of a similar age range (Mervielde, Buyst, & De Fruyt, 1995).

Relation Between Categorized Natural-Language Descriptions and Ratings

The relation between categorized free descriptions and ratings on bipolar scales was assessed by regressing the frequency of descriptors per category on factor scores for each of the six principal components. Each major category had three facets that were further subdivided into high, low, and neutral. This procedure yielded a total of nine predictor variables for each of the first five main categories. Table 10.3 reports the multiple regression coefficients resulting from this analysis.

Each of the five major categories was significantly related to the corresponding components derived from parents' ratings on the 25 bipolar scales. Extraversion, as measured by free descriptions, was most clearly related to Extraversion factor scores derived from bipolar scale ratings. The fifth main descriptive category was comprised of three facets: Intellect, Openness, and Interests. All three facets were regressed on the factor scores for Intellect and for Openness. This procedure might have accounted for the lower multiple correlation coefficients for the last two principal components. Although skewness of the free descriptions limited the magnitude of the correlations to some extent, all the observed multiple correlations were statistically significant and confirmed the convergent validity of free descriptions.

TABLE 10.3
Multiple Regression of B5BBS-25 Factor Scores on Descriptive Categories

Factor	Mult. R	F	P
Extraversion	.60	25.59	.001
Agreeableness	.44	11.23	.001
Conscientiousness	.53	19.98	.001
Emotional Stability	.30	4.70	.001
Intellect	.31	4.86	.001
Openness	.27	3.36	.001

Note. B5BBS-25: Big Five Flemish Bipolar Rating Scales (Mervielde, 1992). Mult. R = Multiple correlation.

TABLE 10.4
Multiple Regression of B5BBS-25 Factor Scores
on Descriptive Categories VI to XIII

Category		EXT	AGR	CON	STA	INT	OPE
VI	Independence	.10	.10	.09	.16**	.10	.14*
VII	Mature for Age	.08	.08	.20***	.05	.14*	.09
VIII	Illness, Handicaps	.04	.10	.08	.08	.09	.08
IX	Rhythmicity	.10	.07	.14*	.07	.12	.04
X	Gender Appropriate	.20***	.05	.08	.03	.07	.09
XI	School Performance	.14*	.12	.24***	.08	.27***	.11
XII	Desire to be Cuddled	.08	.10	.06	.05	.06	.14*
XIII	Relations With Siblings	.03	.19**	.08	.09	.08	.09

Note. B5BBS-25: Big Five Flemish Bipolar Rating Scales (Mervielde, 1992). AGR = Agreeableness; CON = Conscientiousness; EXT = Extraversion; INT = Intellect; OPE = Openness; STA = Emotional Stability.
*$p < .05$. **$p < .01$. ***$p < .001$.

The regression analysis for the other eight categories is reported in Table 10.4. This table shows that the multiple correlations between these additional eight categories and the factor scores on six principal components extracted from the ratings were substantially lower than those reported for the Big Five. Independence was related to both Emotional Stability and Openness. Descriptors referring to a child's maturity, in comparison to children of similar age, were related to ratings of Conscientiousness and Intellect. Maturity was best reflected by ratings of two factors that were the best predictors of school achievement: Conscientiousness and Intellect (Mervielde et al., 1995). Category VIII descriptors were totally unrelated to five-factor ratings and confirmed that parental references to illness and handicaps were unrelated to personality factors. The Rhythmicity descriptors were only marginally related to Conscientiousness ratings. In view of the low frequency of these descriptors, especially for children beyond age 3, it is hardly surprising that they were not related to personality factors underlying adult individual differences. Reference to gender-appropriate behavior was clearly related to Extraversion as rated by parents. Those who behaved in gender-appropriate ways were seen as more active, dominant, and social. School performance, as referenced in parental free descriptions, should be, and indeed was, related to Conscientiousness and Intellect (which have been found to be the best predictors of elementary school grade point average [GPA], Mervielde et al., 1995). The very small category labeled Desire to be cuddled was only marginally related to Openness ratings and therefore was not a good personality predictor, at least for the entire sample from ages 3 to 12. Whether this finding can be interpreted as a genuine effect or an artifact caused by the low frequency of this category (especially beyond age 3) is not yet clear. Finally, Relations With Siblings was a descriptive category that was significantly related to Agreeableness ratings. Children described as getting along with their siblings were rated as friendly and agreeable; those described as arguing and fighting with their siblings were rated as aggressive, unfriendly, and uncooperative.

Joint Principal Component Analysis of Free Descriptions and Ratings

Although the regression analysis reported in Tables 10.3 and 10.4 pointed toward a modest amount of common variance among natural-language descriptions and five-factor ratings, a joint principal component analysis of both types of variables provided the most compelling evidence for the shared variance in both assessment methodologies.

The coded free descriptions per category were converted to proportions by dividing them through the total number of descriptors reported by the parent about the child. To reduce the skewness in distributions as well as the number of near-empty cells, the facets were combined into high- and low-end categories for each of the first five main categories. This procedure effectively reorganized the categorized descriptions into 10 variables based on proportions of natural-language descriptors for both ends of the first five (Big Five) categories, summed over facets.

A joint principal component analysis including the 25 B5BBS-25 rating scales and the 10 proportions was conducted and rotated according to Kaiser's Varimax criterion. Inspection of the pattern of the eigenvalues suggested a five-factor solution.[1] The robustness of this structural representation was checked by separate principal component analysis for two random halves of the sample and within the subsamples of boys and girls. The loading matrix for the joint principal component analysis is shown in Table 10.5. Only 2 of the 25 rating scales had their highest loading on the wrong factor, but both had a substantial secondary loading on the intended factor. More important, all 10 variables based on proportions of free descriptors for both ends of the five main categories loaded on the expected factors. Further, the signs of the loadings were consistently opposite for the low- (evaluative negative) and for the high-end (evaluative positive) category proportions. Consistent with the results of the multiple regression analysis, the joint principal component analysis revealed that the proportions of free descriptors for Extraversion-Introversion loaded on the Extraversion factor almost as highly as did the rating

---

[1]The respective eigenvalues and percentages of explained variance were 5.79 (16.5%), 4.36 (12.5%), 3.13 (8.9%), 2.33 (6.6%), and 1.56 (4.5%).

TABLE 10.5
Joint Principal Component Analysis of Free
Descriptions and B5BBS-25 Rating Scales

Scale	CON	EXT	AGR	STA	INOP
C4: Careless-careful	.85	−.07	.17	.10	.01
C3: Neglectful-thorough	.84	.01	.08	.10	.04
C1: Inaccurate-accurate	.84	−.08	.03	−.01	.09
C2: Negligent-conscientious	.83	−.05	.08	.03	.01
C5: Lazy-industrious	.57	.15	.28	−.12	.11
PFD: Conscientiousness—low	−.54	.05	−.05	.10	.12
I3: Uninterested-eager to learn	.53	.17	−.09	.03	.37
PFD: Conscientiousness—high	.36	−.12	−.03	.14	.01
E5: Introvert-extravert	−.05	.77	.20	−.02	.10
E2: Silent-talkative	−.03	.76	.04	−.08	.18
E4: Inhibited-spontaneous	−.06	.73	.27	.02	.28
PFD: Extraversion—low	.08	−.70	.05	−.05	.07
E1: Timid–self-confident	.03	.63	−.12	.26	.27
PFD: Extraversion—high	.05	.51	−.04	.07	−.14
E3: Submissive-assertive	.03	.49	−.31	.12	.26
A2: Unkind-kind	−.01	.39	.66	−.01	.11
A4: Uncooperative-cooperative	.22	.01	.64	.08	.06
A3: Selfish-unselfish	.02	−.09	.62	.08	.10
A5: Inflexible-flexible	−.03	.34	.58	.15	.08
A1: Cold-warm	−.04	.46	.57	−.12	.14
S5: Angry-calm	.16	−.28	.56	.38	−.02
PFD: Agreeableness—low	−.16	.26	−.46	.03	−.09
PFD: Agreeableness—high	.02	−.01	.42	.02	−.26
S2: Nervy-at ease	.04	.04	.29	.77	.02
S1: Nervous-quiet	.08	−.15	.33	.75	−.01
S3: Tense-relaxed	.06	.19	.33	.74	.02
PFD: Stability—low	.08	−.08	.04	−.51	−.14
S4: Unsteady-steady	.33	.15	−.06	.36	.24
PFD: Stability—high	.02	.02	−.09	.26	−.01
O1: Unimaginative-imaginative	−.01	.18	.20	−.05	.75
O2: Uncreative-creative	.10	.14	.17	−.07	.72
PFD: Openness—high	−.01	−.09	−.02	.15	.55
I2: Unsensible-sensible	.39	.20	−.16	.37	.44
I1: Unintelligent-intelligent	.38	.15	−.20	.36	.42
PFD: Openness—low	−.02	−.09	−.11	−.09	−.15

Note. B5BBS-25: Big Five Flemish Bipolar Rating Scales (Mervielde, 1992). PFD = Proportion of free descriptions for the entire category. AGR = Agreeableness; CON = Conscientiousness; EXT = Extraversion; INOP = Intellect-Openness; STA = Emotional Stability.

scales. In general, however, the proportions of natural-language parental descriptors tended to have lower loadings than did the rating scales, although they never had substantial secondary loadings.

A surprising and interesting result was that the proportions of descriptors derived from the low end of the dimensions loaded in the expected factors higher than did the high-end descriptors (except for the fifth factor). One explanation for this pattern is that high-end parental descriptors tended to be evaluatively positive and socially desirable. Perhaps the positive descriptors were less informative and taken for granted. Once a parent confided less desirable information (introversion, disagreeableness, etc.) in the free description of the child, such information might have been more reliable and salient and hence more consistent with the parental ratings of the child on the bipolar scales.

DISCUSSION

Asking parents to describe their own children in natural language is for most parents an undemanding and pleasant task. It allows them to use their own frames of reference and supplies the researcher with much information that is important from the parental point of view. Such a task has a high degree of immediate relevance and is surely a welcome alternative to filling out lengthy questionnaires. In addition, parents are not forced to answer questions that they consider to be irrelevant or to guess about the meaning or the purpose of some of the questions. They do not have to worry about the researcher's hidden agenda. Once they begin talking about their child, they soon feel at ease with the interviewer and therefore might be willing to supply more information than they would otherwise. All these features of natural-language descriptions undoubtedly contribute to the high face validity of the free-description procedure.

The main limitation of the procedure is its lack of validity. Individual parental descriptions were likely to be selective or biased. Parents focused on a limited number of characteristics. Their selection of content was influenced by both the immediate saliency of certain characteristics and the personal constructs that guide their encoding and retrieval of person-descriptive information. Therefore, free descriptions cannot be considered as a valid procedure for complete personality assessment at the level of the individual. Most parents provided free-description information that was indicative of only two to four of the Big Five domains, but they had no problems in rating their children on each of the Big Five. A collection of free descriptions supplied by a representative sample of parents, however, is much less susceptible to this bias. Our free-description method was used (and intended) to collect information only at the group level.

The individual level of analysis was used in the present chapter, however, to assess some aspects of the convergent validity of the procedure.

The limited correspondence between free descriptions and personality ratings emerging from both the regression analysis and the joint principal component analysis can be attributed in part to the selectivity of the free descriptions and the ensuing positively skewed distributions of frequencies per category. Consequently, free descriptions might not be suitable as an individual diagnostic tool. Aggregated descriptions from a broad sample of parents, however, are a valuable tool to delineate the personality language used to describe individual differences among children. As such they can be considered as a database for the active parental personality language and as a workable alternative for the trait adjective lists derived from dictionaries. Moreover, there was some evidence for a link between free descriptions and ratings of the same child. Although the degree of association between both types of assessment was low and was impeded by the intrinsic measurement problems of free descriptions, it was nevertheless consistent across regression analysis and joint principal component analysis.

The correspondence between free descriptions and ratings on Big Five scales points to a common content tapped by both assessment tools and is a necessary but not sufficient condition for a common structure. Structural analysis of the content of free descriptions requires ratings of children on a common and representative set of items covering the content captured by the aggregated free descriptions. The outcome of these analyses will provide some necessary evidence for whether the Big Five framework can represent individual differences among children. The next phase of the project in each country is to develop questionnaires based on those items derived from parental descriptions, have parents rate children with them, and then assess the construct validity of these new instruments created from parental free descriptions.

REFERENCES

Claeys, W., De Boeck, P., Van Den Bosch, W., Biesmans, R., & Bohrer, A. (1985). A comparison of one free-format and two fixed-format self-report personality assessment methods. *Journal of Personality and Social Psychology, 49,* 1028–1039.

De Raad, B., Hendriks, A. A. J., & Hofstee, W. K. B. (1994). The Big Five: A tip of the iceberg of individual differences. In C. F. Halverson Jr., G. Kohnstamm, & R. P. Martin (Eds.), *The developing structure of temperament and personality from infancy to adulthood* (pp. 91–109). Hillsdale, NJ: Lawrence Erlbaum Associates.

De Raad, B., & Hoskens, M. (1990). Personality descriptive nouns. *European Journal of Personality, 4,* 131–146.

De Raad, B., Mulder, E., Kloosterman, K., & Hofstee, W. K. B. (1988). Personality descriptive verbs. *European Journal of Personality, 2,* 81–96.

Goldberg, L. R. (1981). Language and individual differences: The search for universality in personality lexicons. In L. Wheeler (Ed.), *Review of personality and social psychology* (Vol. 2; pp. 141–165). Beverly Hills, CA: Sage.

Hofstee, W. K. B., & De Raad, B. (1991). Persoonlijkheidsstructuur: De AB5C-taxonomie van Nederlandse eigenschapstermen [Personality structure: The AB5C-taxonomy of Dutch trait terms]. *Nederlands Tijdschrift Psychologie, 46*, 262–274.

John, O. P. (1990). The "Big Five" factor taxonomy: Dimensions of personality in the natural language and in questionnaires. In L. A. Pervin (Ed.), *Handbook of personality theory and research* (pp. 66–100). New York: Guilford Press.

Kohnstamm, G. A., Mervielde, I., Besevegis, I., & Halverson, C. F., Jr. (1995). Tracing the Big Five in parents' free descriptions of their children. *European Journal of Personality, 9*, 283–304.

Mervielde, I. (1992). The B5BBS-25: A Flemish set of bipolar markers for the "Big Five" personality factors. *Psychologica Belgica, 32*, 195–210.

Mervielde, I. (1994). A Five-Factor Model classification of teachers' constructs on individual differences among children age 4 to 12. In C. F. Halverson Jr., G. A. Kohnstamm, & R. P. Martin (Eds.), *The developing structure of temperament and personality from infancy to adulthood* (pp. 387–397). Hillsdale, NJ: Lawrence Erlbaum Associates.

Mervielde, I., Buyst, V., & De Fruyt, F. (1995). The validity of the Big-Five as a model for teachers' ratings of individual differences among children aged 4–12 years. *Personality and Individual Differences, 18*, 525–534.

Peabody, D., & Goldberg, L. R. (1989). Some determinants of factor structures from personality-trait descriptors. *Journal of Personality and Social Psychology, 57*, 552–567.

Pervin, L. A. (1994). A critical analysis of current trait theory. *Psychological Inquiry, 5*, 103–113.

Wiggins, J. S., & Trapnell, P. D. (1996). A dyadic-interactional perspective on the five-factor model. In J. S. Wiggins (Ed.), *The Five-Factor Model of personality: Theoretical perspectives* (pp. 88–162). New York: Guilford Press.

Appendix
Composition of the Seven Samples

Anne-Marie Slotboom
Leiden University

Eric Elphick
Leiden University

SAMPLES

Seven countries participated in this study: Belgium (Ghent), the Netherlands (Leiden), Germany (Bielefeld), Greece (Athens), China (Peking), United States of America (Georgia), and Poland (Wroclaw). Mothers, and sometimes also fathers, were asked to give a free-language personality description of their children. If fathers agreed to participate, both mothers and fathers were interviewed separately (detailed information about the coding of the free descriptions is given in chapter 1). The samples are shown with the name of the country in which they were collected. A detailed description of the samples follows.

TABLE A-1
Number of Fathers and Mothers in Each Participating Country

Age of Child	3	6	9	12	Total[a]
Gender of Parent	F/M	F/M	F/M	F/M	F/M
Belgium	18/76	16/79	14/80	18/65	66/300
The Netherlands	30/43	23/27	20/34	20/44	93/148
Germany	20/54	18/48	16/33	20/37	74/172
Greece	41/63	50/65	55/63	50/62	196/253
China	17/23	55/62	55/57	59/73	186/215
U.S.A.	18/29	13/38	8/30	10/32	49/129
Poland	23/65	20/71	12/68	25/75	80/279

Note. F = father; M = mother.

[a]In the comparison among age groups (chapter 7), included in the data analysis were only those children who ranged in age from 1 year below to 1 year above the age group in which they were classified, reducing the data set from N = 2,416 to 2,241. Therefore, the total shown in Table A-1 might be different from totals in other chapters.

TABLE A-2
Number of Descriptions of Boys and Girls in Each Participating Country

Age of Child	3	6	9	12	Total
Gender of Child	Boys/Girls	Boys/Girls	Boys/Girls	Boys/Girls	Boys/Girls
Belgium	41/53	38/57	50/44	45/39	174/193
The Netherlands	38/35	29/21	25/29	36/28	128/113
Germany	40/34	36/30	24/25	24/33	124/122
Greece	54/50	59/56	62/56	55/57	230/219
China	23/17	69/48	60/52	71/61	223/178
U.S.A.	21/26	24/27	16/22	20/22	81/97
Poland	45/43	48/43	40/40	48/52	181/178

Note. In some cases boys and girls were described by both father and mother. Therefore, the numbers do *not* reflect the number of different boys and girls but the number of descriptions.

TABLE A-3
Age of Child in Months

Age Group	3		6		9		12		Total	
Age of Child in Months	M	SD	M	SD	M	SD	M	SD	M	SD
Belgium	38	6	75	6	110	7	145	7	90	40
The Netherlands	39	5	81	3	116	4	147	5	94	43
Germany[a]	—	—	—	—	—	—	—	—	—	
Greece	41	6	72	9	110	9	139	6	92	37
China[a]	—	—	—	—	—	—	—	—	—	
U.S.A.	37	6	71	8	110	8	141	6	87	40
Poland[a]	—	—	—	—	—	—	—	—	—	

[a]Age in months was not coded; only age group was coded.

TABLE A-4
Demographic Data for Different Samples

	Area(s) Where Interviews Were Collected
Belgium	Ghent, Leuven, and surrounding areas (population range 30,000–100,000).
The Netherlands	Cities in western and southern parts of Netherlands (population range 30,000–100,000).
Germany	Bielefeld (± 330,000 inhabitants) areas.
Greece	Athens and surrounding areas.
China	Beijing (northern China) and Fuzhou, provincial capital of Fujian (southern China).
U.S.A.	Athens, Georgia (± 80,000 inhabitants) and surrounding areas.
Poland	Wroclaw (± 700,000 inhabitants), cities in vicinity of Wroclaw (population range 40,000–200,000).

PROCEDURE

In five of the seven countries, parents were interviewed in their homes. In Poland, parents were interviewed in a room of the school attended by their children. In the United States, parents were interviewed in a variety of settings. Although we do not know whether our results were influenced by these differences in settings, we decided to present general summaries of the results in an order that reflected, to some extent, differences in interview location. Results for the five at-home samples are described together where appropriate, and the two out-of-home samples are described together where appropriate. For each country, the procedure to approach and inform parents about the project, the location where the interviews were held, and the persons doing the interviews are summarized in Table A-5.

Parents were asked to give oral descriptions of their children's personalities. The interviews were audiotaped and transcribed. After transcription, the interview material was segmented into units, each unit consisting of a single person-descriptive characteristic. The interview procedure and coding instructions are fully described in chapter 1.

TABLE A-5
Procedure Followed in Each Country

	Parents Approached Through	Parents Informed by	Location of Interview	Interviews Conducted by
Belgium	Acquaintances/school	Orally	At home	Students
The Netherlands	Kindergarten/primary school	Letter	At home	PhDs
Germany	Announcements	Letter/orally	At home	Students
Greece	Kindergarten/primary school	Letter	At home	PhDs/students
China	Kindergarten/primary school	Orally	At home	PhDs/students
U.S.A.	School/day care centers/camps	Letter/orally	Variety of settings	PhDs/students
Poland	Kindergarten/primary school	Orally	At school	Students

INTERCODER RELIABILITY IN COUNTRIES

In each participating country, intercoder agreement was computed between two different coders by calculating the percentage of agreement
between both coders after consensus had been reached on the identification of descriptors to be coded. Intercoder agreement was computed at
four levels and ranged from the most general agreement over the 14 main
categories of the categorization system to agreement over all (categories
and facets $[5 \times 3] + 9 = 24$ categories), including agreement over assignment
to the high or low end of a subcategory (23×2) [high and low] + 1 [XIV]
= 47 categories; see Table A-6). As is shown in Table A-6, in all seven
countries the highest percentage of agreement was reached for agreement
over the 14 main categories. When subcategories were included, the
agreement was somewhat lower (the difference ranging between 0.7%
and 4.8%). The lowest percentage of agreement was found when the
direction of the coded descriptor (low, neutral [when coded], or high)
was also included. Even with a total of 47 categories, however (70 when
the neutral category was coded), agreement was in the 70 to 80% range
for most research terms.

TABLE A-6
Intercoder Reliabilities for Randomly Selected
Samples of Units of Expression in Seven Countries
(Percentages of Agreement Between Pair of Coders)

	Number of Expressions Coded	For 14 Categories	For 24 Categories	For 46 Categories (Exclusive of Category XIV)	For 47 Categories*
Belgium	1000	84.6	79.8	74.7[a]	63.6[a]
The Netherlands	610	88.7	86.7	83.4[a]	81.4[a]
Germany[b]					
Greece	400	93.7	93.0	91.2	87.8
China	568	98.9	95.6	87.2	*
U.S.A.	200	93.2	89.7	86.7[a]	74.9[a]
Poland	500	*	*	74.4	72.2

[a]In 69 and 70 categories respectively (descriptors were also coded as neutral).

[b]In Germany the intraclass correlation for the boys' data was .89; Cohen's κ for the girls' data was .69.

*Not computed.

Author Index

A

Achenbach, T. M., 95, *101*, 149, *150*, 174, 175, *185*
Ackerman, P. L., 106, *122*, *124*
Ahadi, S. A., 33, 36, 38, *44*, 47, 54, *61*, 70, 76, *82*, 112, *122*, 132, *151*, 158, 164, *165*
Akamine, T. X., 95, *102*
Allen, K., 178, *186*
Allport, G. W., 23, *44*, 88, *101*, 105, 107, *122*
Angleitner, A., 11, *18*, 23, 26, 35, 38, *44*, *46*, 68, 69, *84*, 90–92, *101–103*, 105, 106, 110, 111, *122*, *125*, 145, *152*
Asendorpf, J. B., 37, *44*, 128, *151*
Asher, S. R., 173, *187*
Astone, N. M., 173, 184, *186*
Ayoub, C., 53, *63*
Azuma, H., 131, *152*

B

Bacon, M. K., 160, *165*
Bain, A., 21, *44*
Baldwin, A. L., 56, *61*, 184, *185*
Baldwin, C., 56, *61*, 184, *185*
Bantelmann, J., 111, *125*
Barker, G., 116, *122*
Barry, H., 160, *165*
Bartusch, D. J., 35, *47*
Bates, J. E., 11, *18*, 53, *61*, 111, *124*, 130, 140, 150, *151*, *152*, 174, *186*
Bem, D. J., 54, *61*
Bergeman, C. S., 159, *165*
Berreman, G. D., 172, 173, *185*
Besevegis, E., 17, *19*
Best, D. L., 157, *167*
Biesmans, R., 189, *202*
Birch, H. G., 53, *64*

Bjorklund, D. F., 54, *61*
Blassingame, J. W., 171, *185*
Bleichrodt, N., 73, *82*
Block, J., 51, 52, 55, *61*, 74–76, *82*, 93, *101*, 114, *122*, *123*, 128, *151*
Block, J. H., 74, 76, *82*, 93, *101*, 114, *122*, 123, 128, *151*, 158, 160, 161, 164, *165*
Bloom, B., 128, *151*
Bohlin, G., 33, *46*, 130, *151*
Bohrer, A., 189, *202*
Bond, M. H., 81, *82*
Bontempo, R., 150, *153*
Borgatta, E. F., 51, *61*
Borkenau, P., 161, *165*
Bornholt, L., 131, *152*
Boyle, M. H., 54, *63*
Bracht, G. H., 170, *185*
Braley, K. W., 22, *46*
Brand, C., 106, *122*
Briggs, S. R., 36, *46*
Brokken, F. B., *44*, 105, 106, *123*
Bromley, D. B., 58, *63*
Bronson, W. C., 129, *151*
Burt, C., 32, *44*, 85–86, *101*
Busch, C. M., 51, 52, *63*, 74, *83*
Buss, A. H., 29, 33–38, *44*, *46*, 95–96, *101*, *102*, 111, *123*, 137, *151*, 161, *165*
Buss, D. M., 50, *61*, *62*
Buyst, V., 74, *84*, 113–114, 116, *124*, *203*

C

Cadwell, J., 73, *83*
Camac, C., 29, *48*
Campbell, D. T., 170, *185*
Campbell, J. D., 58, *64*
Campbell, S. B., 53, *61*
Caplan, N., 169, 171, *185*
Caprara, G. V., 90, *102*

211

Carey, W. B., 1–2, *18*, *19*, 72, *83*, 111, *123*, 174, *185*
Carrigan, P. M., 22, *44*
Cartwright, D. S., 67, *82*
Cashmore, J., 131, *151*
Caspi, A., 34, 35, *46*, 54, *61*, 74, 75, *83*, *84*, 94, *102*, *103*, 115, *123*, 124, *125*, 128, *152*
Castaneda, I., 3, *19*
Cattell, R. B., 23–24, 32, *44*, 50, *61*, 66, 72, *82*, 87–88, *102*, 105, 108–109, 117, *123*
Chen, C., 80, *84*, 144, *151*
Chess, S., 1–2, *19*, 32, 38, *46*, *47*, 53, *62*, 64, 71, 73, *84*, 111, *125*, 128, 129, 137, *152*, 173–174, *185*, *187*
Child, I. L., 160, *165*
Chipuer, H. M., 159, *165*
Christal, R. C., 26, *47*, 51, *64*, 67, *84*, 87, *103*, 109, 110, *125*
Church, A. T., viii, *x*, 3, 4, *18*, 95, *102*
Cillessen, A. H. N., *125*
Claeys, W., *202*
Clark, L. A., 33, 43, *47*, 85, 95, 96, *103*
Cloninger, C. R., 159, *165*, *167*
Coan, R. A., 32, *44*, 72, *82*
Coan, R. W., 107, *123*
Cole, R. E., 56, *61*, 184, *185*
Conley, J. J., 51, *61*
Connors, C. K., 174, *185*
Coplan, R. J., 37, *47*
Cosmides, L., 50, *61*
Costa, P. T., Jr., 4, *19*, 25n, 28, 29, 35, 38, *44*–*45*, *47*, 50–52, 59, *61*, *63*, 67–68, 74, 81, *82*, *83*, 92, *102*, 107, 109–110, 112, *123*, *124*, 127, 128, 143, *151*, *152*, 156, 159, 164, *165*
Cotton, S., 131, *151*
Crnic, K., 169, *186*

D

Daniels, D., 160, *167*
Davidson, A. R., 170, *185*
De Boeck, P., *202*
De Fruyt, F., 74, *84*, 111, 113–116, *123*–*125*, 159, *166*, *203*
Dent, H. E., 169, *185*
De Raad, B., 30, 31, 36, 38, *45*–*47*, 51, *61*, 89, 90, *102*, *103*, 105, 106, 110, *123*, *124*, 159, *166*, *202*, *203*
Derryberry, D., 54, *63*
Diamond, S., 22, *45*
Diaz-Guerrero, R., 170, *185*
Dickson, W. P., 131, *152*
Digman, J. M., viii, *x*, 4, *19*, 30, 32, *45*, 51, 54, 55, *62*, 66, 72, 73, *82*–*83*, 112,

114, 116, 121, *123*, 127, *151*, 175, *185*–*186*
Donahue, E. M., 58, *62*, 115, *123*
Durkee, A., 96, *102*
Dye, D. A., 52, *61*

E

Eagly, A. H., 160, *166*
Eaton, W. O., 33, 38, *45*, 137, *151*, 161, 164, *166*
Eaves, L. J., 160, *166*
Eber, H. W., 24, *44*, 66, *82*, 107, *123*
Edelbrock, C., 95, *101*, 149, *150*, 174, *185*
Eisenberg, N. H., 50, 54, *62*
Elder, G. H., 54, *61*
Enns, L. R., 161, 164, *166*
Entwisle, D. R., 173, 184, *186*
Eysenck, H. J., 2, *19*, 22, 24–25, 36, 37, *45*, *62*, 86, *102*, 106, 111, *123*–*124*, 160, *166*, 174, *186*
Eysenck, M. W., 22, 25, 36, 37, *45*, 111, *123*
Eysenck, S. B. G., 2, *19*, 24, 32, *45*, 86, *102*, 111, *124*, 158, 164, *166*, 174, *186*

F

Fan, L., 80, *84*
Feingold, A., 155, 156, 159, 164, *166*
Fiske, D. W., 51, *62*, 67, *83*, 109, 110, *124*
Fleming, J. E., 54, *63*
Floderus-Myrhead, B., 160, *166*
Frame, C., 53, *63*
Freeland, C. A. B., 11, *18*
Freud, S., 65–66, *83*
Freyd, M., 24, *45*
Fruch, T., 160, *167*
Funder, D. C., 161, *166*

G

Gaddis, L., 73, *83*
Garcia-Coll, C., 33, *45*, 169, 170, *186*
Garmezy, N., 176, *186*
Ge, F., *84*
Gelfand, D. M., 131, *151*
Genovese, E., 171, *186*
Gilliland, A. R., *45*
Glass, G. V., 170, *185*
Goff, M., 106, 122, *124*
Goldberg, L. R., viin, *x*, 25n, 26–28, 36, 38–39, *45*, *46*, 49, 51, 52, 59, *62*, 67–68, *83*, 88, 89, *102*, *103*, 107–110, *124*, 127, *151*, 159, *166*, 176, *186*, *203*

Goldsmith, H. H., 38, *46*, 53, *62*
Goodnow, J. J., 131, *151*
Gordon, T., 169, *186*
Gottfried, A. W., 72, *83*, 129, 130, 137, *151*, 158, *166*
Gough, H. G., 107, 110, *124*, 157, *166*
Graham, S., 116, *122*
Graziano, W. G., 50, 54, *62*, 114, *124*
Gretarsson, S. J., 131, *151*
Guerin, D. W., 72, *83*, 129, 130, 137, *151*, 158, *166*
Guilford, J. P., 22, 24, *46*
Guilford, R. B., 22, *46*
Guthrie, R. V., 169, *186*
Gutman, H. G., 171, *186*

H

Hagekull, B., 32, 33, 38, *46*, 71, *83*, 112, *124*, 127, 130, *151*
Hall, J. A., 156, 164, *166*
Halverson, C. F., Jr., viii, *x*, 4, 17, *19*, 38, *46*, 81, *84*, 93, 158, *166*, 173, 175, 178, *186*, *187*
Harkness, S., viii, *x*
Harnishfeger, K. K., 54, *61*
Harris, M., 169, *187*
Haselager, G. J. T., 34, *47*, 55, *64*, 75, *84*, 93, *103*, 115, 121, *125*, 128, *153*
Hauser, R. M., 173, 184, *186*
Havill, V. L., 17, *19*, 81, *84*, 173, 178, *186*
Hegvik, R. L., 33, *47*, 72, *83*
Heilbrun, A. B., Jr., 107, 110, *124*, 157, *166*
Hendriks, A. A. J., 30, *45*, 89, 90, *102*, 191, *202*
Hershey, K. L., 85, *103*
Herskowitz, M., 171, *186*
Hess, R. D., 131, *152*
Hickey, T., 170, *186*
Hildebrand, H. P., 22, *46*
Hinde, R. A., *46*, *62*
Ho, D. Y. F., 80, *83*
Hocevar, D., 112, *126*
Hofstee, W. K. B., 30, 31, 36, 38, *45*, *46*, 51, *61*, 89, 90, *102*, 105, *124*, 159, 161, *166*, *202*, *203*
Hogan, R., 29, *46*, 49–51, *62*, 164, *166*, 176, *186*
Holland, J. L., 159, *166*
Hollet, N., 112, *125*
Hoskens, M., *202*
Howard, A., 170, *186*
Howell, C. T., 174, *185*
Hrebickova, M., *102*
Hui, C. H., 150, *153*
Hultsch, D. F., 170, *186*

Huttunen, M., 2, *19*, *47*, 71, *83*, 94, *102*, 111, *124*, 127, *152*

I

Inouye, J., viii, *x*, 4, *19*, 54, 55, *62*, 72, *82*, 112, 116, 121, 127, *151*, 175, *186*

J

Jaccard, J. J., 170, *185*
Jacklin, C. N., 155, 156, 164, *166*
James, W., 22, *46*
Janssen, A. W. H., *125*
Jardine, R., 160, *166*
Jenkins, R., 169, *186*
John, O., viii, *x*, 2–3, 10, *19*, 23, 25–26, 34, *46*, 52, 54, *62*, 63, 74, 75, *83*, *84*, 90, 94, 95, *101–103*, 105, 106, 115, 121, *122*, *124*, *125*, 127, 128, *152*, 174, *186*, *203*
Johnson, J. A., 51, *62*, 110, *124*
Jones, W. H., 36, *46*
Jung, C. G., 22, *46*

K

Kagan, J., 33, *46*, 58, *62–63*, 128, *152*
Kagitcibasi, J. C., 131, 150, *152*
Kalverboer, A. F., 74, *83*
Kang, T. K., 80, *83*
Kaprio, J., 160, *167*
Kashiwagi, K., 131, *152*
Katigbak, M. S., viii, *x*, 3–4, *18*, 95, *102*
Kent, R. N., 160, *167*
Keogh, B. K., 73, *83*
Khatena, J., 112, *124*
Killeen, M. R., 53, *63*
Kipp, K., 54, *61*
Kloosterman, K., 51, *61*, *202*
Klopp, B., *123*
Knight, R., 131, *151*
Kogan, J., *45*
Kohn, M. L., 56, *63*, 184, *186*
Kohnstamm, G. A., viii, *x*, 4, 17, *19*, 74, *83*, 93, 111, *124*, 158, 161, 162, *166*, 173, 174, 178, *186*
Koot, J. M., *125*
Koskenvuo, M., 160, *167*
Kuhlman, D. M., 29, *48*
Kun, A., 116, *124*

L

Lamberty, G., 169, *186*
Langinvainio, H., 160, *167*

Lanning, K., 11, *19*

Lanthier, R., 38, *46*, 59, *63*, 130, *152*
Leary, T., 51, *63*
Lee, S. Y., 80, *84*
Lemkin, J., 58, *63*
Lerner, R. M., 11, *19*, 38, *47*, 111, *126*, 174, *187*
Leung, K., 150, *153*
Liebler, A., 161, *165*
Lindhagen, K., 33, *46*
Livesely, W. J., 58, *63*
Loeber, R., 53, *63*
Loehlin, J. C., 159–160, *166*
Lounsbury, M. L., 11, *18*
Lovdal, L., 160, *166*
Lummis, M., 80, *84*
Lynam, D., *123*

M

Maccoby, E. E., 155, 156, 164, *166*
Malpass, R. S., 2, *19*
Margalit, M., 158, 164, *166*
Martin, N., 160, *166*
Martin, R. P., viii, *x*, 2, *19*, 32, 33, 37, 38, *47*, 71, 73, *83*, 93, 94, *102*, 111, 112, *124*, 127, 143, *152*, 158, *166*
Masten, A., 176, *186*
McAdoo, H. P., 169, *186*
McCall, R. B., *46*, 62, 130, *152*
McCaulley, M. H., 51, *63*
McClearn, G. E., 159, *165*
McClowry, S. G., 33, 38, *47*, 72, *83*, 158, *167*
McCrae, R. R., 10, *19*, 25n, 28, 29, 35, 38, *44–45*, *47*, 50–52, 59, 60, *61*, *63*, 67–68, 74, 81, 82, *83*, 92, 95, *102*, *103*, 107–110, 112, *123*, *124*, 127, 128, 143, *151*, *152*, 156, 159, 164, *165*
McDevitt, S. C., 1–2, *18*, *19*, 72, *83*, 111, *123*, 174, *185*
McGee, R., 53, *63*
McGhee, P. E., 160, *167*
McLoyd, V. C., 169–173, 175, *186*, *187*
McNeil, T. F., 158, *167*
Mead, M., 50, *63*
Mervielde, I., 17, *19*, 55, *63*, 74, *84*, 113–116, 121, *123–125*, 173, *203*
Mey, J. T. H., *125*
Meyer, W., 116, *125*
Michael, W. B., 112, *126*
Moffitt, T. E., 34, 35, *46*, *47*, 74, *83*, 94, *102*, 115, *123*, *124*, 128, *152*
Morales, A., 169, *187*
Morales, M. L., 170, *185*

Morris, L. W., 32, *47*
Moss, H. A., 128, *152*
Mueller, C. W., 173, 184, *187*
Mulder, E., 51, *61*, *202*
Myers, H. F., 169, *187*
Myers, I. B., 51, *63*

N

Needles, D. J., 35, *47*
Nelson, S. D., 169, 171, *185*
Nesselroade, J. R., 159, *165*
Nichols, R. C., 160, *166*
Norman, W. T., 26–28, *47*, 51, 59, *63*, 88, *103*, 105, 109, 110, *125*
North, R. D., 24, *47*

O

Oberklaid, F., 128, *152*
Odbert, H. S., 23, *44*, 88, *101*, 105, 107, *122*
O'Donnell, K. J., 160, *167*
O'Donnell, W. J., 160, *167*
Offord, D. R., 54, *63*
Ogbu, J. U., 170–173, 176, 179, *187*
Okagaki, L., 80, *84*
O'Leary, K. D., 160, *167*
Olejnik, S., 73, *83*
Oliver, P. M., 72, *83*
Ostendorf, F., 11, *18*, 23, 26, 30, 38, *46*, *47*, 51, 62, 68–69, *84*, 90–92, *101–103*, 105, 106, 110, 111, *122*, *125*, 145, *152*

P

Paguio, L. P., 112, *125*
Parcell, T. L., 173, 184, *187*
Parke, R. D., 173, *187*
Partridge, F., 53, *63*
Peabody, D., 88, 89, *103*, *203*
Pedersen, N., 159, 160, *165*, *166*
Pedlow, R., 128–130, 139, *152*
Peevers, B. H., 58, *63*
Persson-Blennow, I., 158, *167*
Perugini, M., 90, *102*
Pervin, L. A., *203*
Peterson, D., 55, *63*
Peterson, R. R., 175, *187*
Pike, R., 170, *187*
Plomin, R., 29, 33–37, *44*, *46*, 62, 95–96, *102*, 111, *123*, 137, *151*, 159, 160, *165*, *167*
Pluister, C., 74, *83*

Pokhil'ko, V. L., 30, *47*
Poortinga, Y. H., 2, *19*
Posner, M. I., 54, *63*, 70, *84*, 85, *103*
Post-Gorden, J. C., 38, *46*
Powell, G., 169, *187*
Prentice, D. H., 58, *63*
Price, G. G., 131, *152*
Prior, M., 128, *152*
Przybeck, T. R., 159, *165*
Pullis, M., 73, *83*

Q

Quay, H., 55, *63*, 95, *103*, 174, 175, *185*, *187*

R

Racine, Y. A., 54, *63*
Rana, P. G., 169, *187*
Randolph, S., 170, *186*
Rasmusson, I., 160, *166*
Rende, R., 160, *167*
Renmin, Y., 132, *151*
Resing, W. C. M., 73, *82*
Resnick, J. S., 33, *45*, *46*
Riksen-Walraven, J. M. A., *125*
Robins, R. W., 34, *46*, 75, 76, *83*, *84*, 94, *102*, *103*, 115, *124*, *125*, 128, *152*
Romero, A., 169, *187*
Rorer, L. G., 106, *125*
Rose, R. J., 160, *167*
Rosenthal, D., 131, *152*
Rosolack, T., 28, 39, *45*, 51, *62*, 68, *84*
Rothbart, M. K., 33, 36, 38, *44*, *46*, *47*, 54, *61–63*, 70, 76, *82*, *84*, *103*, 111, 112, *122*, *124*, 132, 145, *151*, *152*, 158, *165*, 174, *186*
Rowe, D. C., 159, *167*
Rubin, K. H., 37, *47*
Ruch, W., 111, *125*
Rutter, M., 53, *64*

S

Saklofske, D. H., 106, *125*
Sanson, A., 128, *152*
Sarna, S., 160, *167*
Saucier, G., 25n, *45*, 109, *125*
Scott, R. A., 170, *186*
Secord, P. F., 58, *63*
Serbin, L. A., 160, *167*
Shmelyov, A. G., viii, *x*, 30, *45*, *47*, 114, 121, *123*
Shoji, J., 2, *19*
Shwalb, B. J., 2, *19*

Shwalb, D. W., 2, *19*
Shweder, R. A., 132, *152*
Siebenheller, F. A., *125*
Siegel, I. E., viii, *x*
Silva, P. A., 53, *63*
Smith, R. S., 176, *187*
Smith, T. G., 36, *46*
Sneed, C. D., 161, *166*
Snidman, N., *46*
Stanley, J. C., 170, *185*
Sternberg, R. J., 80, *84*
Stevenson, H. W., 80, *84*, 144, *151*
Stewart, A., 21, *47*
Stewart, S., 37, *47*
Stigler, J. W., 80, *84*
Stouthamer-Loeber, M., 34, 35, *46*, *47*, 74, *83*, 94, *102*, 115, *124*, 128, *152*
Strelau, J., 111, *125*, 130, *152*, 174, *187*
Sung, S., 81, *84*
Super, C. M., viii, *x*
Susman, E. J., 128, *152*
Syrakic, D. M., 159, *165*
Szarota, P., 91, *103*
Szirmák, Z., 30, *47*, 90, *103*

T

Takemoto-Chock, N. K., *62*, 67, 72, *83*, 112, *123*, 175, *186*
Tatsuoka, M. M., 24, *44*, 66, *82*, 107, *123*
Teglasi, H., 33, *47*, 72, *83*
Tellegen, A., 33, *47*, 95, 96, *103*
Ten Brink, P. W. M., *125*
Thomas, A., 1–2, *19*, 32, 38, *46*, *47*, 53, *62*, 64, 71, 73, *84*, 111, *125*, 128, 129, 137, *152*, 173–174, *185*, *187*
Thomas, C. W., 72, *83*
Tonick, I. J., 160, *167*
Torrence, E. P., *125*
Trapnell, P. D., *203*
Triandis, H. C., 57, *64*, 148, 150, *152*, 170–172, *185*, *187*
Tulkin, S. R., 172, *187*
Tupes, E. C., 26, *47*, 51, *64*, 67, *84*, 87, *103*, 109, 110, *125*

U

Uttal, D. H., 144, *151*

V

Valentine, C. A., 172, *187*

Van Den Bosch, W., *202*
Van Heck, G., 106, 110, *123*
van Lieshout, C. F. M., 34, *47*, 55, *64*, 75,
    84, 93, *103*, 114, 115, 121, *125*, 128,
    153
Vasquez-Garcia, H., 169, *186*
Verhulst, F. C., 149, *153*
Victor, J. B., 55, *64*, 73, *84*, 114, *126*, 175,
    187
Visser, J., 74, *83*

W

Wachs, T. D., 53, *61*, 150, *151*
Ward, D., 54, *62*, 114, *124*
Washington, E. D., 169–173, 175, *187*
Wasik, B. H., 169, *186*
Watson, D., 33, 43, *47*, 85, 95, 96, *103*
Webb, E., 32, *47*, 67, *84*
Werner, E. E., 176, *187*
White, J. L., 35, *47*
Wiese, M. R., 169, *187*
Wiggins, J. S., 51, *64*, *203*
Williams, J. E., 157, *167*

Williams, S., 53, *63*
Windle, M., 11, *19*, 38, *47*, 111, *126*, 174,
    187
Wisenbaker, J., 2, *19*, *47*, 71, *83*, 94, *102*,
    111, *124*, 127, *152*
Wood, W., 160, *166*
Wylie, R. C., 58, *64*

Y

Yamamoto, J., 169, *187*
Yarrow, M. R., 58, *64*
Ye, R., 158, *165*
Yik, M. S. M., 81, *83*

Z

Zaal, J. N., 73, *82*
Zarnegar, Z., 112, *126*
Zeidner, M., 106, *125*
Zhou, 144
Zimmerman, W. S., *46*
Zuckerman, M., 22, 25, 29, *48*, 106, 111,
    126, 159, *167*

Subject Index

A

Ability assessment, 106–107
Abridged Big Five Circumplex model, 30, 31, 36, 89, 105, 121, 159, 189–190
Achievement striving, 67
Acting out, 53–54
Active- vs. passive-person descriptive vocabulary, 190
Activity, 7, 72, 130, *see also* Extraversion, facets/factors
  cross-cultural differences, 137
  developmental changes in, 135, 137
  level, 29, 32-34, 38, 42, 137
Adjective Check List (ACL), 107, 157
Affect, *see* Emotions; Neuroticism–emotional stability
African American children, 169–173, 183–185
  dimensions of personality, 176–178
  Five Factor Model approach with, 173–176
  parental descriptions, 169–173, 181, 183–185
    conscientiousness, 181–183
    cross-cultural differences and, 179, 180, 183
    in high- vs. low-risk families, 184–185
    influence of social class on, 178–184
    neuroticism–emotional stability, 182, 184
    openness to experience, 182, 184
Age
  -appropriate questionnaires, 131
  differences, *see* Parental descriptions of child personality, developmental changes in
  effects, 134

Agreeableness, 7, 10, 17, 39, 49–61, 75, 131–141, *see also* Manageability/cooperation
  activity level and, 38
  categories in Norman's taxonomy for, 52
  conceptions of, 49–51, 60–61
  convergent validity, 195, 198, 200
  cross-cultural differences, 56–58, 138, 139, 141
  developmental antecedents, 53–55
  developmental changes and continuity, 129, 138–141
  as facet of Psychoticism, 51
  facets of, 55–57, 60–61
    helpfulness, 7, 55, 139
    honesty-sincerity, 7, 55–57, 139
    manageability, 7, 10, 55, 61, 139–141, 149
  in Five Factor Model, 51–53, 60–61
  in parents' free-language descriptions, 55–58
  sociability and, 38
Anal character, 65–66, *see also* Conscientiousness
Anxiety/fearfulness, 8, 97–99, 145
Approach–withdrawal, 33, 72, 129, *see also* Extraversion
  developmental continuity, 129
Asian attitudes toward education, 79-80
Assertiveness, *see* Dominance
Attention span, *see also* Distractibility
  Thomas–Chess nine-dimensional model and, 71–72
Attentiveness in infants, 71
Australia, 71, 94

B

Baltimore Longitudinal Study of Aging, 52

Behavior
    genetics, 159
    problems, 53
Bible, 49
Big Five-Factor of Conscientiousness, *see under* Conscientiousness
Big Five Model, *see* Five-Factor Model
Big Five Personality Questionnaire
    child self-ratings on, 59

C

California Adult Question (CAQ) Set, 74–76
California Child Question (CCQ) Set, 34,
    51–52, 55, 74–75, 93, 114–115,
    121–122, 128
    ego control and ego resiliency measured
        by, 75–76
    parental and teacher ratings on, 74–76
California Psychological Inventory (CPI), 157
Carefulness, *see* Conscientiousness, facets of
Categorization system of descriptors, 6–18
Category usage, 193
Cattell's 16PF, 24, 29, 66, 107, 157
Cattell's legacy, 108
Child Behavior Check List (CBCL), 95, 149,
    174
Child guidance clinics, 101
Children, *see also specific topics*
    descriptions of others
        focus on external features, 58–59
        free language, 59–60
        spontaneous use of Five Factor Model,
            59–60
    personalities of, *see* Parental descriptions
        of child personality
Children's Behavior Questionnaire (CBQ),
    132, 158
    extraversion and, 33–34
China, *passim*
Chinese parental attitudes, 77–82, 144, 150,
    see also Cross-cultural differences
Coan's Experience Inventory, 107
Coding reliability, 13
Collective cultures vs. individualistic cultures, 172
Compulsiveness, 66
Confidence, *see* Neuroticism–emotional Stability, facets/markers of
Conscience, *see* Superego Strength
Conscientiousness, 7–8, 11, 17, 65–82,
    141–144, 175, 181, 183, *see also* Temperament
    16 PF and, 66
    African American parental descriptions of
        social class and, 181–183
    Big Five-Factor of, 65, 67, 69–70

convergent validity, 195, 198, 200
cross-cultural differences, 76–82,
    141–142, 144
developmental changes in, 77, 141–144,
    149–150
effortful control in infancy and, 70–71,
    76
facet scales, 67–69
facets of
    carefulness, 7, 77–78, 143, 163
    faithfulness, 77
    organization/neatness, 65–69, 81
    will to achieve, 73
gender differences, 162–164
infantile predictors of, 70–71
interpretations of
    Goldberg's unipolar markers, 67, 68
    McCrae and Costa, 67
    Ostendorf and Angleitner, 68–69
teacher ratings and, 74, 75
Thomas–Chess nine-dimensional model,
    71–72
Construct validity, 202
Contact/affection comfort, 9, 11, 198
Content validity of free descriptions,
    191–194
Continuity, 128–130
Control, *see also* Impulsivity/effortful control
    ego, 75–76
Convergent validity, 195–202
Cooperation, *see* Manageability/cooperation
Creativity, 112
Cross-cultural differences, *see also* African
    American children ; *specific topics and
    personality traits*
    in free descriptions of child personalities,
        4–5
    methodology and, 132
    in number of parental descriptors per interview, 15
Cross-cultural research, 2–3, 132, 148, 157,
    161, 171
    difficulties in, 170
    emic vs. etic approach, 174, 176, 191
Culture, 120, *see also* Openness to experience/intellect
Cultural values, 132, 185
Cyclothyme vs. Paranoid schizothyme, 50
Czech language, 91

D

Dependability, 67
Descriptors, *see* Parental descriptions of child
    personality
    positive and negative, 12, 18

Developmental changes, 130-131
Difficultness, 53, 29, 140, *see also* Agreeable-
    ness
Diligence-perseverence, 8, 68, *see also* Task
    persistence
Dimensions of Temperament Survey–Revised
    (DOTS–R), 111, 122
Distractibility, *see also* Attention span
    Thomas–Chess nine-dimensional model
    and, 71–72
Dominance, 7, 129
    gender differences, 163, 164

E

EASI/EAS, 29, 35, 96, 111–112
Ecological perspective, 150, 171
Educational values, 82
Edwards Personal Preference Schedule
    (EPPS), 157
Effortful control, *see* Impulsivity/effortful
    control
Ego control and ego resiliency, 75–76
    measured by California Adult/Child
        Question Sets
    Five Factor Model factors and, 76
Emotionality, *see also* Neuroticism–emotional
    stability; Reactivity
    assessment of, 95–96
    in Buss and Plomin's temperament the-
        ory, 95–97
    fear and anger factors, 95
    negative and positive, 29, 95–96, 98, 129
        compared with neuroticism and ex-
            traversion, 96
    as independent constructs, 96
Emotional stability, 8, 17, 85–101, 144–146,
    182, *see also* Neuroticism–emotional
    stability
Emotions, extraverted vs. introverted, 86
Energy, *see* Activity
Evolutionary theory, 50
Excitement seeking, 29
Externalizing behavior, 53–54, 174
Extraversion (E), 7, 17, 21–23, 27, 28,
    31–35, 39–44, 86–87, 129, 181, *see*
    also Approach–withdrawal; Emotional-
    ity, negative and positive; Sociability
    categories in Norman's taxonomy for, 28
    conceptions of, 21–23, 43
        Cattel's model, 23–24
        Eysenck's model, 24–25
        Five-Factor Model, 25–31
    convergent validity, 198
    cross-cultural differences, 39–43,
        135–137
    descriptions vs. ratings on, 197

developmental changes in, 134–138
facets/factors, 29–35, 39, 43
    activity level, 25, 28, 29, 32–34,
        38–39, 42, 135, 137, *see*
        also Activity
    approach/withdrawal, 33
    dominance, 39, 42, 135
    impulsivity/effortful control, 29, 36,
        70–71, 75, 76
    shyness and, 26–28, 33, 36–38
    sociability, 33, 34, 36–39, 42, 135–136
    gender differences, 160, 163, 164
    parental ratings of infants, 32–33
Extraversion vs. introversion, 21–44, 86,
    134–138
Exvia vs. invia, 23
Eysenck Personality Inventory (EPI), 24, 29,
    86
Eysenck Personality Questionnaire
    (EPQ/EPQ–R), 24, 86, 107,
    157–158, 174

F

Face-validity, 201
Factor-structure, cross-national comparabil-
    ity, 128
Family relations, 9, 17, 198, 199
Fearfulness, 8, 97–99, 145
Femininity, *see* Agreeableness
Finland, 71, 94
Five Factor Model (FFM), 2–3, 59–60,
    107–108, 113–116, 127–128, 189, *see*
    also Big Five Personality Question-
    naire; Free descriptions of child per-
    sonalities; *specific personality traits*
    categorization system, 6, *see also* Free de-
        scriptions of child personalities
    differences in category conceptual
        span/width, 12–13
    rationale for categories, 6, 10–12
    cross-cultural differences and, 30, 193
    teacher ratings, 72–76
Flexibility, *see* Agreeableness; Inflexibility
Free descriptions of child personalities, 2–5,
    14–18, 201–202, *see also* Five-Factor
    Model, categorization system; Paren-
    tal descriptions of child personality
    biases in category usage, 193–195, 201
    case examples of, 133–134
    coding of, 3–4
    cross-cultural and developmental sensitiv-
        ity, 191
    cross-cultural differences, 4–5, 18,
        193–194
    descriptors, 18

(Free descriptions of child personalities; descriptors (*cont'inued*)
  number per interview and breadth of
    coverage, 14–15
  positive vs. negative vs. neutral, 12, 18
  proportion over main categories,
    15–17
Five Factor Model free-description methodology, 3, 6
free-language interviews, 5–6
intercoder reliability, 13
  across countries, 208, 209
parental, disadvantages of, 193
vs. ratings
  categorized natural-language,
    197–199, 202
  joint principal component analysis of,
    199–202
scientific status of, 189–191
scoring categories, coding of, 6–18
validity, 193–194, 201–202
  concurrent, 189
  content, 191–201
  convergent, 195–201
  Five Factor Model and, 193–201

G

Gender-appropriate behavior, 9, 11, 163,
  165, 198
Gender differences, 155–165, 198
  cross-cultural studies and, 157, 163
  etiology of, 159
    genetic-biological model, 159–160
    social-cultural model, 160–161
  Five Factor Model and, 157, 162–163,
    194
  in free descriptions, 161–165
  and personality, 155–165
  research methodology and, 157–158,
    161–165
General emotionality (Burt), *see* Neuroticism
  –emotional stability, emotionality
General intelligence (G), 106
Germany, *passim*
Gewissenhafigkeit, 66
Greece, *passim*
Guilford–Zimmerman Temperament Survey
  (GZTS), 22, 157

H

Hard working, 68
Helpfulness, 7, 55, 139
Hogan Personality Inventory, 51
Holland (The Netherlands), *passim*

Honesty-sincerity, 7, 55–57, 60, 139
Hong Kong, 80
Hostility Inventory, 96
Hungary, 30, 90

I

Impulsivity/effortful control, 29, 33, 35–36,
  70–71, 75, 76
Independence, 9, 10, 17, 148, 163, 198
Individual diagnosis, 195, 202
Industriousness, 68
Inflexibility, developmental continuity of, 129
Inhibition, 33
Intelligence, *see* Openness to experience/intellect
  and personality, 106
Intercoder reliability, 208
Interpersonal circumplex, 51, 194
Introversion, *see* Extraversion
Irritability, 94–96, 129, *see also* Neuroticism
  –emotional stability
Italy, 90

J

Japan, 80, 131

L

Leadership, *see* Dominance
Libido, 22
Liveliness, 33

M

Manageability/cooperation, 7, 10, 55, 60–61,
  129, 139–141, 149, *see also* Agreeableness
  infant, 129
  impulsivity predicted by, 71
Martin Temperament Assessment Battery
  (MTAB), 73, 112
Maturity, 9, 10, 163, 165, 198
Maudsley Personality Inventory, 22, 24, 86
Melancholic type, 21
Middle Childhood Temperament Questionnaire, 72
Minnesota Multiphasic Personality Inventory
  (MMPI), 157

Mundugumor, 50
Myers–Briggs Type Indicator, 51
Mythology, 49

N

N, *see* Neuroticism–emotional stability
Negative affect/negative emotionality, *see
     also* Neuroticism–emotional stability
  in childhood, 93–96
NEO Five Factor Inventory (NEO-FFI) and
     NEO Personality Inventory (NEO-PI-
     R), 29, 35, 38, 52, 67, 92, 107,
     109–111, 114, 157, *see also* Five Fac-
     tor Model, 95, 110–111, 114
  neuroticism facets in, 92
Neuroticism, 24, 85–101, 145
Neuroticism–emotional stability (N), 17, 75,
     85–87, 100–101, 200, *see also* Emo-
     tionality
  adjectives with highest loadings in, 90, 91
  adult content and scope of, 87–91
  African American parental descriptions of
     social class and, 182, 184
  cross-cultural differences, 98–100,
     145–146
  developmental changes in, 144–146
  emotionality, 85–86
     Norman's taxonomy for, 88–89
  facets/markers of, 87–97
     anxiety-fearfulness, 8, 97–99, 145
     emotional reactivity, 8, 97–99,
        145–146
     Five Factor Model and, 92
     Goldberg's, 89
     self-confidence, 8, 97–99, 145
  factor analysis
     using California Child Q-Set, 93–95
     using questionnaires based on
        Thomas–Chess dimensions,
        94–95
  as factor in taxonomies
     Goldberg's, 89–91
  gender differences, 164
  in parental free descriptions, 97–101
Norman's taxonomy, 52

O

Obstinacy, 66
Oedipal conflict, 66
Openness to experience/intellect, 8, 17,
     105–122, 146–147, 175, 182, 197
  African American parental descriptions of
     social class and, 182, 184
  changing interpretations of

Cattell's legacy, 108–109
     factor labels, 110
     questionnaire approach, 109–111
     recurrent and orthogonal factors, 109
  cross-cultural differences, 117–120, 147
  developmental changes in, 146–148
  gender differences, 163
  intelligence, 74, 197, 198, 200
  openness–intellect correlation
     age differences and, 113–114
     parental free descriptions of, 117–120,
        122
     peer nominations/ratings, 115–117
     personality Q sorts and, 114–115
     teacher ratings and, 74, 121
  validity, 122, 198, 200
Orderliness, 67

P

P, *see* Psychoticism-superego control
Parental attitudes
  Chinese, 77–82, 144, 150
  cross-cultural comparison of, 79–81
Parental descriptions of child personality, *see
     also* Free descriptions of child person-
     alities; *specific topics*
  cross-cultural differences, 14–16, 39–44,
     135–139, 141, 142, 144–148, 150
  developmental changes in, 127–129,
     148–150
     agreeableness, 138–141, 149–150
     conscientiousness, 141–144, 149–150
     emotional Stability, 144–146, 150
     heterotypic (construct) *vs.* homotypic
        continuity, 128–130
     openness to experience, 146–148, 150
Parsimony, 66
Passivity–dominance, *see* Dominance
Peer nominations, 27, 88, 115, 121
Peer perception, 121
Persistence, *see also* Task persistence
  in infants, 71
Person perception, 59
Personality
  assessment of
     abilities in, 106–107
     behavioral items in, 107–108
     lexical approach to, 105–107
  descriptions of, *see* Parental descriptions
     of child personality; Self-descrip-
     tions of children
  developmental dimensions of, 129–130
Personality Q sorts, 114–115
Personality Research Form (PRF), 10, 157
Personality traits, *see specific traits*
Philippines, 3, 95

Philothemo, 57
Phrenologists, 65
Physiological measures, 159
Positive affect, 33
Psychopathology, 55, 88, 91
Psychotherapy, 91
Psychoticism-superego control, 24, 51, 86

Q

Q sorts, 114–115

R

Race-comparative research, 176
RBPC, 55
Reactivity/placidity, *see also* Emotionality
    developmental continuity, 129, 130
    emotional, 8, 145–146
        Neuroticism–emotional stability and,
            97–99
    negative, 72
Reliability, 208–209
Reproductive competition, 50
Resiliency, 75–76
Rhythmicity, 9, 11, 17, 198
    developmental continuity of, 129
Russia, 30, 114

S

Samples involved, 13
Sanguine type, 21
School-Age Temperament Inventory (SATI),
    158
School Behavior Check List (SCHOBL), 73
School performance and attitudes, 9, 11, 17,
    198
Self-confidence, 8, 97–99, 145, *see* Neuroti-
    cism–emotional stability, facets/mark-
    ers of
Self-descriptions of children, 59
    focus on external features, 58–59
Self-regulation, *see* Impulsivity
Sensation Seeking Scales (SSS), 111
Sensitivity, *see* Reactivity/placidity
Shyness, 26–28, 33, 36–38, 129, *see also* So-
    ciability
Sibling relations, *see* Family relations
Simple structure model, 30
Skewness of distributions, 15
Sociability, 7, 136, *see also* Extraversion; Shy-
    ness
    agreeableness and, 38
    cross-cultural differences, 136

gender differences, 163
Social class, 4, 172,
    African American parental descriptions
        and, 181–183
Social inhibition, *see* Approach–withdrawal;
    Shyness
Socioeconomic status, 173, 179
Softness, *see* Agreeableness
South Korea, 81
Strelau Temperament Inventory (STI–RS),
    111
Superego, 66
Superego strength, 72,
    teacher ratings and, 72–74
Surgency, 26, 29
Sweden, 71, 94

T

Taiwan, 80
Task orientation, 73
    in parental ratings, 76
    in teacher ratings, 73–74, 76
Task persistence, 71–72, 129, 143, 149, *see
    also* Conscientiousness; Diligence-
    perseverence
    Thomas–Chess nine-dimensional model
        and, 71–72
Teacher Temperament Questionnaire
    task orientation factor, 73
Temperament, 1–2, 71–72, 111–112
    developmental changes in, 130
    extraversion and, 21, 24, 25
    in infancy, 70
    personality ratings and, 112–114
    Thomas–Chess nine-dimensional model,
        71–72
Temperament Assessment Battery for Chil-
    dren (MTAB), 73–74

U

U.S. minorities, 169

V

Validity, 150, 189–202
Vietnam, 80

W

Will (w), 67, 71
Will to achieve, 68, 76